C. F. Rehnborg -
A COLLECTION OF HIS ESSAYS, SPEECHES, AND WRITINGS

PUBLISHED BY
C.F. REHNBORG LITERARY FOUNDATION
Buena Park, California

COPYRIGHT © 1985 BY
THE C.F. REHNBORG
LITERARY FOUNDATION

PUBLISHED BY
C.F. REHNBORG
LITERARY FOUNDATION
5600 Beach Boulevard
Buena Park, California 90622

First Printing 1985
ISBN NUMBER
0-9606564-2-1
Library of Congress Catalog
Card Number 84-62827

Edited by Lee Johnson
P.O. Box 393,
Scottsdale, Arizona 85252

Designed by Roberta Sinnock,
Seven Oaks Studio,
309 S. Roosevelt Street,
Tempe, Arizona 85281

Typesetting by
Dubs Graphics,
P.O. Box 11801,
Phoenix, Arizona 85061

Printing by Bookcrafters,
140 Buchanan Street,
Chelsea, Michigan 48118

Dedicated to
Edith L. Rehnborg,
wife of C.F. Rehnborg,
whose many years of loving support
and dedication were so influential
in bringing his genius to fulfillment.

C.F. Rehnborg

A Tribute to Carl F. Rehnborg

By Rich DeVos, President
AMWAY CORPORATION, Ada, Michigan

Carl F. Rehnborg ... dreamer, creator, visionary, idealist and doer.

For many years Carl Rehnborg was, to me, only a dream as the creator and manufacturer of Nutrilite Food Supplements. We knew him through his product and our belief in that product and in the idea of better nutritional health.

Eventually I met the man himself, at a reception in Chicago. It was then that I discovered the real person and his concern for people. Later on at other functions, I discovered the intelligence, the mind, the insights of a true visionary.

And now through his essays I realize anew the genius of Carl F. Rehnborg, his interest in matters great and small, his faith and belief in what man can accomplish.

You too will make those discoveries in this book. Happy reading.

FOREWORD

By Charles S. Rhyne

EDITOR'S NOTE:

Charlie Rhyne of Washington is known and respected worldwide not only for his legal prowess but also as a strong advocate for the ideal of world peace through law — an ideal he has served for many years as a member and former World President of the World Peace Through Law Center. This organization, which has developed into the largest in the legal profession in all world history, includes more than 140 nations whose members are working together to develop a world legal system for the good of all mankind. He is a former President of the American Bar Association.

A graduate of Duke University, Mr. Rhyne's distinguished career has been highlighted by numerous honorary degrees and specially-conferred offices, including those of Special U.S. Ambassador, United Nations High Commissioner for Refugees, and Personal Representative of the President in 1971. He has served on many fraternal and legal organizations and still serves as a Duke University Trustee. Mr. Rhyne has authored many books and monographs concerning the law, and was honored by TIME Magazine in the issue of May 8, 1958, with a cover story on his career and accomplishments.

Although Rhyne's interests have been generally concerned with law, they have been oriented towards human rights and the betterment of world conditions through peaceful alternatives to nuclear war. Retained by Carl Rehnborg as his legal counsel early in Rhyne's career, the two men became staunch friends and associates in many human rights endeavors worldwide. Their social and political ideals were often on the same wavelength, and it seemed only natural that Mr. Rhyne should be asked to write the Foreword for this book.

* * * * * * * * * *

This volume is representative of the breadth and workings of the great mind of Carl F. Rehnborg. This tremendously accomplished man was a pioneer in the field of food supplements, being singularly responsible for the development and remarkable success of Nutrilite Food Supplements more than 50 years ago. The major theme these essays portray is that throughout his life Carl Rehnborg had one outstanding goal: to make lasting contributions to the betterment of all mankind.

Carl had the most unusual and inquisitive mind regarding nearly all matters affecting humanity that I have ever encountered.

The depth of his concern shows forth in this book, and he strongly believed that the present could only be understood by studying the influences of the past. His views always encompassed the whole of worldwide knowledge then available on any subject upon which he focused his unique powers of concentration. The essays in this book are the result of many hours of personal research, often over extended periods of time and in different languages which he both spoke and wrote.

The reason Carl's views ring with such clarity in today's world is that they are a distillation of the writings of the great minds of history, from ancient times to the most current thinking. He had the ability to absorb the totality of human knowledge on any given subject, yet his conclusions were not influenced by others' thinking but were his own and his alone. Nor did it matter to him that others might disagree; he was able to dig out the most ancient of books in his voluminous library, gathered from throughout the world, to trace the development of any challenged conclusion and to demonstrate the validity of his views.

I first met Carl in the 1940's when the U.S. Food and Drug Administration obtained an indictment claiming that the Nutrilite literature had misbranded the product under applicable federal law. The indictment specifically asserted that sales brochures such as "How to Get Well and Stay Well," and many other articles, misrepresented the true value of the product. The FDA initiated multiple seizure actions throughout the country and began seizing the product through federal court proceedings.

Carl retained my services and gave me a complete report on the history and development of Nutrilite Food Supplements, and the extensive research upon which his claims and conclusions were based. I agreed to undertake litigation to seek a dismissal of the indictment and the seizure actions, and free Nutrilite from the FDA's attempt to prevent the sale of its product.

This is not the place to summarize the years of litigation which I led, and which finally resulted in dismissal of the 11 seizure actions and the indictment. In fact, all litigation was finally concluded by a Consent Decree which was obtained through negotiation with U.S. attorneys and approved by a Federal Court order. That Decree established for the very first time what legally could and could not be claimed for vitamin and mineral food supplements. All my negotiation was conducted under Carl's careful guidance and it was his knowledge that helped to forge guidelines for the developing multi-vitamin-mineral food supplement industry.

I worked with Carl on many other occasions as both friend and legal counsel. He had a brilliant mind and a thorough knowledge of national and international law, as evidenced by his essay on "World Peace Through World Law." His knowledge of jurisprudence invariably acquitted him well, both inside and outside the courtroom.

Our friendship and business association extended far beyond mutual interest in the law. In Washington I introduced Carl to then-President Dwight Eisenhower whom I was serving as Special Counsel. We worked together with the President's Scientific Adviser in handling the ill-fated but famous pre-Thanksgiving ban on cranberries, which had come about because the FDA had mistakenly determined that the cranberry crop had been sprayed with a cancer-causing insecticide. Carl quickly recommended experts who investigated and testified that this finding was erroneous. The ban was then lifted and a program of damage payments was initiated for the cranberry growers. It was necessary for President Eisenhower to solve this problem, because the Departments of Agriculture, and Health, Education and Welfare (of which the FDA is a part) had publicly taken opposite positions on the ban!

When I was President of the American Bar Association I invited Madame Chiang Kai Chek to speak at our annual banquet. I took Carl to meet her, and the two of them had a wonderful time reminiscing about "the China we once knew" so well. She especially enjoyed his China jokes. When Bob Hope, who was also a banquet speaker, jokingly complained because Madame had singled Carl out as one of the most fascinating men she had ever met, she replied that Carl's stories about his life in China were every bit as entertaining as Bob's "one liners." Later Carl and Edith were guests at the prestigious VIP American Bar Association President's Dinner where they enjoyed talking with Chief

Justice and Mrs. Earl Warren, as well as the other Supreme Court Justices and the many famous national and foreign leaders, and their wives, who were present. The highlight of the evening was the Rehnborgs' unique gifts of handcrafted items from Tahiti which were presented to each guest.

I remember our trips to Hemet, California, where we talked for hours about many of the subjects covered in this book. Carl showed me his telescope which at the time was probably one of the largest in private ownership, and helped me to view the moon and various constellations of stars. His description of the moon, so many light years away, and the vastness of the universe, made me feel that no human being would ever visit that far off planet — yet a few years later I watched in wonder as a man walked on the moon!

Throughout most of our lives Carl and I were in touch, usually by telephone. I have spent the last 30 and more years traveling the world in my capacity as President of the World Peace Through Law Center, composed of the World Association of Judges, World Association of Lawyers, World Association of Law Professors, and World Association of Law Students. Carl was of immense aid to me, not only on numerous occasions when I received foreign leaders in Washington but also when I spoke on the same program with those leaders in other countries of the world. My Presidency of the American Bar Association began with its annual meeting in London, where I delivered my first speech as President at a dinner held at London's Guildhall. The major speaker on that occasion was Sir Winston Churchill. I recall how useful Carl's storehouse of knowledge was in writing my own speech, and his aid was equally valuable when I met the first Prime Minister Nehru of India, King Paul of Greece, Pope John XXIII, and the Presidents or heads of state of many other nations with whom I discussed the Center and its World Conferences for strengthening law as a world peace instrument. Carl's knowledge of the nations, their histories, and their leaders was outstanding.

With this background, and having met many of the great men of our time, I can say that Carl Rehnborg was truly one of the greatest. Our earth is a better place in which to live because of his quiet but lasting contributions to all humanity. Few indeed have contributed more. He possessed the attributes of greatness which characterize the leaders of our nation and the world, even though he led the life of the quiet scholar, a multi-faceted and compassionate individual working alone on the critical problems of humankind. He did not reach for headlines but did the hard, difficult research work as illustrated in this volume, which is his trademark of greatness in the history of mankind.

Carl's constant consideration of others and his modest avoidance of argument was typical of this man who was at peace with himself and the world. Yet in making decisions his quiet authoritative handling of any situation almost always prevented disagreement with his decision. Disagreement could rarely be mounted in the face of his complete command of the history and relevant facts of the subject to be decided. He never boasted of his immense knowledge nor took public credit for his truly great accomplishments or fabulous acts of charity to advance the good of humanity, the subject of his greatest concern. Yet his very simplicity and total lack of egotism generated in all who knew him an enormous respect, affection, and above all, loyalty.

Knowing and working with Carl Rehnborg has been a source of great inspiration to me. That his words recorded herein are now available to me for constant rereading gives me a feeling of pride in having known this remarkable man so well, and gratitude that he was my friend. His words will help me on my further travels through life.

— Charles S. Rhyne

TABLE OF CONTENTS

C.F. REHNBORG
-a man with a dream

INTRODUCTION
by Lee Johnson, Editor

C.F. Rehnborg, as he preferred to be known, was — and still is — an inspirational force in the lives of all who knew and loved him, and he has influenced countless thousands of other people in the United States and abroad whose lives have been touched through his achievements. It is not that his achievements were unique in the sense that many other men also have started small businesses based on an idea, and built them into multi-million dollar corporations which contributed to the nation's economy. Rather, it was that the very nature of his idea and its impact on people, combined with his own high purpose and lifelong dedication, gave a special meaning to his work.

What was he really like, this large, genial man whose charisma was such that when he appeared before a convention of thousands of people and began to speak, the auditorium was instantly hushed and still so that not a single word would be lost? What were his thoughts, his attitudes, his beliefs and ideals? To say that he was a genius is not enough; he was much more than that — generous and warm-hearted, wise, witty, and sensitive — and as much at home in dungarees on a sailboat as he was at Maxim's or the Hotel George V in Paris, in the Board Room of any number of large companies, or participating in a native feast on a little-known island in the South Pacific.

C.F. Rehnborg was born June 15, 1887, in St. Petersburg, Florida, and when he died in 1973 at the age of 85, he left a legacy of humanitarian ideals that remains viable still, through the company he founded, Nutrilite Products, Inc., and the Nutrilite Foundation.

"Mr. R," as he was affectionately called by associates and employees, was revered by them, and he returned their love. One of his pleasures was to walk around the plant headquarters at Buena Park or the Farm operation at Lakeview, California, stopping to talk with

vii

employees he met along the way. He was interested in each of them, and although perhaps awed by his status as President and Chairman of the Board, no one could fail to respond to his personal charm and sincerity. Nothing escaped his notice, and nothing was beneath his notice as a keen observer of the human comedy. His whimsical sense of humor was often turned upon his own frailties. The sight of "Mr. R." in his faded Balboa Blues was always a looked-forward-to experience for plant employees. It was also a special thrill for Distributors who came to tour the plant facilities, to catch a glimpse of Mr. R. and perhaps be treated to an hour's conversation with him. On one such occasion the group found him seated under a large pepper tree at the company Farm, and the resulting chat came to be called "The Pepper Tree Talk" which later became a column in the company news magazine, by request.

C.F. Rehnborg had first-hand knowledge of an astounding variety of subjects, and he kept up with state-of-the-art advancements in many fields, especially science and astronomy, through voracious reading — a habit established early in life which never abated. Philosophy, religion, history, politics, astronomy, agriculture, mathematics, chemistry, aerodynamics, human rights, conservation of natural resources, world population growth and food supply, world peace and world government through law, the reforestation of cut-over land, the promotion of profit-sharing in business and industry — these were but a few of his interests, after his first love of nutritional research and development.

Although not religious in a conventional sense, Mr. R. was a keen student of the Bible. He spent nearly forty years researching the life and teachings of Jesus of Nazareth, touring Palestine and Israel and Egypt in the process. He believed in a loving and rational God, and lived according to his high ideals.

C.F. Rehnborg believed firmly in tithing, and with his wife, Edith L. Rehnborg, established the Nutrilite Foundation, to which they contributed the maximum amounts allowable during their years at the helm of Nutrilite Products, Inc. The Foundation improved the quality of life for numbers of people, yet the Rehnborgs remained anonymous donors whenever possible, if given their choice.

Consequently, only a few people were aware that Foundation funds had helped finance a purchase of the Dead Sea Scrolls which have so enriched the study of early Christianity, and also contributed to a "dig" at an archaeological site in Palestine. In 1961 the Foundation paid for a study of the capabilities and needs of Western Samoa that materially affected the establishment of autonomous government for that country as of January 1, 1962. For many years the Foundation administered a program of college scholarships at selected Southern California high schools, and donated several fine telescopes to certain colleges' Astronomy Departments. In keeping with Rehnborg's strong feelings about the preservation of our national forests, a redwood grove was purchased and donated as part of the Prairie Creek Redwoods State Park in California. It is named the Edith L. Rehnborg Redwood Grove, in her honor. The list of Foundation projects is very long.

C.F. Rehnborg remained, throughout his life, an extremely private person and somewhat a man of mystery. It was not that he desired to appear mysterious; it was simply that the complexities of his activities, interests, travels, and hobbies were so time-consuming that he was obliged to ignore the customary social obligations which were, to him, unimportant in any event. He often set enormous tasks for himself, and worked untiringly at them with intense concentration and without sleep until they were finished.

The Rehnborgs maintained a home near Papeete, Tahiti, for many years, and this was one of their favorite getaway places when time permitted. Rehnborg's joy in the simple lifestyle and freedom from routine is reflected in his essays about Polynesia and its peoples. Another great joy was his small observatory in the mountains near Idyllwild, California, where he spent many happy hours observing the stars and planets — often until the wee hours of the morning. He kept notes of his observations, and had begun working on a book outlining a system for locating heavenly objects, which he felt would make it easier for students and amateur astronomers.

Although Rehnborg read and spoke several languages, including Chinese, he had never learned French. At the age of 75, having become frustrated at his inability to communicate correctly with French government officials in Tahiti and Paris, he set out to learn the language — and did so within a very short time.

This remarkable man, who fired the imaginations and widened the horizons of thousands of people, became a living legend, although he would be embarrassed to hear it said. He did it by sharing his dreams and hopes for a better world for all the world's peoples. It began with an idea — a dream — that became the driving force in his life, and resulted in the creation of a food supplement product that is now known worldwide, a leader in its field.

During the 1920's C.F. Rehnborg was engaged as a manufacturer's representative in China. In the approximately fifteen years he spent there, he had ample opportunity to observe the effects of the inadequate diets of the poor people of that country. A man of insatiable curiosity, he made careful notes during his travels and studied all the nutritional literature he was able to get, since the then-new study of nutrition was in its infancy. Gradually he conceived the idea that many of mankind's illnesses might be related to diet — not so much what a person ate, but rather what he did not eat. He believed there must be ways of correcting these inadequacies by making sure that people's nutritional needs were fully met in some form that could supplement their meager diets. The more he saw and learned, the more the idea took hold.

When Rehnborg, along with hundreds of other foreigners in China, was confined to a fenced-in compound by General Chiang Kai Chek's forces in the mid-1920's, he was able to test his theories regarding nutrition. Years later he would relate how, while living within the compound for nearly a year, he supplemented the starvation diet by making a sort of soup, or stew, combining whatever green, leafy plants he found growing in the area with other foodstuffs he was able to persuade the Chinese guards to bring him. He even added rusty nails to his stew whenever he could, knowing that the iron which leached out would be valuable, nutritionally.

He offered his rather ill-tasting soup to friends in the compound, some of whom accepted and some of whom did not. Although the companions who had shared his concoctions thought him rather odd, they were able to survive the rigors of their inadequate diets and walk out of the compound to freedom a year later, while many others could not.

Although C.F. Rehnborg's business in China had developed very successfully, the wars and fighting that raged back and forth across the country during that period had caused the collapse of most of the foreign firms' operations there. Consequently he returned to the United States in 1927 with very little of what he had accumulated in China. He worked at odd jobs for a while, as the idea that had germinated in China began to take shape in his mind. He continued his nutritional experiments at home, eventually renting a sail loft on Balboa Island where he began to make usable forms of the product he had in mind.

Alfalfa had been chosen as the base for his formulations, as it seemed to have the most complete range of the vitamins and minerals that he believed were essential. He added other elements to round out the product and make it as complete as the scientific knowledge of that time dictated. In 1934, when he was finally satisfied with the formula, he gave samples to friends and asked them to try it.

Later when he would go to visit his friends, he would find the product still sitting on their shelves — it had cost them nothing; therefore, it was worth nothing. It then occurred to Rehnborg to charge for the product, and when he did, his friends ate it because they had paid for it! After eating it for a time, they wanted their friends to have it, too, and asked Rehnborg to go see them. He suggested that they tell their friends about the product, and said he would pay a commission when the friends bought it. Thus was born the first distributor system, which later developed into a veritable army of sales representatives.

During the formative years, the company was known as California Vitamins, Inc., and was located on Balboa Island. Then Rehnborg decided to call his product "Nutrilite" and the company became Nutrilite Products in 1939.

By 1939 the company was well established and showing a pattern of strong, continuing success. In actual fact, Nutrilite Products, Inc., developed a sales volume of $7,000,000 per year before any money was spent on advertising; it had all come about simply through word-of-mouth advertising by satisfied customers.

As sales continued to grow, so did the need for more land for growing the alfalfa, and for more spacious quarters to handle the expanded manufacturing and operations activities. In 1946 production facilities were moved to Buena Park, and in 1951 farming operations were moved from Buena Park to the San Jacinto Valley. Careful management of assets had resulted in a strong financial position, so that the young company was able to expand as needed, rapidly creating a business worth millions.

And so, the company which began as a one-man operation became a multi-million dollar business, and one of the pioneer companies in the field of vitamin-mineral food supplementation. It is one of the great success stories of the twentieth century, and a classic example of the American Dream — proof that our free enterprise system is as viable as ever when the ingredients of perseverance, faith, hard work, and good products are combined.

But the story of Nutrilite is not the story of one man alone. Credit must be given to the many other men and women who helped, guided, and gave of their best efforts along the way. Chief among them is Edith L. Rehnborg, who shared her husband's dream and worked by his side through the years. Although it was his genius that developed the products and in the early days even invented or devised equipment required for their production, it was her shrewd money management and investments as Secretary and Treasurer of the company that built the strong financial foundation that later sustained the company when lean years came along. And just as certainly, credit is due the many thousands of loyal distributors and customers who sold and used the products, and so enthusiastically told others about them.

As the distribution and popularity of the product line spread throughout the country, the Rehnborgs no longer had the time to handle the sales end of their business. At first there were sales managers, eventually leading to an arrangement with Mytinger & Casselberry of Long Beach, California, who became Sales Agents for the firm in 1945. Later, with the withdrawal of Dr. William Casselberry from Mytinger & Casselberry, the Mytinger Corporation took over in 1959. Disagreements had developed as to the direction the company should take in regard to product development and merchandising, and in 1963 Nutrilite Products, Inc., purchased all of the assets of the Mytinger Corporation. Once again Nutrilite became responsible for its own sales and distribution activities, in addition to manufacturing.

During this period of turmoil, two young and extremely successful Key Distributors, Rich De Vos and Jay Van Andel, became concerned about the continuing availability of products for their large organization of Distributors. They had formed the Ja-Ri Corporation through which NUTRILITE® Food Supplements were supplied to Distributors and customers. De Vos and Van Andel saw how the Marketing Plan could be adapted to mass merchandising of commodities rather than a specialty line, and they searched very carefully for products to which their theories could be applied. They created a separate company, and beginning with household items such as soaps and detergents, added other products which met their exacting criteria, thus broadening the sales base as it became apparent that their plan for mass merchandising was successful. Their company, which later became the Amway Corporation, grew rapidly and soon rivaled Nutrilite's own phenomenal success story.

Thus it was that as the Amway Corporation flourished, Nutrilite was still struggling to overcome the sales lag that had resulted from the years of uncertainty between 1956 and 1963. Although Jay and Rich and the thousands of Distributors in their Ja-Ri Corporation continued to consume and supply customers with the Nutrilite Food Supplement products, other thousands of Distributors in the rapidly-growing Amway organization began to clamor for such a line, but found nothing equal to Nutrilite in quality or consumer acceptance. The answer was simple: they had to find a way to acquire Nutrilite as a part of their own corporate organization.

Amway's leaders initiated a long series of discussions and negotiations with Nutrilite's principals, including Dr. Sam Rehnborg, son of C.F. Rehnborg and company heir-apparent, to see what could be worked out. The result was Amway's acquisition of the controlling interest in Nutrilite Products, Inc., in 1972, bringing to full circle a business association that had begun in 1950.

Although in the business world ventures such as this are not always highly successful, this one was a 'natural' as it combined the best of two concepts: product excellence and a superior marketing plan. Amway had used the Nutrilite Marketing Plan as a basis, but had changed it to accommodate the great need that existed for a business enterprise that could be used by people everywhere as a part-time or second-income activity, or as a full-time business, depending on the individual's needs. By comparison, Nutrilite's Marketing Plan was product-driven, emphasizing the product excellence that led to business success, while the Amway Marketing Plan concentrated on the business opportunity itself as the motivating force. With the combination of these two elements, Amway, already a corporate giant, has continued to grow at an astonishing rate — and C.F. Rehnborg's dream has begun to approach reality.

Rehnborg envisioned the availability of adequate nutrition for the peoples of the entire world, and dreamed of banishing forever the specter of malnutrition in underdeveloped countries. The first part of his vision is being implemented through the acquisition by Amway Corporation, one of the world's largest direct-selling companies which markets products in more than forty countries and territories. Nutrilite products have begun to move into international commerce in recent years, going first into Canada, then Australia, Malaysia, Hong Kong, United Kingdom, Germany, Japan and Taiwan. Distribution into many other countries is on the horizon.

* * * * * * * * * *

This collection of C.F. Rehnborg's essays has been assembled to reveal his multi-faceted personality and the scope of his thought. This gifted man used his splendid intellect to focus on many of the world's problems, and gave unstintingly of his time and effort — and funds — to help solve them whenever possible. Yet even these writings do not give a true picture of his concern and compassionate regard for his fellow human beings. It was not what he wrote, but what he did, that has improved the quality of life for thousands of people. It was his sincere hope that eventually all humanity might benefit through his ideas and the labor of love that he called Nutrilite Food Supplement. In creating that, he truly gave of himself.

Part 1
THE CONCEPT OF NUTRILITE
-an idea that grew

How I Began To Sell
Nutrilite Food Supplements

No book about the life and thought of C.F. Rehnborg would be complete without his own story of the way in which the company developed from an idea he held in his mind into a multi-million-dollar corporation. Following is the text of an address by Mr. Rehnborg which was given at the Fiesta de Oro Convention in Los Angeles, California, on June 20th, 1964 ... one of his most memorable personal appearances.

When you become a Distributor of products manufactured by Nutrilite Products, Inc., it is quite easy to suppose that the company has always existed pretty much as you find it. This is very far from the fact, however. When the company began, it consisted of just one person, C.F. Rehnborg. I had an idea, but little else, and I stayed with the idea until it clicked. Partly this was because the idea was attractive and appealing, partly because it satisfied my ideals, partly because I am stubborn. I remembered later a boyhood friend, a very successful man, who once told me, "When you are ready to go into business, if you have an idea and the tenacity to stay with it, nothing can stop you."

When we began, I gathered the raw materials, processed them, made the Concentrate (later compounded it with vitamins), packaged the product and labeled the packages, and then went out and sold it. It was only gradually that we began the division of labor which is a necessary part of corporate growth, and it became necessary to treat manufacturing and selling as separate divisions of marketing products. When it did I took manufacturing for my part, and used a succession of sales managers, until finally we made the arrangement with MC. Last of all, as most of you know, we bought out the contract with MC, and with wider interests we now are doing our own selling, as is logical and desirable.

The whole basis for NUTRILITE® Food Supplements itself is an idea, and the idea began in the early 1920's, almost fifty years ago. At that time there was a beginning knowledge that there existed such things as vitamins, but the knowledge was completely fragmentary, and consequently a great deal of research was being done. No one yet really believed in food deficiencies — calories from protein, carbohydrate, and fat defined the idea of food, and only a few scientists were talking of the bad consequences of diets lacking in other factors, some of which had not then been identified as vitamins.

During my years in China I had been able to observe at close range the effects of inadequate diets, and since literature on vitamins and their meaning in nutrition was even then being developed, I followed it all. It seemed to me a perfectly logical idea that there was a close relationship between a balanced diet and the proper functioning of bodily processes, and this idea I carried with me and I never again stopped thinking of it. I gave my European friends in China much advice on what to eat — some of which they followed.

Meanwhile my business in China developed as that of manufacturer's agent, and it was successful. However, this was the period during which modern China was developing. Chiang Kai-shek replaced the many regional governments with a unified government, and began his struggle with the forces which later became Communist. There were wars in which China was harassed and ravaged, and armies flowed around such foreign settlements as Shanghai, which was completely cut off from the rest of the country except by telegraph. Many foreign firms, including mine, lost their business with interior China and were closed out, as I was also. I came back with very little of what I had accumulated in China.

Home again, for a while I had jobs for bread and butter. I have heard a story of a movie producer who had run through his second fortune. When his friends expressed condolences for his being ruined, he said, "Heck, I'm not ruined; I'm just broke." That goes for me, too. But it was clear to me that the time was a natural one for me to develop the notion I had been carrying around for years but had been too busy (and successful) to find imperative.

You should understand, of course, that I did not know clearly how the idea was to be developed. I experimented at home, and one thing followed another until finally I was located in a sail loft at Balboa Island, out of a real "job" and working away at NUTRILITE Food Supplement, absolutely impelled to make it and without interest in anything else. People asked me why I didn't get a job. Actually I had one. It was an all-time job which seemed effortless but which kept me busy every waking hour. There was no way to justify this job to anyone else, but that never worried me.

When I had begun to produce usable forms of product I gave them to friends to try. Then, after a certain length of time, I would go visit the friends to see what results they had obtained, and I found the product that I had made and given to them standing on their bathroom shelves. It had cost them nothing — therefore it was worth nothing. Most naturally it occurred to me that the answer to this difficulty was merely to charge something for the product. When I did that, the friends, having paid for the product, ate it — and after eating it they wanted their friends to have it, too. When they proposed that I talk to their friends about the product, I said instead, "Suppose you tell them, and I will pay you a commission when they buy."

It is for this reason that I tell you reference calls are the most valuable kind of advertising you could possibly have. The names supplied by reference calls are the most worthwhile leads for calls that you can have, because a sale has been all but made before you arrive. Therefore never neglect a reference call, and if you cannot make the call yourself, send it in to the company so it can be given to someone who will be properly located and able to make the call.

Of course in the early days I had only one product and it sold because one user told another, and in fact that was the beginning of the whole sponsorship system of selling NUTRILITE Food Supplement.

Today we have a great many products. However, every one of them is of a kind that can be sold by user recommendation. This is the fundamental basis of Nutrilite Products — quality. Our products, our packaging, our manufacturing controls — all spell quality.

You can be proud of every product presented by Nutrilite Products, Inc. — you don't have to misrepresent — you don't have to "hard sell." All you have to do is to get one person in a household using one Nutrilite Product and you have a customer, and a household full of potential customers for many products.

Our business grew to seven million dollars a year before we spent one penny on advertising, and it made much of this growth by reference calls.

Another point is most important for you to absorb: It is that this company was built from scratch by putting back into it virtually all the profits made from it. When the company, for example, had grown to the point where it made $20,000 net a year, I was paying myself $300 a month, or $3600 a year. The rest was going back into the company.

When we made millions, those millions after taxes appeared as surplus in the company's balance sheet, and were plowed back into the plant and equipment.

In the early days I lived in a corner of the laboratory. I had very monotonous diets, which were designed to nourish but not to interest. For example, I would subsist for considerable periods on corn meal and raisins cooked into a pudding and allowed to harden in a pan and sliced off and eaten with brown sugar for a meal.

The very great reward for building up a business from earnings is in the attitude that it engenders in the people connected with the business itself — and that it makes the business financially strong. NPI, for example, has developed reserves and stability, and the capacity to expand its operations, and has created an establishment worth millions of dollars, all by earned income being kept in the business and not dissipated as either "gravy" or dividends.

One of the obligations of success is, we think at NPI, to pay a tithe of some sort to the Power, whatever it is, that lies behind the universe. Part of our earnings have always been put aside and given to a foundation, called Nutrilite Foundation. This Foundation was begun by Edith and me, setting aside for it nearly a third of the company's stock, and adding year by year from the net earnings of the company.

This Foundation, although it is not large as compared to many others, has chosen its own fields of activity. It founded and still supports the Boys' Club, Buena Park, now affiliated with the Boys' Clubs of America, which has a membership of 1,700 boys in the community of Buena Park, and which has become a community enterprise. Many young people have received grants for college expenses. Schools have received equipment, including telescopes. The Foundation contributed substantial sums to a subsidiary foundation titled Foundation For American Resource Management. Subscriptions were made to the purchases of the Dead Sea Scrolls, which were a very great addition to knowledge of the sources of the Old Testament. The Foundation even paid for a "dig" at an archeological site in Palestine.

Businesses, like all living things, grow by surges. Our business has just reached the point for a vast movement forward. It is now a big little company. In a few months it will become a little big company, and in the course of a very few years will become a big, big company. Our

NUTRILITE Food Supplement business shows steady growth; EDITH REHNBORG® Cosmetics business is growing vigorously; and the NUTRILITE® Household Products business has taken off like a rocket. Nutrilite Products, Inc., has diversified into lines showing steady progress, and this growth lends even greater stability to the company. We have initiated many sorts of sales aids and reactivated recruiting. The feeling at headquarters is of sure and strong confidence in the future.

For me, who has seen our company grow, this is a grand sight. I know absolutely that even greater growth is in the immediate future, and I know equally surely that the advance will come by means of the same simple procedures that meant your greatest advances in the past — to sell by pursuing the "soft sell," with truth and sincerity the guiding principles.

I wish you well, and I am cheering you on.

One up on Dr. Sam: At Nutrilite conventions Distributors and staff members could challenge each other to show their pocket carriers of food supplements or face a mock 'penalty'. At this Fiesta in Los Angeles Dr. Sam so challenged his dad in front of the Ballroom audience, whereupon C.F. Rehnborg whipped out his 'pocket carrier' — a whole box of NUTRILITE® Food Supplement — to the delighted cheers of all present!

Above, at Rehnborg's business establishment in Shanghai in the 20's, he is seated fifth from right, with members of his staff.

Rehnborg is shown at left with staff members in front of his office at 6803 Hoover Street, Los Angeles, in the early 1940's.

6   How I Began to Sell Nutrilite Food Supplements

Why We Selected
The Hemet-San Jacinto Valley
Written Approximately 1958

The Hemet-San Jacinto Valley was selected for our farming operation because it combined the three basic requirements we were seeking for superior plant growth. These initial requirements consisted of (1) soils, highly mineralized, (2) a warm climate with a long growing season, and (3) water in ample supply.

The Hemet-San Jacinto Valley is the silted-in bed of an ancient lake. At the northwest end of the valley, which once was the outlet of the lake, there is a sill of rock rising to the present level of the soil, which formed a natural dam. Behind this dam the lake filled in by slow erosion from the surrounding mountains, over a very long period. The level basin now holds these deposits at approximately the original level of the lake, except where pumping for irrigation has lowered it somewhat. In places the soil deposits are more than a thousand feet deep.

This great bed of silt, sand, gravel, and clay is saturated with water. When this water is drawn to the surface for irrigation, it may be used in any amount desired without depleting the supply, for it will eventually percolate through the soil and rejoin the underground reservoir. The rate of application is limited only by the infiltration rate.

The soils of the valley consist of three different types, each type with its own specific soil characteristics. The Hanford series are recent alluvial soils formed principally from material washed from granite. Our Hemet Ranch* is situated on soils of this type, as is our Lakeview Ranch. The former is a fine sandy loam texture, while the physical structure of the latter is that of a loam. These soils extend to a depth of many feet without appreciable change in texture. The soil at the Hemet Ranch is grayish-brown in color, friable, and contains moderate amounts of organic material. The soil absorbs and retains moisture well but at the same time is adequately drained.

Editor's Note:
*In recent years, due to the location of the Hemet Ranch in the direct path of the expansion of the city of Hemet, it was sold to enable the community's growth. The Lakeview Ranch is more than adequate to meet growing needs.

The Lakeview soil is heavier, darker in color and slightly more alkaline than the soil at Hemet. The geologic background of this area can be partially uncovered as wells are drilled for irrigation purposes. When we dug a well to just over a thousand feet on the Lakeview ranch, at several levels the well drill went through redwood logs. Chips from the logs were brought to the surface, and one log was lying about 750 feet under the present surface, on what was then the shore of the lake.

The original lake was supplied with drainage from the surrounding hills and uplands, and also with underground water. At present there are sections of the valley where the water has different characteristics. At one point it has a high total salt content with a high percentage of sodium salts. This condition is found near a fault line where a recent uplift was experienced. At another point it is high in sulfur compounds, and on the Hemet ranch the water comes from the well at approximately 80 degrees Fahrenheit. There are other places where the water flows at even higher temperatures, and there are hot springs in the hills to the east of the valley.

These are all indications of inflow to the water basin of the Hemet-San Jacinto Valley of large quantities of "new" water from volcanic sources, and the granite, basalt, and lava beds in the surrounding hills indicate the source of this water.

The amount of available water is much greater than the effective rainfall alone would supply. Unless there should be a much greater increase in use made of the water available in the valley, such as drawing it out to other areas, there seems very little likelihood that the water supply for crops will fall short of requirement at present rates of use.

Owing to the high mineral content of the soils in the valley, those soils which have been developed have supported high yielding crops of excellent quality. The east end of the valley consists mainly of apricot, peach, walnut, and citrus groves. Further west, truck crops such as potatoes, onions, and watermelons are grown, usually in rotation with barley and alfalfa. Both the Hemet and Lakeview ranches are used exclusively for the production of alfalfa.

After the lake bed filled in, an uplift created a fault line running for several hundred miles from northwest to southeast, through the center of the valley. This caused a difference in the level of the valley floor, and about half the present valley floor is on the "mesa" and the other half on "lowland" about 15 to 20 feet below.

Our methods of using and improving land are similar to those used by the so-called "organic" farmers, but differ in important particulars. Actually what is called organic farming is the oldest type of all, and is still probably the best. It consists of putting back into the soil as nearly as possible what is taken out, and of increasing its quality when it lacks some of the constituents of fertile ground (as much land in fact does, whether or not it has been farmed).

Much modern agriculture has swung over to the use of chemical or commercial fertilizers, which is a method of mining the ground but not of maintaining it, as opposed to steps used to maintain its fertility over long periods of time by manure and compost, as is typical of old-world agriculture. The old-world type of agriculture has the failing that it does not replace or bring into balance the mineral constituents of the soil, but nevertheless it does attempt to maintain the organic fraction of the soil. Chemical fertilizers result in making a few minerals and some nitrogen available to the plants, but treats the soil as a non-living, completely inorganic body. In light of recent developments in plant hormones and other plant growth regulators, relationship of soil microorganisms to mineral availability, coagulation of soil particles by microbial action, and the buffering effect produced by soil microbiological activity, we certainly cannot ignore the part played by the soil microbial population. However, this is exactly what the chemical farmer chooses to do.

The point is often made by the chemical farmer that the humus fraction of the soil cannot be raised appreciably from a given constant dictated by type of soil, climate, and region. This point is well taken, but it is not a large humus content which we seek in our soil, for this would be impossible under our arid climate. Rather, we strive to achieve the optimum amount of microbiological activity in our soil. The substances produced by these bacteria, actinomyces, fungi, and protozoa, benefit our soil and plants alike. It is estimated there are 3 to 4 thousand pounds per acre of these living organisms in the plow layer of our productive soil, and the substances synthesized by them account for many thousand more pounds.

Our research and experience, then, lead us to make the following points: (1) Soil is primarily an anchor for the plant while it uses the carbon dioxide and water available for growth, although the soil also supplies the small quantity of minerals and available nitrogen the plant requires. (2) Bacteria, worms, and some detritus from previously-living organic forms supply nitrogen and make the proper tilth of the ground by causing it to form aggregates and not colloidal forms of soluble or water-holding clays. (3) The existing mineral content of a soil is not necessarily the best for plants in terms of the kinds of minerals or their relative quantities, so that the additions of compost to the soil should provide humus and the proper amounts of minerals for balance. (4) All minerals have some value in being actually required by the growing plants, but the minerals should be natural rock forms and not chemically changed forms.

In our farming we use composts as the obviously natural means of building the topsoil in which plants grow, following in principle the methods by which topsoil forms under natural conditions. In a natural situation there is a cycle within an area. Plants grow, and some of them are eaten by animals. The plants and the animals and the droppings of the animals return to the soil, and in the other part of the cycle the soil becomes charged with living organisms again. Aside from the leaching effect of rain, that which is in the area stays there, and the production of humus proceeds at a rate which shows some slight gain over the losses by leaching and bacterial action. There is some loss of mineral components, but between volcanic action, erosion of land surface, and dust falling on the earth from the air, the leach loss is compensated, and is not significant over very long periods in any event.

In farming the cycle is broken, because the products of the land are transported to other areas, and much of what came from the land eventually goes to the sea through sewer systems and the rivers. In any event, the crop leaves the area where a cycle is maintained. It is also a fact that the natural cycle is much slower than it needs to be, and it can be accelerated by help from the farmer. The farmer can produce, as well as maintain, the balances in the soil, and can make topsoil much more rapidly than nature does. He can, moreover, put additional mineral elements into the soil. In the best practice, he does this in as nearly a natural manner as possible.

Nutrilite bypasses the long time required by nature, but keeps within the framework of the natural method. To supply the mineral needs of the plants which are to grow in the soil, we add what is required, and we analyze the soil to see how much of each material is needed. These mineral constituents are not commercial fertilizers which aim to supply only the quickly available soluble forms of the most necessary items: calcium, potassium, phosphorus, and nitrogen. Instead we use natural rocks: limestone (for calcium), dolomite (for calcium and magnesium), phosphate rock (for phosphorus), and native rock and naturally occurring forms of the long list of other required elements, including the "trace minerals," bringing these to the land from other points.

To supply the humus of the soil, both the nitrogen compounds and more in addition, we use plant materials and manures, broken down into "compost" by bacterial action. Finally, we mix all these things deep into the soil, building up topsoil in a deep layer of the surface, instead of merely on the surface as in the entirely natural cycle. The result is that practically any soil can be made to have the content and the tilth of a good soil, provided the soil already in place does not contain deleterious substances.

Finally, we colonize worms in the soil, giving them enough organic material at the surface to keep them fed and busy, and they work and aerate the soil. They further fertilize it with their droppings and with their bodies as they die, adding "plant food" at the rate of many hundreds of pounds per acre per year. This kind of soil does not cake, because its particles form aggregates instead of clays, and it holds water and admits oxygen in a way that is favorable to the worms and the bacteria of the soil. Crops grown in such soil are raised under optimum conditions.

Finally, we irrigate this land by overhead sprinkling with quantities of water approaching tropical rainfall, and are able to do this in the Hemet-San Jacinto Valley because the excess water leaches back through the soil to the ground reservoir from which it was drawn. This keeps the soil moist to very great depths and facilitates the growth of very deep root stocks, which in alfalfa go down many feet, thus utilizing the mineral content already present in the soil and recovering the materials applied at the surface and taken down by the irrigation water.

Lastly, the flow of irrigation water down through the soil pumps air deep into the ground, and through the loose character of the composted soil, and the worm burrows aerate the ground thoroughly.

The reason for all this effort to produce the most nearly optimum conditions in the soil is, naturally, tied in with what we want to accomplish. We grow plants for the purpose of getting the raw materials for extraction of as wide a spectrum as possible of the vitamins and minerals in our Concentrate, and selected plants grown under the best possible conditions are the richest source of the desired factors. Synthesis can supply many of the factors, but the factors were found first in plants, and some are not available except in natural concentrates.

In a generalized supplement it is logical to include as many factors as possible, by assuming that they all occur in plant materials to some extent, and very likely, more plentifully in some plants than in others. The materials we use are recorded as containing some fraction of all the factors now known to be essential, and the San Jacinto Valley appears to be the best growing source we have yet found for these materials.

There was no aspect of the growing of raw materials, processing, manufacturing, and packaging that did not receive the personal attention of C.F. Rehnborg. Here he is inspecting the alfalfa crop in one of the fields in the San Jacinto Valley.

Soil Fertility and Plant Nutrition

Written Approximately 1959

In the complexity of civilization, with houses, schools, cars, clothes, and the patterns of social behavior, we very naturally and easily tend to lose sight of our inescapable and absolute relationship to the physical world and the universe of which it is a part. The basic fact is that we live in a universe of chemical substances, and that life itself is a chemical mechanism that uses the elements of which the earth is composed, to build the self-perpetuating living organisms which we observe. We are a part of the earth's living organisms, but we are so used to this fact that we find it commonplace and hardly wonder about it at all.

The existence of life on the earth, however, depends on the most intricate relationships between a number of conditions existing in the physical world; and if any one of these conditions were to be radically changed, life as we know it would probably become impossible. To put it another way, life exists by its very exact adjustment to the conditions of our physical world.

Living things are composed of the elements present in the earth because those are the only materials available, and the process of living is adjusted to the chemical and physical laws of the universe, not as the universe might be, but as it is. Rather than to think that the universe was made for man, or that noses were made to wear spectacles, we should see the fact that man came into being in an already existing universe, and developed in harmony with the laws of that universe.

Living things may be divided into two great groups, (1) those forms which are able to use the raw materials of the universe directly, and (2) those which use these forms in turn as their foods. We call these two groups plants and animals. The division between the groups is not at all sharp and clear, because there are forms which cannot finally be labeled as either plant or animal, but seem to be both, and these intermediate forms may be similar to the very earliest life forms from which both plants and animals arose by evolution.

Plants take the carbon dioxide of the air and water drawn from the ground, and, using the ultraviolet and red bands of light from the sun, in the presence of their catalyst which we call chlorophyll (which gives plants their green color), are able to synthesize formaldehyde, and by condensation to transform this to simple sugars. Next, using sulfur and the many other minerals dissolved in the water from the soil, and nitrogen derived from rainwater and the action of bacteria in the soil, plants can and do build up the enormous and almost infinite number of organic compounds which comprise the trees, herbs, grasses, and other plants, including those we use as foods. The fertile earth is covered with them wherever the conditions are right, for the materials needed for the growth of plants must be present where they grow, and rainfall and other climatic conditions must be favorable.

Only plants can so use the basic materials of the environment. Animals cannot do it at all, but must use the plants for their food. This is true whether the animal is one which eats the plants as they are, or one which eats other animals which eat the plants, and whether the animal lives in the sea or on the land. Simply, if there were no plants there would be no animal life; and since humans are a form of animal life, without plants we would not be here.

This has been generally recognized as a fact since there have been civilizations and languages. Still earlier, men did not bother about such problems or think much at all concerning abstractions. Being omnivorous, eating both plants and other animals, men foraged for food until they found it, and having satisfied themselves, stopped foraging until they were hungry again. Under such conditions men were catholic eaters, eating anything which grew, ran, crawled, or flew, and did not harm or kill them if eaten — or was not too big and fierce or too fleet to be captured! But when men began to live in groups larger than one family —first clans, then tribes — the conditions for securing foods changed radically.

Basically, group living grew up around the idea of cooperation. It was easier for a group of men to collect food, and at the same time to protect one another from animals and other men, than for any one man to do the same things alone. For it must be remembered that until man lived in groups, he lived alone or in a family — and he lived only by continuously fighting for survival in a world which was much more unfriendly than friendly.

The growth and development of the mechanisms of civilization has brought us to the stage where most of the primal dangers are never met, unless we put to sea in a small boat, or hunt big game with a bow and arrow or only a club. But our remote ancestor lived by his agility and his wits, and he rarely lived much longer than it took to mature, or perhaps to mature and mate and wean a brood, and he lived a rough and not very happy life. It is even probable that men had developed civilization to a fairly advanced stage before they learned to laugh. All mankind now lives in groups, but even yet the thing most amusing to a member of a primitive group is an unexpected accident happening to someone else.

After the basic invention of group living, for which men perhaps saw the model in the herding instinct of some animals, men very slowly invented animal husbandry as a branch of agriculture, with the accompanying domestication of animals, and they invented the division of labor, or specialization. In turn, agriculture either suggested, or itself resulted from, the idea of storing foods at lush times for use at leaner times. Perhaps man had already learned in the hunting stage to store meat by drying it. These three things — group protection, specialization and division of labor, and the storing and sharing of foods — are still the basic elements of even the most complicated civilization.

But agriculture itself introduced new problems — what to grow; and how to make the selected foods grow best. We can imagine that the foods to be grown were first selected for the ease with which they could be stored, and second for their taste appeal. Almost universally the grains were selected as desirable foods both for men and domestic animals, because they could readily be dried and stored almost indefinitely for famine years as well as for winters, and because the men and animals eating them thrived in health. The taste appeal may always to some degree have been secondary. Men tend to develop a taste for foods according to the form in which they must be used for best storage results. Cheeses, poi, and yogurt are good examples.

The problem of how to make the selected foods grow best was more difficult and was solved much more slowly. At first men burned off a forest section, scratched the ground, and planted their seed. Then, in a few years, when crops began to be of poorer quality, or even to fail, they moved on and cleared a new area. In Yucatan, where thriving and advanced civilizations failed and disappeared, it is probable they failed because the men did not get beyond this primitive step, and there simply was not enough food after the ground became exhausted and the forests were gone. The same thing was true of the tobacco growers of colonial Virginia, and it is still true today in some parts of the U.S.

At some relatively late stage, when the great river civilizations developed along the Euphrates and the Nile, men learned to fertilize the ground. All the methods were partial and imperfect, and were only successful in such valleys because annual inundations by the river constantly deposited new silt washed down from the uncultivated areas up river. The same sequence occurred in China. Men eventually learned the value of cover crops, of composting, and of crop rotation, and apparently they learned these things before the dawn of written history.

Yet, strange as it may seem, all the farmers of all the centuries between then and now, up to the most recent decades of the long history of human civilizations, did not learn anything new or original beyond these items of ancient lore. No one ever used the knowledge — because no one ever acquired the knowledge — that there was a fundamental relation between the constitution of the soil and the ability of the soil to grow good plants and good food, until the modern science of chemistry was extended into the field of agronomics.

It is as obvious as anything can well be that since there is an exact and complete correspondence between plants and the soils in which they grow, good plants and good food values cannot be produced on poor soils. The farmer is completely aware that some soils will produce sixty or more bushels of wheat to the acre, while other soils will only produce ten, and yet other soils will not produce any. He calls these soils good and bad, and what he says is obvious and true; but until recently it was not clearly known that, grain by grain, the ten bushels of wheat produced on poor soil are inferior as food to the sixty bushels produced on the good land.

Since the beginning of this century scientists have increasingly recognized these differences, and have learned that by adding nutrients to the soil we are also adding to the food values of plants grown on those soils. Much of this awakened interest was due to the growing awareness that the soil is a chemical factory producing food — that the growth of plants is not miraculous and incomprehensible, but a scientifically logical result of conditions which can be analyzed.

It came to be recognized that the new science of ecology, the dynamic relationship of all the elements of a given environment, whether one field or the whole of a continent, was particularly applicable to agriculture —and that soil condition, bacterial population, climate, water supply, and types of plants are all parts of a complex, varying in quite definite ways with changes in the basic conditions.

Prior to 1900, only a few articles on soil care were published in the agricultural books and magazines. Today, however, volumes of information are available discussing the relationship of plants to the quality and composition of the soils in which they are grown, and regarding their relative values as foods because of this relationship.

Research scientists in the fields of agronomy, animal husbandry, botany, chemistry, horticulture, and microbiology have all contributed to the study of soil properties, and the results of their investigations have enabled us to formulate an overall pattern of what constitutes a good soil structure and composition. The researchers have also demonstrated that all food plants which grow are not necessarily good food, and that the good food plant can only be good if the conditions which promote its best growth are all completely satisfied. A plant which grows under conditions which are not the best will not have the expected food value, a fact just as simple as the fact that you cannot fill a ten-quart pail with eight quarts of water. Further, the use of such substandard foods will produce conditions of dietary deficiency in the user. Strangely enough, however, this understanding has been easily reached and generally accepted as it applies to farm animals, without equal perception of the fact that it also applies to the human beings who live on the farm or eat the produce of the farm.

Plants grow in soil. Soil is a natural nutrient medium in which plants can germinate, take root, and grow. It can be naturally fertile and can remain fertile if the cycle of growth and decay is not disturbed — if the things which grow on the soil die on the soil and decay back into it, and nothing is removed. But if, as in agriculture, the material which grows is removed, then part of the fertility of the soil is taken away in the crops. If this is not restored (and it almost never is), the fertility of that soil will decline and it will become a progressively poorer medium for the desired crop. In addition, the crops which are produced will become progressively poorer as sustenance for man or any other animal form, volume for volume and weight for weight.

Modern practice, therefore, is a continuing study of the best means for returning all constituents to the soil as they are removed; and this study is extended to devise means for making marginal soils fully productive. Unfortunately, the availability of knowledge is no criterion of the extent to which it is applied, and it takes a very long time to induce the average grower to see the wisdom and the economic feasibility of using the best methods. It is true that it is practically impossible to put more into the soil than one can take out as return, but it is quite another thing to convince a man doing marginal farming that he should invest the necessary funds from his meager store to prove the point for himself.

There is probably nowhere a perfect soil. There are only better and poorer qualities of soils. When the soil chemists and agronomists undertook the systematic examination of soils they quickly recognized this fact. But just as definitely scientists have always recognized that nature operates in terms of the mean, the middle point, the average of conditions. The adjustment of natural forms is between the extremes to be met in the environment, and husbandmen long ago recognized that they could improve on nature and produce superior forms of domestic plants and animals by protecting them from extremes of the environment. Our domestic crop plants and our domestic animals are greatly superior for special purposes to any naturally-occurring forms, but they could not survive in a natural environment, subjected to its extremes and in competition with wild forms.

Agriculture, throughout its development, has been the setting up of a more or less artificial environment by man, which he uses and maintains, and modern agricultural science simply sets out to build and maintain an optimum environment in which to produce more nearly perfect forms of plants and animals. The scientist states, quite simply, that it is possible to do this. The first requirement is soil which within practical limits is perfect; and theoretically, it is possible to use any soil whatever as a base for a perfect soil. It may require either simple or very elaborate procedures, but it is possible.

The new science of hydroponics is a valuable tool in this effort. Tanks of solution, or of some inert material such as quartz sand wetted with solution, become the growing medium, and then under controlled conditions the requirement of plants for minerals, organic components, hormones, and vitamins can be determined very exactly. The next step is to determine how nearly a given soil of a region or area comes to meeting these requirements, and what steps will be necessary to bring the characteristics of the soil up to the condition which will satisfy all the requirements completely. This may be a relatively simple procedure, or it may require such elaborate procedures that it is not feasible for economic reasons — but it is always possible.

Actual farming, as it is done by farmers of every type, varies from the ground-grubbing of the primitive sharecropper to the scientific methods and procedures used on fine fields of well-improved lands, but it nearly always falls short of the achievable possibilities. The combined efforts of government agencies, agricultural colleges, and individual scientists are constantly directed towards educational efforts to persuade the farmers as a class to use improved methods, with varying degrees of success.

The economic pressures of the world's constantly burgeoning population will eventually force mankind to make the optimum use of the land, but meanwhile, land by the millions of acres is being degraded in use each year, and the longer an approach to proper use of the land is delayed, the longer will be the road back when mankind awakens to the terrible urgency of the problem.

The Secret of Normal Health and Well-Being

The following presentation was written by C.F. Rehnborg in approximately 1944, and later formed the basic outline used in a booklet that the early Distributors of Nutrilite Food Supplement could give to prospective customers to read. It is included in this book to illustrate his universalist approach to man's relationship to the earth, and to the entire cosmos — an integrated oneness that brings all living things together, in a wonderfully simple yet complex explanation.

It is an open secret — this information is available to everyone, everywhere. As you read this booklet you will see that what is said is logical and reasonable. Much of it you will recall as something you have heard before, or read somewhere in a book or magazine. But perhaps you have never before tied it all together and seen that it applies to you and me — not to some other people in some other places.

If everyone, everywhere, clearly understood and applied the principles set forth to their own living, many of the health problems or conditions we accept as inevitable would probably cease to exist.

Do you think it is inevitable that human beings are subject to health conditions that lessen their full enjoyment of life, or lessen their energies and strength? Do you believe that people have the responsibility to live in such a way as to insure their own normal health and well-being? We all know, instinctively and positively, that it is NORMAL to be well and vigorous, and abnormal to be anything less than that. Then, let us investigate what is involved in this.

The Origin of Man

Whenever a chemist or biologist sets out to discuss the subject we are going to discuss — the relationship of men to the earth on which they live — he is aware that to many people there seems to be a conflict between science and what to them are cherished and honored beliefs. Usually the scientists do not mention this fact, but they show it either by pussyfooting in what they say, or by being very positive and firm in the way they state the case of man's origin.

Therefore, let us at once face the fact that scientists do not accept the account of man's origin given in Genesis as a verbatim account of events. They would say that the account given is correct in principle but not scientific. The earth evolves from the void and first there is water and land, then the simplest forms of life, then more complex plants and animals, and finally man. Science agrees — it only does not agree that it happened in six days, or that it happened approximately six thousand years ago. Let us then merely accept the time element as an honest difference of opinion, and proceed with our discussion.

The Earth, The Sun, And The Universe

We live on a planet which revolves around the sun, and is one of a family of such planets which are satellites of the same sun. Our sun is a star. It is so near to us that it seems huge, and it is hot and life-sustaining, and intimate with us — but it is similar to the other stars which we see at night and, as suns or stars go, is rather small and unimportant — except to us. ·

The sun is a member of an enormous group of stars, numbering several hundred billion, which are called a galaxy. In our case, the galaxy is called the Milky Way. This galaxy is so huge that light traveling 186,000 miles per second requires about 200,000 years to traverse it from side to side, and about 60,000 years to travel across its thickest part. Out in space, beyond our galaxy, there are other galaxies. The nearest of these, in the constellation Andromeda, can be seen with the eye as a faint blob of light and is about a million light years distant. Most of the observed galaxies are so distant that they must be observed in a telescope by exposing a highly sensitive photographic plate for many consecutive nights. There are over a million of these known galaxies, some of them at distances of 500,000,000 light years, and the number we see is limited only by the size of the telescope we use to see them. The new telescope at Mount Palomar will see galaxies that no present telescope is large enough to reach.

A marvelous instrument called a spectroscope can take the light from the sun, or from any of the stars of our galaxy, or any of the galaxies scattered through space, and by passing it through a slit and then through a prism, can make an analysis of the materials of the source of the light, which is the star or galaxy. In turn, chemistry has identified for us the elements of the earth, and when these elements are made radiant in an arc, they can be analyzed in the same manner as the light from the sun and the stars.

Analysis and comparison of this type tells us this fundamental fact about the earth, the sun, and the universe: They are all composed of the same elements from the earth under our feet to the most distant observable galaxy of stars — THE UNIVERSE IS ALL OF ONE PIECE.

Furthermore, when the same analysis is made of living things, they also are found to be composed of the same elements. There is nothing in a mouse or a plant or a bacterium which is not also in your body. There is nothing in any living thing which is not also in the earth; and nothing in the earth which is not also in all living things.

We all show that we know this in a general way when we accept the fact that our bodies are composed of the foods we have eaten. But the correspondence is even more exact and complete. We, and the earth, sun, stars, and galaxies, are parts of one great whole. We are not merely on the earth, we are of the earth — parts of the earth, intimately related and tied to it — and parts of the whole universe.

The Origin of Life

The simple, plain fact concerning the origin of life on the earth is that science does not know anything about it. The Bible says that God breathed the breath of life into the dust of the earth, and there has never been a clearer or better explanation. Science has to beg the question, by saying that life probably is innate in the universe; that wherever life can be, life is.

Evolution

The question of the evolution of the various forms of living things is the most controversial of all — but not to the scientists. The scientists have assembled what is generally accepted as incontrovertible evidence that life on the earth started as the most simple of forms, and evolved by mutation and natural selection into more and more complex forms; and that the whole process consumed much more than a thousand million years.

Scientists also believe two other important things about life; one, that it has been a continuous process from its beginning until now, and second, that it is all interrelated. The first means that life has not started and then stopped and then started again, or made a fresh start for each special form of life represented, but has proceeded continuously from the beginning. The second means that every living thing on the earth is related to every other living thing, from bacterium to plant to man — not unrelated but all of one piece, as is the universe itself.

Adjustment to Environment

The principle of adjustment to environment sounds more difficult than the facts it represents will actually be found to be. It means, simply, that since all living things are made of the substances of the earth, these substances limit and determine the chemistry of the living things. If that doesn't sound simple, let's try again: the elements which comprise your body — the carbon, oxygen, hydrogen, nitrogen, and various mineral elements — were always used and are now used to build your body, because they are all that is available with which to build it. Since there is nothing other than the substances of the earth available anywhere for use, the nature of the earth determines the nature of your body.

Early in the evolution of living organisms there was a separation into the two great branches of life which we call animal and vegetable. Down near the source, among the simplest forms, it is difficult to draw a clear line between these two divisions. There are single-celled plants which have animal-like characteristics, and animals which have plant-like functions, but in higher levels it is easy to distinguish the difference, say, between a plant and a man. The basic cellular structure of both is the same, but the man moves and the plant does not, and the plant can organize the simple elemental substances of the earth into a living form, and the man cannot.

The result of this inability to make "organic" substances from "inorganic" elements — living substance from non-living — has been that from the beginning, animals have been dependent on plants. More accurately, animals, including man, are parasites on plants. Without the plants they cannot continue to exist, but the plants can exist without the animals. The life economy of the plants is complete and self-contained, while that of the animals is not. The animal, then, is made of the substances of the earth, but the plants must intervene to modify the simple elemental substances into compounds which the animal can use.

The result is that the chemistry of the life process of an animal is determined by the chemistry of a plant. What is made by the plant for its own life process is appropriated by the animal and used just as it is, either by eating the plant or by eating another animal which in turn has eaten plants.

The Life Process of a Plant

The fundamental routine of living is the same for all things. All living things are composed of cells, and each living thing reproduces itself in its descendants.

The plant starts as a cell, and is as complex in its final organization as the corresponding level of animal life, but it "eats" primary substances and, for the most part, those plants which serve as "foods" for animals and men organize all their substances in their leaves.

In the leaf of a plant, the carbon dioxide of the air and water from the ground, together with nitrogen fixed from the air by certain bacteria or by electrical discharges in storms, are "organized" by certain wavelengths of light from the sun in the presence of the chlorophyll of the leaf (which acts as a "catalytic" agent) into the sugars and starches, fats, and proteins which are the building units of living things. The details of this process, simple in outline, are enormously complicated in operation, and are still further complicated by the need for mineral elements, both as structural materials in some cells and for controlling the "osmotic pressures" of the fluids in the body of the plant (or man) which control the chain of chemical reactions of the life process.

When the plant has manufactured the various "organic" materials it uses, these are transported by the fluids from the leaf where they were made to the other parts of the plant, and the plant grows, matures, and produces its fruits. Its fruits, in turn, are the seeds of the next generation of that type of plant.

The ground in which the plant is rooted serves as an anchorage and as the source of the necessary water and traces of minerals which the plant will use, which are in solution in the ground water. The ground itself supplies only a tiny part of the bulk of the plant — much less than one percent — and the greater part of the plant is built of sunshine and water and carbon dioxide.

In its own life process, the plant builds and uses all the components of what we call food — carbohydrates, fats, proteins, vitamins and minerals. It builds these for its own life process, not for ours. This is a fact of the highest importance. It is the absolute basis of any real understanding of our relation to the plants and to the earth. The plant does not make for us the organic substances of which it is composed, and which it uses to grow and continue living, and to perpetuate itself. It makes them for itself, and we merely appropriate what is in the plant, or root, or fruit, or seed, at the moment when we eat it.

The Materials of Our Bodies

These, then, are the materials for our bodies — the only possible materials for our bodies. Ever since there has been life, the plants have made certain substances for themselves from the simple elements and inorganic compounds that are available in the earth, and its atmosphere and water. Then the animals have appropriated these substances from the plants and have used them to build their own bodies.

Since these are the only possible materials with which to build such animal bodies, the character of the materials available has determined the chemical character of the bodies built from them. This point has to be stressed again and again — and again — because it is fundamental and final. We are chemically as we are now because the plants have set the pattern, and the plants are what they are because the nature of the materials available in the earth have determined their structure. All the universe is indissolubly tied together — galaxies and stars and planets and living things are all parts of one great pattern, and composed of the same materials.

The Ascent of Man

All the grand-scale geological history of the earth — written in terms of millions of years — is read from the record of the rocks, where the fossils of earlier forms have left their traces. This record is consecutive and continuous over the whole period recorded, and proceeds in an unbroken evolution from the simple to the more and more complex forms of living things.

Man appears very late in this record, and in the same manner as all other life forms, shows progression in development. The first records are of sub-human forms, and then successively of more and more "human" forms, culminating in man as we know him now. The living forms of the present day are not necessarily the highest possible point of organic development, but man has taken "dominion over the earth" and will continuously interfere with natural evolution.

Scientists report that the record of man goes back apparently for several millions of years, and the forebears of man's forebears will, when all the record is clear, trace a sequence back to the beginnings of life. In all this sequence, there has been the continuous relationship between food and life chemistry, between animal and plant, between plant and the earth, and man has always been made, essentially, of the leaves of plants.

Civilization

Finally, and recently in terms of geological time but a very long time ago in terms of man's written history, men stopped living in a completely primitive manner and began to develop cultures and civilizations. The anthropologists tell us that this development was associated with the development of man himself — that as he changed his posture he changed his physical form, until his more erect carriage permitted the development of a better brain-case and a better brain. The better brain in turn permitted the growth of language, the development of social habits, comprehension of abstract ideas, and "civilization" as we know it now.

In the process, men learned cooperative activities. The primary basis for a social group is mutual protection, the producing and husbanding of food, and the division of labor. Men learned these activities in time. Actually they adopted them, because such behavior runs all through the organization of animal life. Wild grazing animals know the use of a group for mutual protection. Ants use all three principles in the organization of the ant-hill. But man developed them logically.

Along the river valleys he began to cultivate foods and developed his first "civilizations." This made it possible for larger and larger groups of men to live in the same areas of land. Where free-ranging forebears of man may never have numbered more than a few tens of thousands over the whole of the earth, the same areas now support civilizations of over two billions of men.

The Foods of Human Beings

Primitive human beings eat chiefly meat, when available, and only incidentally eat fruits, roots, seeds, or leaves of plants. Civilized human beings select and develop plants which produce seeds such as rice, wheat, millet, and barley, and these seeds become the "staff of life" and the basic food of the civilization. They are supplemented by other selected plants which produce fruits, roots, and others of which the leaves are eaten; and civilized men feed plants to selected types of animals and then eat these animals. Men in groups also learn to store, cook, and process foods.

In effect, men in a "civilization" stop living in a natural environment, and instead build up a new selected environment which may or may not correspond to the natural environment. Please note this with close attention and remember it, because it is a fact of the highest importance — vital to the whole consideration of why men have sometimes developed nutritional deficiencies. The environment to which man must adjust himself has been changed, but not his chemical requirements — and the result is maladjustment.

The Cultivation of Foods

When primitive men were free-roving, they ate what they could find. They foraged for the next supply of food, eating if they found it and going hungry if they did not. The human body — and in fact all animal bodies —show this adjustment to a hard necessity. If we get no food we can live for a considerable period on our stored supplies, and if we eat too much our bodies store it and we grow fat. On the other hand, air, which is always and everywhere normally available, cannot be stored and must be available continuously; while water, which is generally but not always instantly available, we can do without for a limited period of time.

The first natural concern of groups was to avoid the necessity for foraging for foods. The first thing developed in group living was a method — any method — for storing foods. Men selected foods which could be stored as they were — notably the grains — and they learned to salt and dry and pickle other foods. Dried meats and grains are the commonest types of foods stored by primitive groups.

This selection of foods for specific qualities, mainly storage convenience and taste appeal, and not, except as guided by instinct, for the foods of highest nutritional value, greatly changed the variety of substances eaten. Primitive men eat whatever does not poison them, learning the list of poisonous substances by trial and then passing the knowledge on. Civilized men eat a restricted list of specially selected foods, and the list differs with each different section of the earth's surface.

The Cooking of Foods

There is no existing group of people, however primitive, which does not know how to cook foods. Probably this knowledge is as old as the knowledge of fire, and knowledge of the use of fire is probably as old as the history of the human race. The most ancient traces of humans and sub-humans include the remnants of their campfires and the cracked bones of the game they roasted and ate there.

But as civilization developed, men also learned to cook with water. They parched grain as they had roasted meat, and ground it up and baked it in cakes, but eventually they learned to cook these and other foods in water.

At first the cooking pot was probably a gourd. Water and food were put into the gourd, then hot stones were dropped in the water to heat it and cook the food, and the food was fished out and eaten. Lastly, the water and the cooking stones were thrown away. Later, when metal pots were devised, the food still was fished out and the water thrown away. The habit has persisted until now because men are very conservative creatures and only reluctantly give up any custom. It is quite probable that no group has ever made a habit of drinking the cooking water, although in the last few thousand years men invented soup. We know now that this discarding of the cooking water is an almost fatal error, and that much of the value of our cooked foods has always been thrown away.

The Processing of Foods

Processing foods is a relatively new development. Salting, pickling, and drying — particularly drying — of foods are old tricks in terms of man's written history, but processing foods in the modern sense is a development chiefly of the last few centuries, and especially of the last hundred years.

We still salt and pickle and dry foods — "it has always been done." But we also refine molasses, which is a "natural" food, into white sugar, which is not. We remove the hulls and middlings and germ from wheat and produce white flour. These two items — sugar and flour — comprise 20 to 30 percent of our total diet. We blanch and dye foods, add preservatives to them, store enormous quantities of our foods in tin and glass (after making it "pretty" by peeling it and soaking it in acids or alkalies and coloring it), remove the peels or outer leaves from fresh foods in our kitchens — and we still throw away the cooking water.

Everything we do with foods is designed, in effect, not to increase but to decrease their nutritional value.

The Transportation of Foods

Our civilization has become so complex that practically none of us grow the fresh foods we will eat. We buy aged meat from the store, calling it better to make a virtue of necessity. We buy much of it from the grocer in tins and cans, still good but not as good as when it was fresh. The fresh foods we do use are bought from the corner grocer, who bought from the jobber, who bought from the handler, who bought from the farmer, who shipped the food from a point a few miles or a few thousand miles away a few days or weeks ago. And from the moment the food was gathered from the place where it grew, it has progressively deteriorated through oxidation and the action of bacteria.

To offset this slow spoilage, we use refrigerated trucks and cars, and at home we store the foods in a refrigerator. These are great conveniences and surely notable improvements over unprotected transportation of foodstuffs, but still, in essence, they are merely conscious attempts to delay the progress of deterioration and decay long enough for us to eat the food before it has spoiled utterly.

The Fertile Land

Yet all these wrongful things we do to foods are enumerated with the implicit assumption that they would be good foods if we could get them quite fresh, and eat them fresh after cooking them scientifically, without altering or processing them except to the minimum extent necessary, such as washing sand from the potatoes. But this assumption is not true, because the food is not always "good" even when it starts on its journey towards us.

Some foods have been grown in land which has been depleted year after year of the important trace elements which were removed with the crops and not scientifically replaced. Examples are iodine, selenium and zinc.

From ancient times men have known enough to return organic mineral materials to our cultivated fields — the chaff from the threshing, manure from our domestic animals, cover crops plowed back under. In certain cultures, even sacrificial animals were killed and buried in the newly-plowed fields, in the spring.

But we have never learned, although we are now beginning to learn, to fertilize the fields we use in a scientific manner. It is still chiefly knowledge in the government agencies and agricultural schools — not in the fields — that before we grow crops we should make sure the land contains all that the plants will require; and we should put back into the ground all — every quantity of every element — that our crops take out.

So What?

Let's suppose that you say now, "What has this to do with ME?"

It has everything to do with you. YOU depend on the quality of the foods offered to you to buy. YOU eat a selection of foods which is a matter of habit, and has nothing to do with the problem of whether they are the BEST AVAILABLE food materials. YOU join in the habit of processing and preserving foods. YOU cook your foods unscientifically. YOU never consider that the uncomfortable or dangerous things that may happen could be your own responsibility.

We live in an infinite universe of infinite supply. When men strike for more pay, the often desperate conditions against which they strike are no fault of the universe, but usually of a human — a purely human — institution. When you are in less than optimum health, it is no fault of the universe — germs, viruses and accidents notwithstanding. Your body was designed to function perfectly and you were meant to be well. If you are not, it is your fault and my fault — the fault of the human race and its habits, and not of the earth.

The Solutions

There are actually two solutions to the dietary problems of those of us who have deficient diets.

One solution depends on cooperation from all of us — a solution which will be slow to accomplish.

The other depends only on ourselves.

The first solution is to change our basic food habits: to fertilize the ground in which our foods are grown with all the skill of our scientific knowledge, to select and grow the foods which have the highest nutritional value, to shorten the interval between the gathering and eating of such foods, to avoid processing completely, to use scientific methods of preservation and cooking rather than chemicals, to eat natural foods in their natural form so far as possible, to eat a very wide variety of foods — and to feed with equal scientific precision the animals which we propose to use for meat. You can figure out for yourself how long that will take, and whether you can afford to wait for it to be done.

It will be done eventually — that is as certain as tomorrow's sunrise — but it will be a slow process of education and changes in procedures over many years.

The other solution, which depends on yourself alone, is to get the things which your present civilized diet may not give you, and add them to that diet, so that your body which is organized to function in a natural environment, will, wherever you are, secure all the factors of a natural environment which are required for an adequate diet.

Diet Deficiencies

To the extent that they are known, our product attempts to supply these required factors in the diet. The knowledge on which the product depends is new. It depended in turn on the development of the modern sciences, biology and chemistry particularly, and in turn on the chemistry of living things, called biochemistry.

It is certain knowledge that foods are not merely substances which please your palate and fill your stomach, but organic fuels for a chemical machine which you call your body.

It is certain knowledge that these true foods are composed of classified types of organic and inorganic substances called carbohydrates, fats, proteins, minerals and vitamins, water, and oxygen — ALL of which are necessary in various but specific quantities for normal functioning of the body's chemical machine. Some of these required substances are not always present in our ordinary civilized diets, in the quantities which meet the body's needs.

It is certain knowledge that the various things which civilized people do to foods do not substantially harm the things which we can see — the bulk of the food, the carbohydrates, proteins, and fats — so that men have been slow, first to suspect and then finally to learn precisely, that certain deficiencies could be due to things NOT eaten in the needed amounts. They saw the food. It was still there after the processing, drying, pickling, or cooking. They could not at once suspect that parts of the food too small to see, but equally as vital as the part they could see, were being partially removed or destroyed by the methods used on the foods, and that the ailments from which they suffered as a consequence were sure and certain results.

It is certain knowledge that the things which we do not get, due to ignorance or carelessness about our diets, can cause deficiencies.

The Distributor

The Distributor who hands you this booklet has an answer to offer. He knows that the principle of the product is right, and believes you will recognize its rightness. He will answer all the questions he is able to answer, but he may not answer all your questions because no one yet knows all the answers about the relationship between nutrients and deficiencies.

Among other things, your distributor will tell you that there is no known means of deciding whether a particular condition or discomfort is due to a deficiency. You cannot be certain that this product will help you. What he can tell you with certainty is that if you eat this product as suggested, you can be assured of an adequate intake of the vitamins and minerals now known to be essential in human nutrition.

The Nature of Nutrition: A Universal Concept

The following talk was given before a large group of Nutrilite Distributors at a meeting in New York, N.Y., on June 7, 1958, by C.F. Rehnborg. It is an interesting discourse on his view of nutrition as related, not just to man alone, but to the earth itself and in fact, to the whole of the great universe and its immutable laws.

I intend, in more than one talk with distributors, to discuss the meaning of what we, as a functional group, are doing. This includes background. If at first you think you are listening to a lecture on astronomy, have patience. There is a clear connection, although this time the background picture is very wide.

We call our product Nutrilite Food Supplement. Since food means the substances used in the nutrition of a living organism, we are also saying that Nutrilite is an additive or supplement in nutrition. But "nutrition" itself is a word which we use casually, as if we all knew exactly what it means. Like all words we use in a general sense, however, the word "nutrition" has meanings we do not commonly examine in detail. Yet for us it is a word which deserves very careful examination indeed. Let us give it such an examination.

We live in a universe. Our earth, on which we live, and on which the human race probably will always live so long as it endures, is one of the satellites of a star which we call the sun. The work of the cosmologists (who are the astronomers specializing in analysis of the character of the universe as an orderly system) leads them to believe that a very high number of the stars or suns in the universe may have satellites; and that, if the conditions for the maintenance of life are favorable on a satellite, life will occur.

Our sun apparently has only one planet capable of maintaining life in the exact terms which apply to us. One of the other planets, Mars, seems to show evidence that perhaps it sustains plant life of a low order, at least; and another of the planets, Venus, may be at the evolutionary stage of development at which the earth stood a billion or more years ago. None of the other satellites of our sun could sustain life as we know it. It is proper, also, to assume that in any case only a few stars or suns have planets. But there are many suns.

Our own sun is a member of a galaxy. Its nearest neighbor in space in its own galaxy is approximately 25 trillion miles away; or, measured in light years, 4-1/3 light years distant from us. This means quanta of light traveling 186,000 miles a second (as compared to Sputnik's speed of five miles a second), second after second, or over 11,000,000 miles a minute, minute by minute and hour by hour for 1500 days. And this is the *nearest* of the other suns.

Our galaxy is something like 200,000 light years in diameter, arranged in a great disc with trailing arms, which at the center is of the order of 60,000 light years in diameter. In this volume of space, even at distances from star to star averaging the four-plus light years which separate us from our nearest neighboring star, there are something like 100 billion stars and an equal volume of the dust and gas from which the suns were formed.

Extended through space in all directions about us, to at least the distance of about two billion light years, or the range to which the great telescope on Mount Palomar can reach, there are billions of other galaxies, each containing approximately as many stars, or suns, as does our galaxy. In all these swarming myriads of suns, astronomers are inclined to believe that some proportion have planets capable of supporting life. They disagree only on the proportion this represents. But if we considered that only one star in a million was accompanied by a planet in most respects similar to the planet Earth, in the universe there would still be countless billions of planets constituted as the earth is constituted, capable of sustaining life, and therefore inferentially the home of living things of some sort.

In all these worlds of life the problems of animal nutrition would be essentially the same as they are on the earth. This conclusion follows because of the very nature of the universe itself. There is not any endless variety in the constitution of the stars and of the planets which might revolve around them. Instead, the universe is all of one piece. Every star in the billions of stars in our galaxy, and in the billions of stars in the yet other billions of galaxies which surround us, is made of exactly the same materials: the 92 elements of the periodic table, plus some occurrence of the higher orders of elements such as those which scientists have recreated on the earth in their laboratories to constitute the atomic fission and fusion bombs, and the promise of boundless energy for the future.

The combinations, or compounds, of these 92 elements of the periodic table tend to follow patterns. All the life there is on the earth, for example, is built around the carbon atom and the capacity of the carbon atom to form molecular compounds, and with these to form molecular systems which can continue themselves as living entities by the intake of energy-bearing materials and the oxidation of these materials to produce the energy required in living. It is probable these same combinations of chemical elements, and of their inherent or "natural" patterns of organization, would always produce living things which we could recognize as following the same chemical pattern as we ourselves follow in the organization of our human bodies.

In accepting this fact, we should let ourselves be convinced that there is nothing supernatural or "unnatural" in the whole of the universe. The universe is a completely organized and unified system, consistent and interrelated in all its parts, and constituted throughout of the same materials, with the same characteristics as these materials have here on the earth on which we live. In the same way, wherever we found life it would represent a type of chemical organization already familiar to us. This would mean, not that we knew what "life" itself is, because this is a continuing mystery, but that we would recognize life anywhere as being dynamic entities of chemical organization, separated from the environment but in flux and in balance with it. Each entity would be capable of ingesting supplies and of using these supplies in the function of living and of reproducing itself — and the living system has to reproduce itself or it does not even continue to exist as the continuing chain of entities which we call life.

This system of using a flow of ingested supplies, and of effecting duplication or reproduction of the form which lives, are included in the word "nutrition." The problems of nutrition would be the same wherever we found them, and would be the key to the continuation of life itself. Further, since the materials of which the universe is constituted are the same in all parts of the universe, and since these materials or elements tend to be combined in a limited range of patterns, the constitution of living forms, whatever their variety in form, would be essentially the same everywhere, because of the similarities impelled by the "alikeness" everywhere of the materials from which life could be constituted. The diversity in the forms of life we observe on our earth, for example, is a diversity of complex patterns, not a diversity of materials.

In the stars, on and in the planets, and in life, there are always and *only* the elements of the periodic table; and only the particular combinations or compounds into which these can enter. This means, always, that living things are made of the same elements as the earth and the stars. No element is found in a living thing which is not also found in the earth and in the stars.

Simply, living things are made of the materials of the universe, and not ever of anything else. This means, also, that the materials to be ingested or taken into the living system will be always elements and compounds from the materials of the earth, and *nothing* else. The ancient poets epitomized this truth when they said that man was dust and returned to dust. He cannot be made of anything else but the substances of the earth, and he cannot disintegrate into anything but these same substances.

What we call life is the use of the energy from our sun, or star, built into organic molecules which require the energy of the sun for their formation and in the process of living. This process is built around the use of carbon dioxide and water, plus the energy of the sun, and degrades again into carbon dioxide and water as we use the energy from the sun, whether in the motion of the body and its resulting use of heat, which are part of the living process, or in the construction of our living bodies and the disintegration of our bodies after we have ceased to live. There undoubtedly is more to a man and to his mind than the chemical exchanges of the living process. We cannot, for example, "explain" individual awareness of self or moral values as a chemical process. Yet all of the tangible material facts of the living process are explainable as chemical exchanges between atoms of elemental substances, and all of this process is integrated completely with the matter and energy of the universe in which the life occurs.

Now, and only now, do we come to the point at which we can consider the chemical organization which we call life, and its method of sustaining and reproducing itself which we call nutrition. On the earth, life has differentiated into the entities which we call plants and the entities which we call animal. Further, on the earth only the plants have the capacity to use elemental atoms and inorganic compounds to build the *organic* compounds containing carbon which are the basis of our life process. Man does not, nor does any other earthly animal, have the capacity to perform this first and vital step.

In the strictest sense, then, all animal forms are parasitic on the vegetable forms, whether on the land or in the sea. The only exception is that we can use water and simple inorganic salts, one as the carrier, and the others as additives to the chemistry of the life process. Animals, then, are constituted of, and maintain themselves with, organic compounds constructed in plants, plus air and water and a few inorganic salts entering into structure and into cellular functions. All animals, including man, must secure these organic substances from plants, or from animals which have eaten plants.

Now let us look more closely at the chemical machine which is the body in which each of us lives.

You are to see your human body as a tremendous community of some tens of trillions of cells, or thousands of times as many cells as there are human beings on the earth. These cells are themselves individuals, or entities. We call the collection of about two and a half billion human beings on the earth the human community — the world population — or, in smaller groupings, parts of it are called France, or Great Britain, or the United States, personified as Uncle Sam, and John Bull, and Marianne. The enormously greater number of cells which constitute the body of an individual human being we call a personality — John Robinson or Henry Smith or whatever — but, in the final analysis, each individual human being is a cell or member of a world community, and his body is in turn a community of separate cells.

Each of these cells in the body which is the human entity, in the same manner as each of the persons in a human community, lives as an entity, and as a function of living, performs in addition a service to the community. Just as in a human community an individual is both Henry Smith and a shoemaker, or doctor, or grocery salesman, so in the body's community of cells each individual cell both lives as an individual, and also performs a special service for the body community. All of the body's cells are basically alike, but some function as brain cells, or muscle cells, or bone cells, or fat cells, or even as the red and the white corpuscles of the blood stream.

A doctor, in checking on the health or physical condition of the whole community of body cells, gives a test known as a metabolic test, or determination of the rate of energy requirement for the whole community of cells in the body. When this test is made, the average result shows that a total of about 1200 calories of food per day is needed merely for the business of continuing to live as an individual. An additional allowance of calories, ranging from about 400 calories for a sedentary worker to 4000 calories, or even more, for a man doing heavy physical labor, is required to do the work of the whole community of cells — the human individual — over and above the amount required merely to stay alive. This gives us a picture, in the case of the sedentary worker, of 75 percent of the total energy requirement devoted to the business of keeping the cells of the body alive, and 25 percent devoted to the specialized community activities of these same cells.

Further, just as the world community of human individuals requires a continuous supply of the necessary quantities of the whole required range of food substances merely to stay alive, and an additional quantity with which to do the work of the community, so does the personal community represented by each human body and its trillions of cells. In both cases, the community requires the food, but cannot itself synthesize or manufacture it. It must be secured from outside, from plants or from other animals, and it must be secured in full variety of all the factors required in nutrition, or some disorder or malfunction, representing a level lower than the level of normal health and full function, may result. If the individual cell or human being does not receive a supply greater than its basic requirement, it can do no community work. If it receives less than its basic requirement, then over a shorter or a longer period of time it ceases to live.

The range of these necessary foods, each factor of which is necessary to the continued existence of the organism, is a very large range. It includes various types of sugars and starches, all of which are converted in the body for utilization as simple invert sugars; a range of fats and oils, all of which are broken down in the body to various fatty acids and glycerol and recombined as human fat; a variety of proteins, all comprised of various proportions of some 23 nutritionally-significant amino acids, which are separated in the digestive system and recombined as human protein; inorganic mineral salts over a range nearly as wide as the range of the periodic table; and a great number of complex organic substances initially derived from plant substances, and including the vitamins, which serve as component parts of the catalysts triggering the chemical processes which together constitute the process of life.

Now we have man in his setting. To begin with, man is a physical entity in the universe and himself a part of the universe. He is not a "visitor." He fits where he is. Next, the basis of all our science or "knowing" of the universe is an assumption called "the law of the conservation of matter and energy." This law states that the total of matter and energy, which have an equivalence to one another, remains forever the same in the universe, and that nothing can be subtracted from the universe or added to the universe. As nearly as any assumption can be proved, this assumption is proved. The observed natural "laws" of the universe conform to it. Further, all these natural laws of the universe apply to the whole of the universe and to every atom in the universe. They all apply completely to you where you stand. Neither you nor anyone else can separate you from the universe nor hold you free from any law of the universe, for it is a universe of law and reason, integrated and interrelated in every part, and you yourself are a part of this universe. You can obey or not obey the laws of the universe, but you cannot break them. If you conform, you are in adjustment. If you attempt to disobey, the *law* is not broken. The law breaks *you.*

But you will note that if the law breaks you, you will have been the cause of its happening. The laws are inexorable, but they are beneficent, and they can be trusted. This is their beauty, and the glory of man's identity with them. All that is yourself was in the universe before you were a conscious being. All that you are will be in the universe when others think that you are gone, even the things that we call spiritual, because any words making the universe both natural and supernatural are man-made and arbitrary. All that is in the universe is forever an integrated part of the universe.

Now you, as an entity in the universe, are integrated with the universe, and your conformity to the laws of the universe is automatic and instinctive unless by intent, or by inattention, or by accident, you set yourself counter to those laws. Your body, as a physical entity integrated with the universe and existing in the web of its laws, represents an implementation of those laws, through the process we call evolution. Evolution produced more and more complex forms of animal life, culminating, so far as the earth is concerned, in the highly complex mechanism called man, with the capacity for thought concerning abstractions, and gifted with what is called a "soul." This body obeys natural law as exactly and as inevitably as water boils when heated to 212 degrees Fahrenheit at an atmospheric or gas pressure of about 15 pounds to the square inch.

The whole of this physical attunement to the laws of the universe is embraced in what we call nutrition. Nutrition is the process by which the laws of the universe operate to construct your body, to maintain it, to duplicate it, and to renew it, and the materials so used during the course of your life amount in bulk and mass to many times the bulk of your physical body at any given moment. It is the variety and quantity of the various necessary materials, entering into the nutritional aspect of their use, which determines whether this physical community of cells called yourself has been well or badly adjusted to the terms of the life process. Because our knowledge of the physical factors and the natural laws involved has become so much greater than it was earlier in man's history, you have now more than ever before the choice of determining whether the physical mechanisms of your body have been supplied with the necessary factors in its nutrition, or have not.

Perhaps we can formulate a definition of nutrition. Let us say nutrition is the process by which the living organism receives and uses all of the supplies required for its growth, maintenance, and reproduction.

Man cannot create these supplies in the form in which he uses them. He must receive them from what he breathes, and drinks, and eats. Without air, or water, or food, he ceases to live. Furthermore, "food" is not a specific single substance. It is a complex of many separate organic substances, and a few inorganic substances in small quantity, each of which is essential and cannot be substituted for another, and all of which man must receive in quantities which are great enough to supply his requirements.

Much has been learned as to what, exactly, these requirements are. Until the most recent century, it was assumed as a self-evident fact that anything which had a satisfactory taste, and satisfied the feeling of hunger, and did not disagree with one, could be considered as food, and that there was a wide element of choice as to what could be used habitually as food. Simply, there was no reasoning about food as a problem. Now we know better.

Now it is understood that food represents the requirements of the body for its growth, health, and maintenance, and that, next to lack of food itself, lack of any of the specific constituents of food is the most serious problem with respect to food as a source of necessary supply. It is known that food is comprised of several basic groups of organic materials: proteins, carbohydrates, fats, vitamins and vitamin-like substances, and various inorganic minerals. It is known further that these organic substances have their origins in plant substances; that they constitute a great variety of substances; and that, of course, even the knowledge concerning them is still limited. It is known that all the factors of foods must be received, preferably as they occur in nature, in quantities which are adequate for the requirement of the physical organism, and that they cannot be substituted for one another. Further, it is known that *all* the required substances, and not merely some of them, must be ingested in quantities which are adequate to the need, or the intricate mechanism of the body will suffer malfunction of various degrees of severity.

Almost none of the standard diets eaten by various regional groups of human beings is scientifically devised to supply the required and balanced amounts of the necessary substances. Instead, most human diets are the result of ages-long patterns of habit. Some were instinctively right, but none of them was ever planned. Regional and national diets grew into being as a result of the kinds and varieties of food substances available locally for use. In the main, since man is omnivorous, and since all of the living things on the earth, plant and animal, which could serve as foods, obey the same chemical laws of constitution, and are all constituted of the same basic materials supplied by the earth, there has always been in all areas of the earth, a general correspondence between the things which were required and the things which could be secured from the habitual diet.

But in time the habitual diet became even more restricted by preferences for certain foods, or taboos, or regional prejudices which classified some foods as undesirable. Finally, as mankind in larger groups has become civilized, he has chosen certain foods as preferable because of convenience in handling and storage. He has learned various methods of processing foods. For economic reasons he has tended to prefer those foods which could be most reasonably and economically produced, and which could best be stored. In this way, it has come about that many diets have become severely restricted, and the results of the restrictions have been disregarded because the effects of the changes and restrictions of the diet were general to the whole area occupied by the particular group, and therefore were the usual thing, and so were unremarkable to the group.

New scientific knowledge takes a very long time to percolate down through all the levels of any human group, or down through the whole of the human population of the earth. Habit is much stronger in its daily effect than is new knowledge. People and governments have only begun to comprehend that the question of *quality* of the food supply is the one to which the world of men must give constant and unremitting attention and concerning which there must be positive and constructive and consistent action. Our group is a group of missionaries of this particular idea.

Now, the picture I have wanted to give you is of the entity or organism which is a human being, existing, not merely at a specific location on the earth's surface, but in and as a part of, the whole of the greater world which is the universe. The picture is of a universe which is a system of law, wholly integrated as one great unit of unknown and incomprehensible size. This size is incomprehensible to us, only, as limited human beings, but the immensity of the universe is not irrational, since it is the sum of its ordered parts and an expression of its Cause. We can disregard this size, but only if we remember it is there; and that the laws of life, like all other natural laws, are universal and cannot be anything else; and that all human beings, as inseparable parts of the universe, are meshed into these laws by the nature of their bodies as chemical machines.

In this ordered and consistent universe, man exists on one planet of one sun, subject to, and integrated with, all of the universal laws. He can decide whether he will be a Republican or a Democrat; or what particular job he will fill to earn his living; or whether he will buy a new house or car, or not; or if he will go to the beach next Sunday, or not; or what he will do about, or with, or for his neighbors, because these are matters of free will. He cannot, however, decide whether or not he will obey the natural laws of the universe concerning his nutrition, because these are beyond his control and are inescapable, and there are penalties for non-observance.

Freedom of arbitrary or capricious choice, with respect to the elements of diet, whether the choice is man's own, or is a choice due to the habits of the regional population, or of a social group, or of a family, is out of order. Diet *must* conform to the universal physical laws which control man's being, and enough is known to make this course of action feasible. Whether feasible or not, however, it is essential. If habit *cannot* produce the patterns of diet which satisfy the requirements of man's physical body, science *must*. It is the essence of science for someone to produce for the use of human beings a supplement which will to some degree compensate for the inadequacies of judgment which habit and inertia of certain human groups, with respect to their diet, allow to exist. One such product, the one we sell and the one we believe in, is Nutrilite Food Supplement. The more people we can tell about it, the better, because too many people to whom we tell our story have not as yet found the answers for themselves.

Food And The Life Processes

Written Approximately 1955

When you sit in your garden on a quiet afternoon, the calm is not really static. In every leaf of every plant there is tremendous activity, all below the level of our ordinary perceptions.

In the millions of cells of each leaf, a bewildering variety of chemical reactions are using the energy of light to transform carbon dioxide and water into organic compounds, to increase the structure of the plant. There is a ceaseless flow of materials within the plant, with perhaps as many individual events of construction and exchange and circulation as in a city the size of New York, as the plant makes its growth and develops its seeds — and quite incidentally gives us the pleasure of watching its growth and flowering.

When you decide to turn your hand and look at your palm, the action seems quite simple, but it is in fact most·complicated. The thought is made an order to the muscles. As an electrical impulse, it travels to the cerebellum, and there, in the instant it requires to bring about the movement, the cerebellum has sorted out the individual messages. Since a muscle fiber either contracts or does not (that is, gives its whole force or none), it is necessary for only a few fibers in each muscle to contract to build up the force necessary to turn over your hand.

The cerebellum in that instant has determined the thousands of individual fibers in the muscles of the neck and arm and hand which shall contract, and the fibers in opposing muscles which shall preserve the tonicity or tenseness of drag to be kept, so that the hand does not merely flop over or the head drop slackly as you look at your hand. And the cerebellum sends all these individual messages by individual fibers of the nerves to the corresponding muscle fibers, without error.

Moreover, in each tendril or fiber of the nerves transmitting these messages there are a myriad of nerve cells, and the messages must be relayed from cell to cell at the synapses where they are in contact with one another. At each synapse the exchange of the electrical impulse is effected by chemical reactions involving exchanges of phosphate radicals in enzyme chain reactions, perhaps a hundred thousand molecular reactions for each exchange.

The ingestion of nutrients has been an element of the life process since life began on the earth. Man, as a member of the animal kingdom and a part of the life processes of the earth, has eaten foods since first there were men. Although eating is as old as mankind itself, the Science of Nutrition is very new. The knowledge of the relationship between foods and the normal functioning of man's body as a chemical machine has only been coordinated within the last sixty to seventy years. The newest part of this science is the knowledge of the constituents of foods — the proteins, carbohydrates, fats, vitamins, and minerals — and their separate functions in the metabolism of the body. This most recent knowledge has all been developed within this century in which we live, and the value of this knowledge has only now begun to be properly realized.

The vitamins have only become well known within the past thirty years. Before that they were largely unknown, both to science and to the lay public. Vitamins are essential to life. They have always been essential to life, even when they were not known to exist. The saving fact for man, as for all life, is that they are normal components of foods, so that the instinctive act of eating things which were edible supplied some proportion of what was needed to all creatures.

But now that we are well informed concerning the various factors of foods, and innumerable experiments have been conducted to establish scientifically the proportions of the various factors necessary in full nutrition, we know also that throughout history there has rarely been any complete balance between what was required and what was obtained in the foods eaten. What we know as vitamin deficiencies, which means an inadequate supply of one or many vitamins, have produced deficiency diseases and subclinical disturbances of health over the whole of history in very large segments of the world's population. Although deficiency diseases as such are rare in the United States today, there are still some deficiencies and sub-clinical disturbances in civilized societies. However, because it is virtually impossible to change accepted eating habits, usage of supplemental additions of vitamins and minerals to the ordinary diet has been accepted by only a small percentage of the world's population.

In a completely primitive environment, such as may have existed from time to time in the early history of man, in an isolated location with no movement of people in or out of the area, the condition may have existed wherein foods were balanced to nutritional needs. The vegetation grew and then decayed back into the soil; the animals eating plants lived and died in the environment, returning to the earth the products of their metabolism and finally the bodies in which they had lived. The primitive men of the area ate plants and animals, and also, like the other animals, returned to the earth. In such an environment there was a continuing balance between the things eaten and the eaters, especially for the mankind of the area when they ate the flesh and fish and fowl and fruit to which they were adjusted.

But under conditions of civilization men grow a narrow selection of foods by agriculture, and eat a selected list of domesticated animals and fowl. In addition they cook and preserve foods — they do not even eat them as they are, but modify them in various ways for eating by washing, peeling, and discarding all but selected parts. They throw away the wash water and the cooking water. Foods are shipped into the area, and other foods are shipped out to other areas. Foods are stored for short or long periods. The wastes do not return to the soil, but are buried in cesspools or dumped into the sewers and swept away in rivers to the sea.

All these, while natural to a civilization and necessary because of the numbers of people involved, are an impoverishment of the immediate environment. Furthermore, the extremely important vitamins are the factors most readily sacrificed. Some vitamins which are soluble in water are discarded in wash and cooking water; some are destroyed by heat and oxidation in cooking and storing; the parts of foods richest in vitamins are frequently discarded; and the foods selected by a civilized group are not always the foods which best supply these factors.

As a result of these conditions, which apply to practically every civilized economy in the modern world, there is almost no area where the diet of all the people is completely adequate. Many of the people living in civilization eat diets which are to some degree deficient in some or many of the vitamins and minerals. A notable exception, perhaps, are the Hunzas who live as an isolated community in the Himalayan Mountains. There are few such communities. For many of us, the difference between the vitamins and minerals we get and what we should have is just possibly enough to produce subnormal health — for it is the belief of many nutritional experts that many of the vague malaises and degenerative illnesses suffered by civilized men are, in the final analysis, the results of improper dietary habits.

In a very large section of the world there are deficiencies of other kinds. For example, it has been reported that perhaps two-fifths of the world's population does not get sufficient protein in the diet. For all, undernourished nations and well-fed nations alike, there is the overall condition of partial lack of vitamins and minerals, unless steps have been taken to supplement the ordinary diet of the area.

In certain areas some of the existing deficiencies are being made up by governmental action. This takes the form, for example, of "fortifying" a staple food, such as putting back into white bread some part of the vitamins removed in milling the flour. But this is only a partial answer; partial both in the extent of the list of the vitamins so supplied, and partial because the quantities so restored are not great enough and are not an enforced part of any individual's diet. The true and complete answer is scientific supplementation.

It is important to make clear that vitamins and minerals are not drugs. They are natural and normal components of foods. They do not "cure" anything; but the individual who receives enough of them tends to function normally as a living being, and to be normal is by definition to tend to be free from any condition caused by lack of such nutrients.

This brings us to the Nutrilite Concentrate. It is a concentrate from plant and fruit materials that supplies many of the vitamins and minerals needed in human nutrition. Fundamentally, NUTRILITE Food Supplement is an attempt to improve the nutritional status of the human population by fortifying their diet with vitamins and minerals that may be lacking for any number of reasons.

There are something more than two billion people in the world. They did not suddenly appear from nowhere, fully equipped to function as individuals and independent of the earth on which they live, but instead are today's representatives of a chain of evolution that goes back to the beginning of life on the earth. No one witnessed the beginnings of life on the earth, but all the biological sciences unite in telling us that it began as simple, single-celled forms. Very early in this development according to the scientists, life differentiated into animal and vegetable form, of which the vegetable form probably preceded the animal form, and throughout the history of life since this first differentiation, animal life has been dependent on the vegetable kingdom. All living forms, plants and animals alike, are composed of extremely complex organic substances, and only the plants have the power to synthetize these complex organic substances from the simpler inorganic materials of the earth, the atmosphere, and water.

All these forms of life have remained interrelated and intricately adjusted to one another, and to the earth on which they all live. All of the substances of which living forms are composed are compounded of the materials supplied by the earth. There is nothing in any living form which cannot be found in the earth, and which did not originate in the earth.

This interrelationship and interdependence is called adjustment to the environment, and only those forms of life which are adjusted to the environment continue to live. Man is the highest form of animal life on the earth, but man is just as dependent on this adjustment to environment as is any other form of life. Man as an animal, like any other animal, eats food or ingests food and excretes waste to maintain the intricate chemical mechanism which is his body.

The sequence of living forms on the earth has been continuous since the beginnings of life on the earth. At some stage in this development, perhaps a billion years ago, half way in the long history of life on the earth, the vertebrate arose, and we belong to this phylum. Some special branch of the fishes, perhaps the lung fishes, gave rise to the amphibian living partly on land and partly in the water. These in turn gave rise to the reptiles, and the reptiles to the mammals and birds. One branch of the mammals, the anthropoids, gave rise to the monkeys and apes which live today, and somewhere along this line a side branch developed into sub-human men, and finally into men as we now know them. Scientists indicate there have been men on the earth approximately as we know them now for something of the order of a million years, so that if the whole sequence of life from the beginning has taken two billion or more years in its development, as is the consensus of the paleontologists, men have been a part of it for only about a thousandth of the total time. And there have been historical records of mankind for only about a two-hundredth of that million years, or about five thousand years.

During all this immense span of time, all forms of animal life have eaten plants or have eaten other animals which have eaten plants, and the plants grew in the earth and were forms of the earth, so that the earth and all the living things on it have been one unit. In other words, men are made as they are simply because they are constructed of the only materials available. The corollary of this fact is that all the materials provided by plants are essential in the construction of animals.

The science of nutrition is relatively new, so that we have only recently begun to recognize the intricate and exact relationship between the chemical constitution of plants and the chemical constitution of animals, including men. We are only really beginning to comprehend the extent of our dependence on the compounds synthesized in plants. For countless ages food has meant, to men, anything that filled the stomach and satisfied hunger, and was not poisonous. But in modern times and collaterally with the growth of modern science, we have developed a knowledge of the constituents of plants and have classified and analyzed the various organic compounds which together make up the total of what we can properly call food. First we learned of the major components of food — the proteins, fats, and carbohydrates which make up the bulk of the things we eat, and which constitute the structural materials of the body and its sources of energy. Even more recently we have learned of the vitamins and minerals, and of their importance in the total diet.

But even this degree of knowledge is a little short of the idea represented by such a product as Nutrilite. Let us state, as we see it to be possible, the overall concept on which Nutrilite Food Supplement is devised.

All over the world men still eat the things which are most available as food, sometimes the natural products of the land and sometimes food grown as crops cultivated by men themselves. These foods usually are not selected for the highest possible value, but are selected because of taste appeal, or because of convenience in cultivation, harvesting, or storage, or perhaps all three of these factors.

All over the world people eat diets which are approximately but not exactly representative of what they need to eat. The result is that a great many people, whatever their culture, may be somewhat undernourished. Nearly all men in primitive societies secure enough carbohydrates, but some do not secure enough fats, and a great many do not secure enough protein. In advanced societies, men consume the wrong kinds of carbohydrates (sugars), too much fat, and sometimes insufficient protein. In addition, many people, civilized and uncivilized alike, secure less than adequate quantities of all the vitamins, and sometimes of all the minerals.

The problem of correcting diets high in carbohydrates but low in fats and proteins affects such immense populations and such tremendous areas of the world's surface that it could only be met by the individual countries, or by a world government. But in the areas where there is good supply of all three of the major factors — proteins, fats, and carbohydrates, such as our country — the problem is only one of supplying additional quantities of vitamins and minerals, and this can be done by supplementation when people feel their diets may be deficient.

As a result, in our country for example, there has grown up a whole new industry concerned with the problem of supplying these additional quantities of vitamins and minerals to be added to the ordinary diet of the American population. The size and success of this new and tremendous industry is evidence of the fact that the need is recognized and that the method is generally advantageous. However, even this falls short of the mark because this industry is based on supplying only those vitamins which have been identified, and synthesized, and which can be produced in large quantity by methods of chemical manufacture. This is not necessarily a correct conclusion.

The basic idea at Nutrilite is that all of the factors required in nutrition are nearly always found in plant substances, and therefore it is proper to use a plant source to secure the nutrients which are required. As time has gone on, some forty vitamins and vitamin-like factors have been found to exist and there are probably many more which must still be rated as unknowns. Most of these occur in plant substances to some extent, but even of the known factors only about one-third can be chemically manufactured. The others must still be secured as concentrates of natural substances.

All of the vitamins occur in foods in very small amounts, but of those now known, to the extent the fact can be proved that they are necessary in human nutrition and essential for health, some are hundreds of times as bulky as others in the quantities which are significant in nutrition. For example, the amount of vitamin C held to be required daily in human nutrition is one hundred thousand times greater by weight than the amount of vitamin B12 required daily. It therefore has happened, following the discovery that vitamins existed, that the ones which could be isolated and analyzed and finally manufactured chemically were those occurring in the largest quantity and found necessary in the largest quantity, such as vitamins A, B1, B2, C, Niacin, and others. The discovery and identification of the others has had to wait for enormously extended experimental work, and the development of more and more refined procedures for isolating and identifying the factors. But all the time this progression in skill of the chemical procedures for discovering and identifying the vitamin factors has been in progress, there never was a time when they were not available in plant materials.

Our company started and continues on the theory that if proper concentration of plant materials can be achieved, all the vitamins in the plant material will be present in that concentrate, and therefore available for use in supplementation. It is not known, of course, whether our food supplement or any other does in fact supply all the required factors in necessary quantities, and any such knowledge will have to wait for an indefinite time until more has been discovered concerning the vitamin factors, their occurrence in natural substances, the methods for concentrating them, and the facts concerning their requirements in human nutrition. But the overall concept is still sound, still logical, and in practice, still effective.

Careful initial examination and experimentation in our laboratories determined that the most suitable sources of these plant factors for Nutrilite's use were alfalfa, watercress, and parsley. Later on selected yeasts, kelp, acerola cherries, and certain other natural substances were added. There is no absolute assurance that these are the best substances for the purpose, out of all the plants which grow, but they are the best known to us, and the literature on the characteristics of these materials seems to support this opinion.

Nutrilite Concentrate, therefore, was originally a concentration of the desired factors using alfalfa, watercress and parsley as the source. When concentration of this material was first done by us on a commercial scale, there was little general interest in the subject — practically none, in fact. In the laboratories the thousands of great scientists who have since isolated and synthesized the various vitamins were still carrying on their work of discovery, and the present great industry had not arisen because there were no man-made vitamins.

As the man-made vitamins were manufactured and became available, they have been added to Nutrilite food supplements to enhance its potency in these particular factors — but the Concentrate itself was manufactured, and is still manufactured, because it represented a generalized source of other factors.

It is not possible to assert a value for an unknown factor. It is assumed that there are unknown factors and that they may have significance in human nutrition. Repeatedly this has been shown to be true. At one time for example, folic acid, Vitamin B6, Vitamin B12, and biotin were unknown factors; they were not even known to exist. But they have since been shown to exist and to have definite, significant value in human nutrition — and they were present in the Nutrilite Concentrate before we knew they existed.

As a result of research done in our own laboratories, we have published information in a scientific journal concerning a still unknown factor which occurs in the Alfalfa Concentrate. We still do not know what it is and we still do not know whether it is important in human nutrition, but the chances are that some years from now this new factor will have a name and a known function in human nutrition.*

*EDITOR'S NOTE: In the early years of research and development, it had been noted that there was apparently an active factor (or factors) retained in the alfalfa residue fraction (the water-washed pulp remaining after extraction of the juice) which seemed to have a significant effect in counteracting the results of toxic substances fed to laboratory animals. This factor was unknown, and was apparently distinct from any of the then-known nutrients. It was called the P.R. factor, for Plant Residue. This research done by Dr. Benjamin Ershoff of the Department of Biochemistry and Nutrition, University of Southern California at Los Angeles, was supported in part by grant-in-aid from Nutrilite Products, Inc. A paper was published in 1957 on his investigations. ("Beneficial Effects of Alfalfa and Other Succulent Plants on Glucoascorbic Acid Toxicity in the Rat, No. 23319, printed in the PROCEEDINGS OF THE SOCIETY FOR EXPERIMENTAL BIOLOGY AND MEDICINE, 1957, v95, 656-659), which states in part: "Considerable data are available indicating that alfalfa contains one or more factors, apparently distinct from any of the known nutrients, which are essential for optimal growth and psychologic performance under various experimental conditions (3, 4). The effects of alfalfa supplementation are particularly marked in animals exposed to certain stressor agents (2, 5, 6) . . . The protective factor (plant residue) was distinct from any of the known nutrients and was retained in the alfalfa residue fraction (water washed pulp remaining after extraction of the juice). This is the same alfalfa fraction that was active in counteracting the inhibitory effects of alpha-estradiol on ovarian development (6), in prolonging survival of hamsters fed highly purified diets (7), in promoting growth of guinea pigs fed a mineralized dried milk ration (8), and in prolonging survival of rats fed massive doses of desiccated thyroid or iodinated casein (9)."

A second paper written by Dr. Benjamin H. Ershoff under the auspices of the Institute for Nutritional Studies, Los Angeles, CA 90034, and printed in the December 1972 issue of PROCEEDINGS OF THE SOCIETY FOR EXPERIMENTAL BIOLOGY AND MEDICINE 141, 857-862, under the title "Comparative Effects of a Purified Diet and Stock Ration on Sodium Cyclamate Toxicity in Rats, No. 36889," also gives credence to the apparent protective effect of a stock diet incorporating the P.R. or Plant Residue factor. The Summary states in part: "Immature rats were fed graded levels of sodium cyclamate in conjunction with either a highly purified diet or a natural food-stock ration. On the stock ration, sodium cyclamate when fed at levels of 2.5%, 5%, or 10% of the diet had little, if any, adverse effect on weight increment and none on gross appearance. When fed at comparable levels in the purified diet, however, sodium cyclamate caused a significant retardation in growth which was proportional to the level fed, an unthrifty appearance of the fur, varying degrees of alopecia, extensive diarrhea; and at the 10% level of feeding, death."

There is no evidence that alfalfa concentrate would produce the same effect when fed to humans. The proportion of alfalfa concentrate in the diet of the animals was far in excess of the amount that would be tolerated by humans and, because of the severe nature of these tests, it is doubtful they would ever be performed on human subjects.

The Fabulous Fiesta

Because the annual Fiesta de Oro convention of distributors was held in Los Angeles, C.F. Rehnborg appeared and spoke there perhaps more often than in other cities — it was close to his beloved Newport Beach and Lakeview Farm homes. Following are excerpts from his talk to Distributors at the Fiesta, given on May 3, 1958, edited to emphasize the inspirational part of his message.

I'm rather moved. It has been a very long time since I have had a chance to talk to a group of Nutrilite Distributors. And, as a family man should, I am telling you that I have missed you very much.

I think what I have missed most is this feeling of warmth between us, because this is not just a group of people thumping the tub to appear enthusiastic, but a group of devoted believers rekindling the fire of conviction and purpose.

What we are all doing together, in our distribution of Nutrilite Food Supplement, is nothing less than a sustained drive to convince every human being who lives, beginning with the persons next to us each day, that health and well-being are not things merely to be regained when lost, but rather gifts to be maintained with all our power, on a regular and constant basis.

I've heard people compare our meetings to revivals, to describe the intensity of purpose. Perhaps — but there is an element these people miss. Revivals and some sales meetings depend on noise and confusion and some degree of mass hysteria for effect. But we are not hysterical. We shine because we know, and wonder why it should be necessary to argue the point, that living in this universe is a wonderful experience if we are well enough to enjoy it. And we know the way to be adjusted to the universe and to enjoy it.

We live in a social system in which the only way to carry out a continuing and self-sustaining campaign to bring a product to the people who may need or want it, and to take care of the ordinary needs of those who devote themselves to the effort, is through a business organization which makes a profit. We are, therefore, organized — all of us — as a business group ... I refer to you, by the way, most fondly as the most beautiful bunch of grocery salesmen in the whole world.

What we move in this way to the people who want it, is a relatively small package of organic and mineral substances — one package for the use of each person. This product, Nutrilite Food Supplement, is not just a package weighing a few ounces — it is a physical manifestation of a powerful ideal, the conviction that it is truly and really and actually the means by which any one person may make his or her adjustment to the conditions of living. It is the instrument by which each person may overcome the nutritional handicaps unwittingly caused by man himself in his choice and use of his foods — the substances which, when added to his foods, may provide the things quite possibly missing from his ordinary diet.

I said that this package was an expression, a physical expression, of an ideal. It is. Once in a while I think we all get the impression that practical people consider ideals to be something impractical and fuzzy-minded. They could not be more wrong! Ideals are the only dependable and trustworthy drives for human effort. They are the motive power for all the advances of the human spirit, whether in what are called moral values, or in the arts and sciences, or in government, or in the rearing of our families, or in business!

I can best drive home the thought that your product is the expression of an ideal . . . I'll try to re-state it in a few words. The reason for our effort is our product, and the reason for our product is the ideal on which it is built. This ideal is of good to the human race. For this particular time a product is offered by a group of people who believe in it, and who can feel that the exchange of the product for its price in the market is morally justified. It is as good as it says it is. So let us determine our course and dedicate ourselves to take this message to the world . . . let's tell everyone!

Family gathering: At Fiesta de Oro banquet are Dr. Sam Rehnborg, Edith Rehnborg, and C.F. Rehnborg.

Nutrilite — The Expression of An Ideal

The following address was given by C.F. Rehnborg at the Chicago Pow-Wow on November 8, 1958, to a large group of Distributors. It was warmly received and long remembered as one of his most inspiring talks. Although edited to reduce his discussion of astronomy as illustrating universal laws, it still expresses Rehnborg's cosmic view of the universe, and his belief that the same laws that govern the creation of a galaxy in space may also apply equally to the world of men and the achievement of ideals for the benefit of the human race.

It is always an inspiring and productive experience to talk at these meetings of regional groups about our tremendous organization of Nutrilite distributors. The atmosphere that exists in this room, of warmth and comradeship, and of deep and genuine enthusiasm — a deep-rooted belief in ourselves and in the integrity of our work together — is far more than simply the holding of a sales convention.

All of us — those here representing Nutrilite Products, Inc., and you as thousands of independent direct sales business people — are not here just because of the need to devise plans for selling a product. We are here because of a great and shining ideal — the dedicated undertaking of doing something which perhaps may improve the nutritional status and well-being of human beings. This kind of effort, and the earnest intensity we bring to it, can only be the expression of an ideal.

What we are attempting to do can only be done through business organizations by business methods, but the business form is for us the instrument for giving reality to the ideal. Finally, it is altogether right to have a successful ideal. Finally also, the ideals have to be based on a philosophy, and the philosophy cannot exist all by itself without foundation, but has to be based on the facts of the universe.

All of us are looking at what we are doing as the practical and concrete expression of these ideals, whether we are conscious of this fact as we look or not. It seems to me, however, that our reasons for what we do could make it much more concrete and rewarding to us if we analyzed for ourselves the reasoning behind the ideal and its relationship to all the other facts of living.

Once you have started to examine the system of logic behind a specific sort of ideal, it is amazing how far it will take you in the search for its roots. The particular philosophy which concerns us is the philosophy of success. This as an idea has to be based on logic and reason, and the reason has to be the order of the universe — and the order of the universe has no final meaning unless we can believe it to be a result of cause and of purpose.

Many of the things I have to say on this subject are generally supposed to be applicable only in Sunday School, but I assure you that I do not have this opinion. I think that whatever the faith by which a man lives, it has no value whatever if it only holds good in one place and not another. It must be a belief which dominates every waking moment of a whole life if it is to be effective, or if it is to have meaning.

The many great and shining leaders of the spirits of mankind have made it abundantly clear, one after the other, that they considered that belief in something more than merely material values was to be a lifelong habit, and in control of one's thinking all the time and not just some of the time. Therefore, I want to discuss, concerning the business of living, the intangible values — without substance but as real as chairs and tables —which are component parts of human spirit and drive; and particularly I want to put this together as an expression of the philosophy of success.

I think it is fair to ask, as is asked constantly, whether these values are real or whether the statement of these values is merely a set of words designed to build up courage — something like whistling in the dark in what might really be an unfriendly universe. I think the answer depends on how the universe is made; that is, whether it is indifferent or neutral, or whether it is beneficient. Let us take a look at this question from a new angle.

The universe is immense beyond comprehension by a human mind, but we can deal with it if we consider it as a unit. Now, considering the universe as a unit, we have to begin with consideration of the origin of the universe. It is undeniable that the universe exists, but (1) Is it real, or do we in some way merely imagine that we perceive it? (2) Did it arise spontaneously out of nothing? Is it infinite in time as well as extent, but never had a beginning? (3) Was it created? and, (4) Is it meaningless, or does it express order and purpose?

These questions have no direct answers, but at least we can say that what we can see and experience of the universe is "real" to the extent we as human beings are able to determine, and we communicate to one another the obvious fact that we all share the same perceptions concerning it.

Let us start by assuming what we all assume: that the universe was created, and that it has order and purpose. When we examine the universe and admit that all probability indicates it is not an accident, but was created, we find confirmation for our belief that the universe was created by a Creator of purpose: it is, throughout, a system of order. Everywhere in the universe matter and energy have basically the same characteristics, and the basic laws of interaction show cause and effect operating in orderly and invariable sequences. Science itself is possible because this is true — we are in a universe of law, and the laws are universal and can be trusted.

So much for the material universe. But all the great teachers of humanity have insisted that this same rule of law extends into the realm of the spirit, and that the laws of the spirit, also, are real and can be trusted; and they have made spirit equally a part of a beneficient universe, together with matter and energy. All the great teachers have said the same thing in essence: Jesus of Nazareth, Lao-tzu, Kung Fu-tze (or Confucius), Gautama, Zoroaster, and many others.

We call these laws of order in the universe the "laws of nature," and so put the word "nature" as a buffer between us and the ineffable. But Jesus, who put the matter in its clearest light, called them simply the "Laws of God," partly because the relatively simple language of the area in which he taught did not include such a concept as Nature, and perhaps because the word "God" was the word he intended to use. In fact, Jesus, who clearly conveyed the idea that he was speaking of a system of order, did not at all deal with this order in the realm of the material universe, but dealt exclusively with the subject of the laws of the human spirit.

He taught a system of adjustment to the universe, and to the laws of Nature, or God, and he built them into a formula for achievement and success. In fact, I am amazed, for myself, to realize that the description of this formula is so clearly set forth in the record, and yet has been so effectively neglected by the world of men.

I have had as an avocation since I was young, the study of the teachings of the great teachers. Let me put into words of today what I think it was that they said in common, but that Jesus said best.

Jesus was asked, you remember, by a Pharisee to name the greatest of the laws of the universe. You are to remember that the Pharisees were not hypocrites and rogues. Their name itself meant that they were "set apart," and their own definition of this was that they were set apart to preserve the purity of their Mosaic religion. The only quarrel Jesus had with them was that he said most of their rules of conduct were man-made and not divine. At any rate, Jesus made a serious point to answer the question.

He said that the greatest of the laws was that one was to love God with all his being, and that the second law was exactly like the first law in principle: that one was to love his neighbor as he loved himself — that every law of human activity depended on these two.

The Pharisee then asked another question. In effect he said, "All right, but just who is my neighbor?" And Jesus gave his answer in the form of a parable. He told the story of the Good Samaritan.

Now you must understand that the Jews hated the Samaritans, and that the Pharisee was a Jew. The story therefore was both bitter and pointed. The Samaritans were a mixed stock of Jews and Canaanites and other races, living in the area between Judea and Galilee, but not regarded by the Jews as belonging to themselves. They had what the Jews considered to be the unbearable effrontery to declare that they, the Samaritans, followed the ancient laws of Moses of the Jewish religion, and that the Jews themselves were apostate. The Jews therefore could not believe that there was such a thing as a "good" Samaritan.

The story Jesus told was of a traveler on the road up the defile from Jericho to Jerusalem, who was set upon by bandits and robbed and beaten; and how a priest, a leader in the temple at Jerusalem, the center itself of the Jewish religion, and a Levite, a member of the hereditary clan who gave service at the altar, had each avoided trouble by walking around the injured man and proceeding on his way, while a Samaritan going along the same road had stopped to give aid to the injured man. He had bound up his wounds and then taken him to an inn to recover, and had paid his lodging. And then Jesus said to the Pharisee, "And who think you was neighbor to the man who fell among the thieves?" And the Pharisee answered, honestly, but still not mentioning the word "Samaritan," "The one who gave aid to him."

This principle so stated sets the basic rule of human conduct. In a world of neighbors there would be no injustice, nor deceit, nor basic selfishness. One would, in simply the terms of reciprocal conduct, achieve adjustment to the universe itself, and to its Cause. There would in all this be no interdiction against material success, but rather the reverse.

For some reason one feels a little timid or abashed, in our society, to speak of spiritual values as if they had real meaning, instead of going along with the general attitude that they are impractical and perhaps fuzzy-minded. It may be this is because the values cannot be proved as one proves a mechanical or chemical problem. Yet the real leaders of the human race have always been those who argued the spiritual values only, and in the light of so much evidence from genius, we ought perhaps to realize that modern pragmatists could very well be mistaken.

Certainly, the purely practical values do not of themselves produce the principles and standards of conduct that mark the higher types of human society, and we ought to be able to accept the word of the sages that they were talking about real things and talking about good sense, when they gave reality and substance to spiritual values. The great teachers themselves eschewed all human possessions, because the business of expounding their great perceptions of the underlying laws of reality demanded complete self-abnegation to the business of conveying those teachings to other human beings. There was no spare time for the teacher to devote to the routines of ordinary living. The ordinary individual such as you and I could live a normal life of family and social responsibility, without being dedicated to the business of conveying the teaching, but only dedicated to observing the basic laws of human conduct.

This conviction is fortified by the fact that elsewhere and at another time Jesus taught the formula for success.

To paraphrase this teaching, you will remember that he said that whatever thing you will to have, if you believe that already it is yours, it will be yours. He said, "Ask, and you shall receive. Search, and you will find. Knock, and the door shall be opened to you." And he added, "But it is he who asks who receives, and he who searches who finds, and he who knocks to whom the door is opened." In other words, there was a purposeful act by which you moved towards the desired end. You were not merely supinely ready to accept, but did your part to get what you wanted. The belief and confidence you felt keyed the results to your belief, in some way definite and sure, but still quite mysterious to our limited comprehension, and yet to be trusted because it was a law. Perhaps, as a guess, in some way the belief and desire are themselves guides in a choice of action, but I do not know. I am content that the law exists, and that it works.

I prefer to believe that, in fact, belief and desire are guides in our choices of action. An attempt to utilize these laws is an adventure in amazement and wonder. Things have a way of happening as if by coincidence that cannot be made to look like coincidence. To each need there is always an answer. Perhaps the naturalness with which the desired end seems just to happen can be illustrated by a simple example.

If one walks down a street and comes to an intersection, there are three directions in which to proceed, and it is quite clear that in some ways the overall results of each of the three courses of action will differ in some particular from the others, and that the detailed sequence of subsequent events will in that case differ to some degree from each of the others, and yet two choices are abandoned in taking the third. Now, if some pattern of purpose impelled the choice, the results which followed could be and would be completely natural, but one choice would lead in the desired direction and the other two might not.

Perhaps it is this simple. Certainly it seems to be natural, and certainly it works. Even insuperable obstacles turn out to be signposts for a change of direction, and the whole thing is instinct with purpose and orderly as a sequence.

Perhaps this seems to be stretching the search for purpose. That is not the idea I wish to convey. One cannot find, anywhere in the universe, purpose expressed in words of a language, but only by the analogy of experience. But the experience itself simply does not make sense if it is imagined to be accidental, and it certainly does not seem to be accidental. So many of the great teachers have averred the reality of the laws, that perhaps we can take their word for it. I myself prefer to do so, and perhaps you would also.

Every pep talk to a sales group, every determined effort to win a race or achieve success, is an indirect acknowledgement that these laws exist. Thousands of men have written inspirational books which likewise are an acknowledgement that the laws exist, but without crediting the statement of law to the true discoverer or discoverers. But would it not be better to accept the body of the law as a coherent whole, completely inclusive in spite of the fact that it can be so simply stated, and to recognize that the laws proceed from the highest authority, as interpretations of the meaning of the universe itself?

I think that I, in moving to achieve adjustment and success, would rather feel that I was observing the laws of the universe than to feel that I was following the suggestions of the Chamber of Commerce. I am certain you would also. The laws are there, ready to help you use them.

These things can happen in a world filled with tensions and with enormities of misconduct against the liberties and rights of men, with war and strife and discordances everywhere we look. Yet one can see that the simple principles of brotherly love and reciprocity, if applied, would cause the welter of strife to melt away like fog. Maybe the thing wrong with the world is simply and only the lack of that consideration for the rights of others, which would be corrected if mankind in some general way followed the principles of the Golden Rule. It is unfortunate that so simple and logical a concept has to be on the defensive instead of in the ascendancy.

I think it would be the perfection of hope if all human beings in their enterprises could intend adjustment to the basic laws, even if this cannot be fully achieved. Every time that any group of human beings or any individual human being reaches such a basic decision, no matter how feebly or how partially they carry it out, the world of men itself has moved a long step toward peace and adjustment and achievement. It is a matter of intent, only and simply.

No human being ever did a perfect job at anything. Merely, we are only able to achieve percentage gains toward perfection. Whatever intent we have toward achievement of proper ideals, we can always, individually and collectively, intensify it. It is worth trying, and it works — and it enriches life proportionately as it is attempted.

All ideals are greater than the people who attempt to express them. Our ideals are greater than we can express, but I cannot help feeling that in explaining what I think is the philosophy of success, I have also been describing what it is that all of us feel in this sense of connection and common purpose we all have toward one another in our meetings. They are certainly not just sales meetings, and quite certainly ours is not just a manufacturing and sales organization. It is much more. I think that the warmth we feel for one another is a proper expression of what we believe, so deep down that it is hard to express in words, and it is the thing which will crown with success everything we have undertaken or will undertake.

Chicago Pow Wow always drew a full-capacity audience; this was the 1953 Convention.

A Tribute To Our First Lady of Cosmetics

When Edith Rehnborg Cosmetics were introduced May 19, 1958, they received an enthusiastic reception. On May 19, 1959, a year later, it was announced that sales volume had grown from 'zero' to nearly three-quarters of a million dollars per month at retail — testimony to their success. Several of the products have been incorporated into Amway's ARTISTRY line and continue to sell, carrying on the basic concepts involved in their creation. On the first anniversary of the line's introduction, the following article was written by C.F. Rehnborg and printed in the company news magazine in honor of Edith Rehnborg.

Edith Rehnborg Cosmetics are new. We have made them only a few years. But the art of cosmetics is as old as civilization, going back almost ten thousand years — maybe longer.

Today's cosmetics are based on modern scientific knowledge of materials, but there may be lost secrets in the cosmetic jars and pots that archeologists uncover in the graves of ancient civilizations. Those oldest cosmetics were made of oils and waxes furnished by the immediate environment — palm oil, sesame oil, fats and greases, mixed sometimes with aromatic herbs.

Even the most primitive people are accustomed to using vegetable and animal oils and fats for skin conditioning. The beginning of the use of these materials as definitely cosmetic would be difficult to determine. However, when they were compounded and put into jars and pots, so very long ago, with aromatic herbs and even with colored minerals — black to shadow the eyes and red to color the cheeks, as in ancient Mesopotamian cultures — women had already made them their own as cosmetics and were using them to enhance beauty as well as to condition the skin.

Cosmetology as an art has flourished wherever and whenever the arts and sciences have been part of civilization. The golden ages of history have all been noted for the importance attached to personal grooming, and to health and beauty. Cleopatra was heir to all the thousands of years of culture in the Nile Valley, and famous for her art in compounding and using cosmetics. The Greeks made a cult of physical perfection and the care of beauty. At one time they even fined any woman who was negligent in her dress or the care of her person.

The luxurious grooming of the Roman beauties is mentioned in the works of Horace and Ovid. As recently as the Renaissance period in Europe, women were so lavish in their use of cosmetics that it is still noted as a time of painted faces and powdered hair, and extreme fashions. They didn't know about today, did they?

In our own day cosmetics have become mass-produced items in business, and as they have done so, the ideas simply of skin condition and beauty have run into problems of competition and economics. There is much science, but also there are examples of ingredients used chiefly to enhance the appearance of the product itself — its color, body, smoothness, consistency, and sometimes its keeping quality. As competition sharpens, to some degree the function of the cosmetics takes second place to commercial attractiveness.

The time has come to get all the way back to the primary idea of cosmetics as skin care and aids to beauty — cosmetics designed to DO something. Oddly enough, this purpose produces cosmetics which have their own charm of appearance, just as precious gems are not merely rare and costly, but more beautiful than more common and less valuable stones.

Edith Rehnborg Cosmetics has its own objective — to find by research into all natural ingredients the things now known and the things long forgotten about the craft of cosmetics — the relation between various cosmetic materials and the skins of womankind — the things that encourage health and good condition of the skin and the things which enhance its beauty and texture — even the ingredients that add the touch of art to beauty just for beauty's own sake.

When we set out to develop the Edith Rehnborg line of cosmetics, we were also developing an idea. First, we were sure cosmetics would open doors for distributors and add to their incomes. Second, was the matching of inner care with food supplements to outer care with cosmetics. It is our belief that all the substances used should have value as cosmetics; that they should all be natural; and that there are many natural substances which either have not been used or else have been forgotten and are not used now. As we follow out this line of development, we will have finer and finer cosmetics and the world of men will recognize their quality.

Nutrilite Seen In Retrospect

The following has been excerpted from a memo written by C.F. Rehnborg in October, 1967 when he was 80 years old. He had been thinking about the changes in technology that had taken place since the Nutrilite Food Supplement product had been developed in the '30's, and this summary illustrates his concept of the rationale for and purpose of the product.

When Nutrilite Food Supplement was first being developed, there was no vitamin industry as such, and no vitamin products. Our product became a "vitamin product" through being swept along by our sales agents and the public news media.

When we started, we were not selling a "vitamin product" but rather a "food supplement," and except for the "vitamin" label under which it is now sold, it is still a "food supplement." We should begin once more to talk and think in our own idiom and get back into our own business of food supplements.

We can almost start again from the beginning, and in a very practical way we can re-study our process reasons and process steps. When I began, there were no crystalline vitamins other than in experimental laboratories. Some vitamins were known and were called by letters as provisional titles, such as A, B, C, D, E, and G, but it was not yet known, for example, that B was not a single-unit substance, but a complex of several factors. B-1 was a single factor, but B-2 required additional subscripts, B-3, B-6, and B-12, for example. And these were not exact until the chemical structure of the various vitamins was known, and then they began to be called by their names as organic compounds: thiamine, riboflavin, and so on.

Even then there was further juggling of names as the vitamin designations were seen to be multiple designations for a smaller number of true entities. Up to now it has not been possible to make a final statement that all of the micro-factors are known and identified, and that all their relations to food factors or their interactions among themselves are finally clarified.

From our position, none of these bits of information are uniquely necessary. We are properly committed to extracts and concentrates of plant and fruit materials. The many new items of discovery in the science of nutrition act as the dots in an electrotype which reproduce a picture in printing. The picture is the whole relationship of life to its environment. Instead of these details, we need only to look at the whole concept.

Food, and the animal which eats it, are equivalent to one another. The adaptation of the animal to the environment is a matter of specific use of the total environment by a life form, and the environment to a certain extent determines the character of the life form. The life forms we know are conformed to the physics and chemistry of our world as a unit of the whole universe.

In turn, when man in his cultural development invents the means by which the physical facts of nature are ameliorated for the comfort, convenience, and safety of mankind, man needs also to make the physical and chemical facts of his new environment fit his own biological requirements. The Eskimo eats the contents of the stomach of the walrus for his "salad"; the Chinese eats bean sprouts for his Vitamin C.

But mankind living in a greater degree of civilizing culture gives less authority to nature, and breaks her finally unbreakable laws by his arbitrary choices of foods, based on his own preferences and convenience, as well as his ignorance at all levels of the culture. Such ignorance is not even yet dispelled — especially in his choices of the foods which must be stored after accumulation for some interval between harvest and the time they are used. This is a matter of trial and error until his sciences are developed and the new knowledge is disseminated among the society, and there have been many errors throughout history, including the present time.

Even now, when the sciences are becoming a more exact degree of general knowledge, habit and ignorance stand between man and his full adjustment to his environment. Various major inadequacies in accustomed diets produce massive deficiencies affecting millions of people, who suffer and die when they could thrive if kinds and quantities of completely available food were used by them to correct their inadequate diets.

Our own nation is the best fed nation in the world, yet our Department of Agriculture says that 40-odd percent of all Americans eat diets which are deficient in one way or another for various necessary food factors. And these deficiencies are not in quantity only, or even generally, but in quality of nutrients. Most of the actual deficiencies in diets are due to poor choices of foods eaten, including both economic and habitual choices.

It usually happens by ignorance that most of the substances for which deficiencies occur — other than deficiencies for bulk protein, meat, and milk, for example — are for complex carbohydrates, minerals, and vitamins. Yet all of the mineral and vitamin components for these substances can be extracted and concentrated from many common organic materials, and do not need to be secured from the organic substances in the actual diets being ignorantly used through local or class habit. As an example of this, consider the French-fried potatoes and Coke for lunch of hundreds of thousands of school kids, or the hominy and sowbelly of some Appalachian mountain people.

A substance such as Nutrilite Concentrate, for example, taken from plants, yeasts, and other materials, will contain an undifferentiated total extraction of essential vitamins, minerals, and trace elements ordinarily secured from a well-chosen total diet, even if not the diet customarily eaten by the ill-fed individual. As a food supplement, such a concentration makes up for many diet deficiencies, whether caused by poor choice of diet or by the many things done to food substances to increase their marketability.

Simply, as I have tried to say in so many ways as to become monotonous, the chemical components of a human diet are well known in principle. In addition to animal and vegetable proteins (meat and beans, for example), fats and carbohydrates (oils, sugars and starches) which in nearly all diets are present and familiar to all eaters of foods, human nutrition also requires for normal function of the chemical machine which is the human body, small amounts of a group of factors including the vitamins and a wide group of various compounds of mineral elements, as well as many organic compounds in the substance of the food plants.

All these substances are soluble in the body's fluids and fats, and the amounts required in the human diet represent a rather small volume in comparison to the bulk of the food vegetables and fruits from which they are taken. This small volume of the factors which should be contained in an adequate diet can even supply them to a surplus of the required amount. These organic materials can be secured from vegetable materials even richer than those which are normally part of the human diet, and as a concentrate or in tablets may be added to the intake of food as a food supplement to prevent deficiencies from occurring.

It is not even necessary to be so limited and selective as to the particular plant sources of the concentrates or extracts. All the wanted factors occur to some extent in all the plants used. There are also available specific plants known to be especially rich in particular factors, such as A (carrots), B (grains and yeasts), C (acerola cherries and other fruits), E (wheat germ oil), and so on.

Organic substances in general contain some quantity of some or all of the required factors, as well as other compounds of value in nutrition, in a broad list of possible sources. In the same way the extracted material, the food supplement, also is not specific but generalized as a source of vitamin and mineral food factors and a wide range of organic food components, and is added to a deficient diet without the bulk of the fresh vegetable and fruit sources from which it is extracted.

It is not possible now, and may not be for a long time to come, to know exactly what deficiencies occur in a particular poor diet, nor is it necessary to know. So far as present knowledge extends, NUTRILITE Food Supplements contain an adequate daily ration for each of the trace factors required in human nutrition. If a known factor is the particular substance required in a given instance, it is included in the product.

NUTRILITE Food Supplement is not merely a vitamin and mineral product. It is a food supplement, intended to round out and complete any deficient diet, so that its use is an insurance against simple deficiency.

We may need professional assistance in composing the statements used, but these statements need only to convey the fact that all the universal components of a diet which enter into the construction and maintenance of a human body do so as organic compounds, whether the facet of life involved is bone structure or muscle movement; that there are deficiencies in some areas of territory and in some regional diets; and that all of these can be supplemented by a diet supplement containing dietary factors obtained from fresh plant materials.

The fertile soils and ample water supply of Southern California's San Jacinto Valley made it the ideal location for growing alfalfa, watercress, and parsley used in the NUTRILITE ® concentrate.

Right, recent photo of Buena Park manufacturing plant shows the expansion and growth that has taken place.

Below is an aerial view of the Buena Park plant taken in 1952, when it consisted of nine structures.

NUTRILITE

An Idea

On the following pages a series of "then and now" photos illustrate the dramatic changes not only in size and capacity of the various types of equipment used in both processing and manufacturing, but also in the complexity and

The first alfalfa farm at Hemet, California, above, may be contrasted with the rolling acres of the present Lakeview Farm, at right.

Early Farm Office at Lakeview, above left, has been greatly modernized and expanded, as its present sleek appearance shows, at left.

Fondly remembered is the original Quonset hut in which Carl Rehnborg first began to make usable forms of his products. It was kept for its sentimental and historical value and now houses the Nutrilite Museum, having been moved from Buena Park to Lakeview.

That Grew

refinement that has developed as the demand for products leads to ever newer and more efficient technology. If he were alive today, C.F. Rehnborg would be proud indeed of these improvements.

In the very early days C.F. Rehnborg did everything himself, even going to his growing areas and cutting fresh alfalfa with a scythe, then quickly transporting it to his laboratory. In recent years only the most modern Field Queens are used to harvest the alfalfa crops, at left.

This one small building held the early-day dehydration equipment, and the process took 24 hours.

The dehydration process now takes place in minutes, in a huge, slowly-rotating cylinder that removes moisture from the plant materials at a very low temperature, thus preserving all possible nutrient value.

After dehydration a slurry is made of plant materials and then the bulky materials are extracted. Above are the extractors originally used, as compared to present-day extractors, below, which operate in tandem with clarifiers.

Although this Concentrator and Vacuum Pump, at left, were considered state-of-the-art in their time, they are obsolete compared to the giant Turba-Film Evaporators now in use, below.

Plant material reduced to a paste by the evaporating process is now spray-dried by tumbling in air, which transforms it to a powder. The former drum dryer, above, has been replaced by the huge new spray dryer, left. The powder is then put into containers and transported to the Buena Park manufacturing plant. Additional materials are blended in to form the Nutrilite Concentrate.

Former Fitz-mill Grinder, right, has been replaced by an automated Chilsonator and Fitz-mill Grinders, below, which greatly increase the amount of materials that can be processed in the same period of time.

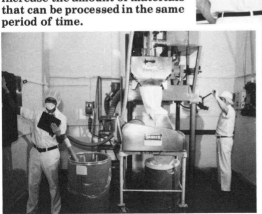

After final formulation, the supplements are compressed i tablets and then coated with NUTRILOCK®coating which seals in nutrients. At left, a Quality Control inspector is examining the coating. These machines have also been replaced by efficient, high-spee "Hi-Coaters" which are totall automated and can coat up to o million tablets at a time, belov

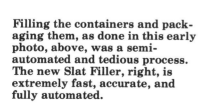

Filling the containers and packaging them, as done in this early photo, above, was a semi-automated and tedious process. The new Slat Filler, right, is extremely fast, accurate, and fully automated.

Nutrilite — A Chronology of Events

1915-1933:   C.F. Rehnborg lived and worked in China during the period 1915 to approximately 1927, as follows:

   1915-1916: Accountant with Standard Oil Co., Tientsin.
   1916-1918: China American Trading Company, Tientsin.
   1918-1919: Comptroller, Lone Star Shipbuilding Corp.
   1919-1923: Manufacturer's Representative, American Milk Products Company of New York, Carnation Company.
   1923-1927: Operated his own business as representative of Colgate Products Company. Was a member of the Shanghai Volunteer Corps.

   During this period he had ample opportunity to observe the results of poor nutrition among the people of China, and he conceived the idea of a food supplement for home consumption. After being confined to a compound in Shanghai by the revolutionary forces for nearly a year, C.F. Rehnborg returned to the U.S. in 1927 and set up a small laboratory in a sail loft on Balboa Island, California, determined to develop a method for concentrating nutrient-rich plant materials.

1934:   After several years of trial and experimentation, Carl Rehnborg finally produced and began to sell his first multivitamin/multimineral product. The company was named California Vitamins, Inc.

1939:   Company operations were moved to Slauson Avenue in Los Angeles, and the name was changed to Nutrilite Products. A preliminary version of the sponsorship method of distribution was established.

1940:   Packaging and shipping operations were moved to Hoover Street in Los Angeles, as more space was needed.

1945:   In September C.F. Rehnborg, Dr. William Casselberry, and Lee Mytinger established their business association, with Mytinger & Casselberry, Inc. as exclusive distributors of Nutrilite Food Supplements. This was officially the beginning of the Marketing Plan.

1946:	Production facilities were moved to seven acres of land which had been acquired in Buena Park, California. Improvements were made to the Marketing Plan Refund Schedule.
1948:	C.F. Rehnborg continued to develop and improve his product until he was satisfied with all aspects of quality, performance, and shelf life. An improved product was introduced, and it was called Nutrilite XX. It made the company famous.
1949:	Jay Van Andel and Rich DeVos became Distributors of Nutrilite Food Supplements and began to build a thriving organization. During the next few years sales mounted rapidly, and Nutrilite Products, Inc. became a multimillion dollar corporation.
1951:	Farming operations required expansion and were moved from Buena Park to the San Jacinto Valley with the purchase of a 100-acre farm at Hemet. The extraction and concentration facilities were moved from Buena Park to the Hemet Farm.
1953:	Still more acreage was needed to grow alfalfa, so a much larger tract was purchased at Lakeview. Construction began on new processing facilities.
1955:	Under the direction of Dr. Stefan Tenkoff as Vice President-Production, the extraction and concentration facilities were moved from Hemet to Lakeview.
1956:	Acerola cherry orchards were established in Hawaii.
1958:	Edith Rehnborg Cosmetics were introduced and immediately became popular.
1959:	Jay Van Andel and Rich DeVos founded the Amway Corporation and adapted the Marketing Plan to the sale of household products. In that same year Dr. William Casselberry retired and Mytinger & Casselberry, Inc. became The Mytinger Corporation.
1963:	Nutrilite Products, Inc. purchased the assets of The Mytinger Corporation, and once again production and distribution were united.

| 1962: | Dr. Stefan Tenkoff was elected President of Nutrilite Products, Inc., with C.F. Rehnborg continuing as Chairman of the Board. |

1962:   Dr. Stefan Tenkoff was elected President of Nutrilite Products, Inc., with C.F. Rehnborg continuing as Chairman of the Board.

1963:   Nutrilite Products, Inc. purchased the assets of The Mytinger Corporation, and once again production and distribution were united.

1964:   Sam Rehnborg, son of C.F. Rehnborg, received a Ph.D in Biophysics from the University of California at Berkeley, and joined the company's staff at Buena Park.

1970:   Acerola cherry orchards were leased in Puerto Rico, insuring a continuing supply of natural Vitamin C with better growing conditions and additional plantings.

1972:   After a long period of negotiations the Amway Corporation acquired a controlling interest in Nutrilite Products, Inc. With the resultant expansion of the Distributor base, sales of Nutrilite products increased many times over.

1973:   C.F. Rehnborg passed away in his 86th year, having been very active both mentally and physically up to that time. He had only recently returned from a trip to Micronesia.

1974 to present: In keeping with C.F. Rehnborg's fondest hope, Nutrilite products were introduced in other countries. Canada was first in 1974, then Australia in 1976, Malaysia and Hong Kong in 1977, the United Kingdom in 1983, and Germany, Taiwan, and Japan in 1984.

1975-1978:   Dr. Sam Rehnborg spent three years circumnavigating the world, studying the customs and eating habits of various cultures.

1976-1980:   Robert T. Hunter was elected Chief Executive Officer of Nutrilite Products, Inc. During this time all operational facilities were improved and greatly expanded to meet Amway's increased sales demands.

1977:   An additional 400 acres were purchased in Naguabo, Puerto Rico, in order to meet the growing demand for Acerola Concentrate used in Nutrilite Food Supplements.

1978- present: Dr. Sam Rehnborg was named Senior Vice President of Nutrilite Products, Inc. in 1978. In 1981 he became Executive Vice President and Chief Executive Officer, and in 1983 he was named President and Chief Executive Officer.

1979: A special facility was constructed at Buena Park for the production of Nutrilite Daily.

1981: A food bar facility was built and put into production at Buena Park.

1983: A powdered nutritious drink facility was established at Lakeview.

1984: Joining with the Amway Corporation which celebrates its 25th anniversary in business this year, Nutrilite Products, Inc. commemorates 50 years of producing quality nutritional products based on the genius of C.F. Rehnborg, and dedicated to his dream of improving diets of people throughout the world.

Part II
RESEARCH AND DEVELOPMENT:
ideas for the future

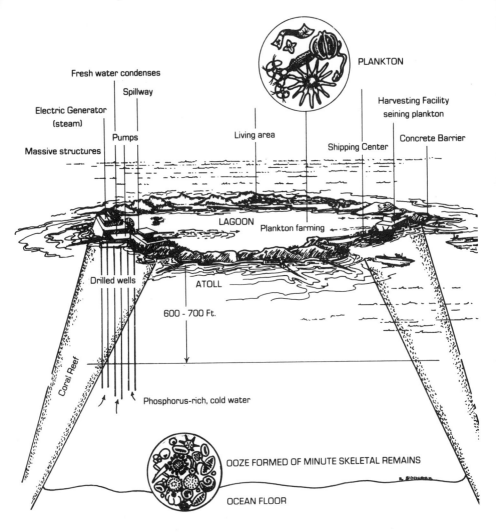

PLANKTON

Fresh water condenses

Spillway

Harvesting Facility
seining plankton

Electric Generator
(steam)

Living area

Concrete Barrier

Pumps

Shipping Center

Massive structures

LAGOON Plankton farming

Drilled wells

ATOLL

600 - 700 Ft.

Coral Reef

Phosphorus-rich, cold water

OOZE FORMED OF MINUTE SKELETAL REMAINS

OCEAN FLOOR

Farming the Sea for Food

The following was taken from a series of memos from C.F. Rehnborg to Dr. Sam Rehnborg, dated in April and May of 1966. Rehnborg's concern with overpopulation and dwindling world food supplies had led to research on plankton as a source of protein, carried out by Nutrilite Products, Inc. during 1954 to 1958. This in turn stimulated his inventive mind to consideration of ways in which the sea could be harvested for both plankton and fish, and of ways in which the yield could be increased and made commercially feasible. His idea for "an unlimited energy source," described in this chapter, was one result.

While we had the Acania as a research vessel, we were one of the first to produce plankton meal as a protein source. We were only ahead of our time. Now we should re-explore the possibilities, both of fish or plankton meal and of the various plants of the sea, both plankton and various seaweeds, as raw materials for protein meal and as sources of various vitamin groups.

What is really most needed for us as a group is actually to get the picture of the facts. The sea may be the place life started, and man is basically attuned to its chemistry and its rhythms. We ought to be able to enrich human existence in yet unknown ways through the chemistry of the sea. Certainly the sea is going to be the reserve source if we survive, rather than to breed ourselves to extinction as a race.

What we had in mind was to farm the sea for plankton and fish, by having a nuclear device at the floor of the sea sending up a thermal column of phosphorus-rich water to the surface, where the plankton would proliferate, increasing the population of small fish and food fish, sort of jack-in-the-box fashion. And then, we would fish the area continuously with extra-large fishing and processing ships. Or alternately, we might use an atoll as a farm by enclosing its lagoon completely and bringing in deep-sea phosphorus-rich water, and use the temperature gradient to operate the processing plant with a low-pressure steam plant supplying power.

To draw sea water from the depths requires no power at the water surface, because the water from 1,000 feet down or more expands as it rises and warms. It is also less saline than at the surface, and approaches the zero centigrade temperature of the deep sea bottom. As the water rises and warms, however slightly, it becomes a convection current within the continuous pipe of ten-foot diameter. Additionally, the difference in temperature of the rising water permits use of the warm surface water to generate low-pressure steam, and for the cold deep water to condense it. The electric current from a low-pressure turbine could operate the facilities of the processing plant.

Phosphorus is the limiting element in the proliferation of life, both on land and in the sea. The phosphorus in the deep water of the sea is the detritus of earlier life forms. It stays in the deep water, it has been estimated, for upwards of a thousand years before it gets to the surface and is again used by a living plant or animal. Some of this deep water rises to the surface where an ocean current hits a continental slope, and then there is an explosion of marine life such as is observed off the west coast of South America, for example. The phosphorus-rich water which thus comes to the ocean surface each year is the agency for the deep sea phosphorus to again form part of the biosphere.

The Acania was purchased in the 50's and equipped as a research vessel in connection with the company's project for exploring the feasibility of harvesting plankton as a source of protein for the world's hungry people. A voyage was made from California north into Alaskan waters with good results, but the project was put on hold for economic reasons. Later the Acania was donated to Scripps Institute of Oceanography at LaJolla, California.

An Unlimited Energy Source

Written May 4, 1966

The world is becoming aware that the growth of its human population is within one or at most a few centuries of becoming a catastrophe. Unless we find we can control population growth, and do so, our planet will become our catafalque.

There is, in fact, no intrinsic reason for any singularly human being to live on this planet, or for us to possess it, and if we cannot be wise enough to justify our lives, the universe can and will continue without us.

If we move effectively to limit and control population, we will yet need some time to make the required changes, and so should possess a reserve food supply.

The only place we can find such a reserve food supply, after the arable land surfaces have been committed, is in the sea, and it exists in the sea as if it had been planned and provided from the beginning to rescue us from the results of our stupidity and ignorance.

Life in the sea, all life, both the eaters and the eaten, is basically a chemical process occurring in a solution in water. Life most probably began in the sea, where the necessary elements and compounds are in solution, and where the greater part of life still exists. The automatic control on the natural growth of life is the available supply (or lack) of one element — in this case, phosphorus.

Life occurs in the top five or six hundred feet of the water, where there is light to support photosynthesis for the basic plant forms in the life chain. There are some scavenger fish at the bottom of the sea to eat the dead who drift down from the surface, but the rest of the water of the sea and its mineral content are effectually in storage for a matter of centuries, mixing slowly with the surface layers, and so returning to use in living forms.

If the stored water mixed more rapidly with the surface water, the total of life in the surface water would increase. Therefore, to increase the availability of food is as simple as to increase the rate at which phosphorus is recirculated from storage to the zone of life at the surface. There could be new and other limiting mineral factors as phosphorus became more available, but since these in turn are already in solution in the water of the sea, there probably would not be any other check to the total of life. It is phosphorus which is the worldwide brake and control on the total of life.

The problem is therefore to increase the flow of deep water to the surface of the sea. There is no problem as to the return of the soluble minerals to the storehouse in the sea. All the water in circulation in the world returns to the sea again and again. All that is spent in each circuit is the solar energy which powers photosynthesis and which lifts the vapor from the sea, which falls as rain. The total of life on the earth, the total of water in circulation and in the sea, and the total of mineral salts in solution in the water, change only within very narrow limits.

This is the "perpetual motion machine"; and the energy which (as in all such machines) powers the operation of the machine is the sun's radiation falling on all the surface of the earth.

The problem of increasing the quantity of soluble minerals, especially phosphorus, in the upper level of the sea is a solvable problem. It is perhaps too easy, constituting a danger unless controls are worldwide and under international control.

The upper level of the deep-water 'storage' is upwards of 700 feet from the surface of the sea: above that level there tends to be a phosphorus deficiency, below that a phosphorus surplus, or at least more than at the surface. The problem is to have some of the deeper water mix with the surface water. When it is drawn towards the surface, its natural character will end in its mixing properly. Then there will be more phytoplankton (minute vegetable forms) which will feed more zooplankton (minute animal forms) which, again in turn, will feed larger and larger animal forms. Briefly, the basis of life in the sea is vegetable, as it is on land. Increasing the volume of food forms, even some of the minute animals, is automatic if the mineral supply of the water is increased properly.

The richer water is brought to the top naturally in a number of locations: the arctic seas, places where ocean currents strike precipitous shores, such as Peru, and so on. At these places there is an explosion of sea life, and the plankton even support such large forms as the whales.

To induce currents of deep water to rise to the surface by intent, can be done by several methods: first, one could sink a thermal source (such as a nuclear device) to the bottom of the sea, where it would warm water and thus create a thermal column of water; second, by making a channel for warmer water to rise.

This last is with some danger of overdoing a good thing. At any precipitous underwater slope, such as a coral island for example, a closed aqueduct, either bored through the coral or laid down as a pipe, could reach from below the rich water level to near the surface. This deep water is very cold and dense. As the water was started toward the sea surface, its lower salt level and the gradual warming by upper levels of water would cause the flow to become continuous: once begun it would continue indefinitely.

The upper end of the water column could be surfaced within a lagoon or at the sea level from land. The mixture of deep water and surface water would support increased life, and the increase would occur naturally and spontaneously. It would be as simple as increasing the facilities for harvesting the sea within a circumference around the welling deep water. The number of such sources for deep water rising to the surface would be one-time projects, and in numbers only limited by the engineering effort expended one time only for each well.

Further, at each 'source', the surface water, several tens of degrees warmer than the deep water, could be used to produce low-pressure steam to generate electrical current, and the deep cold water could be used in a condenser before being released at the surface. The production of current would be continuous and could continue forever.

Now, to return to the human population for which the food supplies need to be thus increased.

Human population tends to increase geometrically, and now, in the absence of natural checks such as accidental death or death by disease or warfare, it is geometrically increasing at a net increase in numbers of 4 to 5 percent annually, or a doubling of population between four and five decades. This rate of increase will now be continuous forever unless checked by a decrease in the human birthrate. There has been a first recent doubling in the lifetimes of the people now living, and there will be another doubling by the year 2000.

This means that then there will be a human population twice as great as the present population, and then in successive periods of about thirty-five years, doubling again, and again, up to the limit of numbers which can find food to eat, to the pending near-death of the whole human race.

We can say we now have a possible way to feed greater numbers of human beings than are being fed at present — and even now the pressure of human population leaves much of the present population on less than a full or even adequate diet.

There is no assurance that the human race is not now on its way out. At whatever desperate cost, the human race must save itself or soon disappear. It is humanly possible to check and reverse the present course to destruction, but any course of salvation will be less and less desirable the longer population increases are not controlled.

No one speaking through the public press does more than to offer solutions against starvation during the next doubling of population. But there is no period of grace for defense against annihilation; the crisis is here and now. All we can hope for is a delay made possible by increasing the available food supply, and that delay should be regarded as already expended, or as less and less with any meaning, unless the corrective procedures are put under way immediately.

Staff research and development meetings were held frequently in the company's library, which was considered one of the finest technical libraries in the area.

Protein From The Sea

The following is a memorandum written by C.F. Rehnborg on April 29, 1967, while he and Mrs. Rehnborg were at their home in Tahiti, in response to material which had been forwarded to him on research into the production of protein powder from marine sources. Although it was later amended by a second memo stating that "...we must recognize that this kind of project is completely out of reach for us as far as the financial resources necessary are concerned," it is nevertheless fascinating for the originality and scope of the ideas expressed by Rehnborg.

The material concerning the process of preparing protein powder from edible but less popular kinds of fish was of much interest, but does not address the point of my previous memorandum of a week ago.

The future problem will be one of feeding perhaps billions of people a supplemental ration; the key to the ration is a protein powder, preferably animal protein, added to any inadequate ration. The proposal was to skip an obvious loss of protein in a natural marine food chain, and thus to add a hundred or a thousand times as much protein to the available source by using the plankton directly as a source of protein. There are fisheries which net fish from the sea, such as hake and sardines, and use the fish for oil and fertilizer, but only to a smaller degree for human food. This is a more wasteful step than will be permitted in a worldwide protein deficiency, but to use the zooplankton (animal protein) directly calls for a development which has no earlier precedent, and for a different approach wholly.

In the natural food chain of the world's seas, ten pounds of phytoplankton become one pound of zooplankton, but this is unavoidable in large part since the phyton, because they are microscopic, are virtually impossible to separate from the sea water (which is the 'soil' in which they grow). These, the 'vegetables' of the sea, are also sometimes poisonous, although the animal forms that subsist on them are not, except rarely and detectably, in which case they are not used as a protein source.

The animal food chain begins with the zooplankton, which are usable as a human food source of protein, and of which ten to ten thousand times the weight of the final product, food fishes, are lost to the fishes in any emergency food source using protein from the sea.

Everything living in the sea, because the 'vegetable' step is of small and largely invisible forms, seems to eat some smaller animal and to be eaten by some larger animal. This apparent chain, beginning with the zooplankton, has many variations but is typified by the one in which ten pounds of zooplankton become one pound of other planktonic forms, either fish larvae or permanent plankton; ten pounds of planktonic forms become one pound of herring or mackerel or sardines; ten pounds of small fishes become one pound of food fishes such as are caught by fisheries —a chain of 3 powers of 10 among many types of food and chemical cycles.

The only reason the very small animal forms do not fill the sea solid, and so become easy for us to collect, is that certain essential minerals of animal forms in the sea, and of the phytoplankton at the very base of the food chains, are in limited supply. Therefore, fairly early in each "bloom" or active growing season of the sea, these minerals become locked in the life forms and are no longer found in solution, and growth stops. This is a most important limitation on the growth of life in the sea, and important also in our problem of getting protein from the sea as a food additive. What we want to get done does not interfere with the normal use of the elements locked in the life forms, and each of the life forms in the food chains is an efficient user of the general supply; better than we, in fact. We could not, for example, match the efficiency of a baleen whale sieving the water through his fringed plates to sort out the planktonic forms at the rate of tons per day. But the marine animals consume only a part of what is available, yet convey to us only a fraction of what they consume.

Part of the life-chain in the sea is the existence of the great currents at the surface of the sea, which flow as if between banks held in place by water differences in salinity and temperature. The surface water finally goes below the surface, and deep water rises to take its place. There is complicated stratification by density and temperature in the great mass of the sea, and it is estimated that on the average each gallon of surface water disappears into the depths for anything between one hundred and one thousand years. It takes with it the inertly floating plankton, which dies in the dark and cold of the depths and rains down on the benthonic life forms on the sea floor, forming part of their life cycle, or decays into simpler chemical forms and joins the ammonia and phosphorus stored in the deeps, rising many decades later again to the surface.

The water which rises to the surface renews the supply of the mineral factors which limit the seasonal growth at the surface. Areas like the land masses at the north of the Pacific and around Antarctica, and the specially shaped coast of South America, where this deep water rises to the surface, have a permanent 'bloom' and support a tremendous surface water population, including a replacement of the plankton which died in the water which sank to the depths.

When we talk about farming the sea for protein, we really mean farming at the points where the deep water rises and the "bloom" on the surface multiplies the total of life made up of the protein we want to get as a food additive. We want as well to concentrate the planktonic forms for convenient harvesting, but there are inconveniences in the climatic conditions of the upwellings near the poles, and the "bloom" around the west coast of South America is too diffused over too great an area for economical harvesting. The harvesting would have to be done from a ship, which would inevitably be less efficient than to harvest from a land surface.

We need to set up a vertical current from the bottom to the surface, and the current has to start from a fixed point and rise practically straight up, if it is to create a dependable source of supply of the chemicals for life. The more the problem is studied, the more evident it becomes that an atoll used as a farm is the most practical present solution. On an atoll all the now-foreseeable problems have answers.

As if created especially to meet our problem, an atoll is a tropical island roughly in the form of a ring, with a lagoon within the ring extending at the interior side of the ring to the mountainous island at the center of the ring, or to the opposite side of the ring if the mountain has subsided below the level of the sea. At times the coral ring is wide enough for a coral island to form on the ring, or a series of islands virtually at sea level, formed of coral sand held in place by the root systems of coconut trees.

The floor of the sea, at the outside of the ring, is down at an angle sometimes very steep, and the floor of the sea is fairly to very deep. Darwin worked out in detail the origin and growth of an atoll: the reef of an island rising as the volcanic island subsided, until the reef was well separated from the island or even until the mountain at the center had subsided below water.

There are thousands of approximately circular atolls in the Pacific tropical zone. The reef tops are level and sometimes wide. Sometimes the outer reef joins the shore-side reef for part of its circle. The lagoon of the reef is our farm; the tide-level reef itself the perfectly level site of the necessary manufactory works. The tropical sun speeds the growth of the planktonic raw material, and the sun's heat can be used in the protein process. And the phosphorus-rich water is steeply down from the outside edge of the reef, very deep and very cold, (perhaps 45 to 40 degrees Fahrenheit or even less) to be used as condenser water for the low-pressure turbine of the electric plant and then as the only necessary fertilizer for the continuous 'bloom' of the water of the lagoon. It will supply also, with the steam condensate of the generator turbines, all the fresh water necessary for both a factory and a small town. (Any town or complex in the South Seas could generate electrical power and secure pure fresh water in the same way.) There is no need to seed the lagoon 'farm,' which will initiate the growth of the living crop of protein from the spawn bed of the sea itself.

Let's develop this matter of the generation of electricity as a general example of how specifically the idea of a 'farm' operation for production of a good additive of protein fits a tropical atoll. The atoll is always in a surface current of the ocean. The phosphorus-rich seawater of the deep sea, on the side of the atoll facing the surface current, is within a thousand feet of the surface. It is drawn to the surface by a pipe or pipes going down to the deep water along the steep slope of the island. If the deep water, which is less saline than the surface water, is made to start to flow to the surface with an outlet at sea level, it may be assisted and speeded by fan-type pumps near the surface, but in any case it will continue permanently to flow.

The whole idea, in fact, is based on essentially simple facts. We are using the energy of sunlight in several facets of the project, and we are indirectly producing edible protein from the source of power in the sun shining on an ocean. The atoll, as if from the first designed for the project, serves to enclose a segment of the warm ocean within very massive walls. The sun shines every day of the year to warm the water and supply energy for the growth of the food source and to synthesize the organic compounds which will be the protein we need for the human ecology. It is the tremendous size and scope of essentially simple processes which makes the project so impressive.

The particular 30-mile atoll which is our frame of reference has a band of level ground around its circumference, varying in horizontal width from a few dozen yards to fractions of a mile, made up of coral sand held in place by the roots of trees and brush. Rain of heavy volume at some seasons of the year fills the surface ground by subsoil flow with brackish fresh water. The ocean surges break up on the outer part of the reef, and except in some extreme storms the land of the islets along the reef almost at sea level is not wet except by fresh water from the sky. There are some thin spots along the massive reef where the surge can wash over from the sea into the lagoon of the reef, but there is only one open passage to the sea, about two hundred yards wide and up to a hundred feet deep. There the water of a one-or-two-foot tide flows into and out of the lagoon, twice each day, as an immense and very swift current.

All the structures to be put on the reef will be extremely massive, including all roofs and towers, and almost level with the reef-top, so that the usual activities of the complex will proceed without any change due to storm or season. There will be a heavy concrete barrier, almost at the inner edge of the reef, with shallower ridges between the barrier and the breakers of the sea, to break and soften the impact of the waves directly off the ocean. At the site of the electric plant there will be a row of drilled wells near the inner edge of the reef, straight down through the massive reef, and far enough down and matched to the seaward contour of the reef bottom, curved to drill out to the vertical face of the reef wall for the bottom opening of the well into the phosphorus-rich water of the deep sea.

The amount of water brought up by these open-end wells can be whatever is decided by increasing the size or number of wells drilled. All this cold water will go through the extended condensers of the low-pressure steam boilers and then through channels in the reef surface ending into spillways where it flows, after being thus warmed, into the lagoon as the essential and only fertilizer for the great culture beds. In these culture beds the permanent plankton forms grow to produce animal protein. Warmer water from the lagoon surface, pumped into shallow ponds on the reef, is further warmed by passing through arrangements of mirrors on V-shaped carriers canted to the angle, east-west, of the sun's latitude at each day or season, requiring only small change per day. The water then goes into a covered or sub-surface storage area before going as feed-water into the low-pressure boilers of the power house. The whole power system is at high vacuum, depending on the chilled bottom water from the pump-wells to maintain the highest possible difference of temperature between the heated water from the lagoon surface and the chilled deep water from the sea.

All the power needed by all the facilities on the reef will be electric, and supplied from the powerhouse, in excess of requirements. There will be no need for oil, except lubricants, and there will be no dust or dirt from the project buildings or machinery. There should be no pollution of sea or lagoon.

It will be the eventual intent, or even from the first, that the present open sea channel into the lagoon will be the entrance into the docking facilities. The inflow and outflow of the lagoon, with the need of a tide-flow ended, will be stopped and the harbor structures will take its place. The land structures will be massive, in keeping with the tropical potential of storms, but there will be no ocean surge to disturb the mooring of the ships. Not more than a few hundred tons of supplies will be shipped in as cargo, and the product of the manufactory will be powder in bulk, so ships can be turned around in a few hours, if desired.

Extra water can be taken into or discharged from the lagoon through the water gates, but the inflow from the wells will probably take care of water replacement to any extent necessary. The managed outflow through the harvesting facilities where the planktonic forms are strained from the outgoing water will best be done in a current which is not swift, and which goes to the ocean or back into the lagoon. Every type of facility can be multiplied around the almost hundred-mile length of the reef, and doubtless it will be best to have the harvesting facilities in smaller units rather than one big plant. The pace of the harvesting can be increased by the use of net trawlers inside the lagoon, if desirable, to match the breeding rate and swiftness of growth of plankton, and there will be long-range capture of large plankton users or of pests such as pelagic sharks.

It is the nature of a reef that an electric-powered transportation will conveniently serve all the working parts of the complex, beginning from the ship harbor, but it can be expected that one massive complex on this scale can supply the world demand for protein products, including things outside the food additive enterprise.

It is my feeling that at this point there should be some discussion of this project by the Board. It is an enormous project requiring government-sized participation, but as to which government should depend on the interest shown in the subject. At present no government and very few groups have shown any pressing interest in population explosion, but it is in fact an emergency matter with overtones of catastrophe.

I can imagine the project including an autonomous colony of the men operating the project, and their families, with its land farms of sandy soil generously fertilized with organic waste from the project, adequately and even generously watered by condenser water from the warm water boiling in the low-pressure boilers of the electric plant. It might even be necessary to irrigate the land with some proportion of seawater added to the condenser water, to include minerals for flavor in the drinking water and for the irrigation water put on crops.

Certainly we could get the cold deep water and sun-warmed water together, and generate electric power at a low cost, only on an atoll or similar island. Rains occur on an atoll, but in the main the sun shines every day and there are almost no seasonal changes. A most interesting detail is that the cold and hot water brought together on an atoll in a powerhouse means ample fresh water for all purposes in a very clean ambience, and about the cleanest industrial area possible.

A fearless underwater explorer even in his 60's, C.F. Rehnborg and his son Sam are shown on a trip to Alaska which involved some deep-sea diving.

In this photo Rehnborg has been outfitted in diving gear and is awaiting the placement of his helmet, at left on small boat seat.

Notes On Research

This memo was written to Dr. Sam Rehnborg by C.F. Rehnborg, on April 26, 1966, when he was 78 years of age. His strongly-held belief in the value of food supplementation was often demonstrated by memos suggesting new research projects, and the addition of products. His interest in this field never waned, and he kept current with all developments in the science of nutrition.

In another memo of this same date, I have noted an idea which I think should be examined carefully in laying out lines of projected research: That in man's history and pre-history, living in a culture made possible by agriculture, his ideas on food have been dominated by his culture and not by physiology.

By one means or another he learned to gather and then to cultivate grains and other plants, of which the fruits could be dried and stored for later use. These foods were selected for their convenience value, and because they were adjusted to their particular location. Social and religious ideas became associated with the foods. There were foods which could not be eaten at all, merely because they were taboo. Travels between locations were also taboo, except in an organized way for conquest, and new foods came into a given culture very slowly.

The ancient cultures each had a very nebulous idea of the existence of the other, and various cultures developed on the several great continents. The concept of relationship between cultures came very slowly, and the present state of a world society did not even exist until recent times.

As a consequence, nothing caused any group to examine or question such things as the chemical connections between diet and well-being. Tradition about foods was handed down from generation to generation for very long times, but a direct knowledge that foods varied in their values and their relationships to bodily functions was linked only with medicine men. Food was merely an edible substance, and some foods had better taste than others, but in general, food was food in an uncomplicated way, and when hunger was satisfied everything necessary had occurred.

The complexities of foods in their relationship to health awaited modern growth of the sciences, and better contact between peoples. These in turn developed knowledge of the sciences, especially chemistry and medicine, and especially in the more recent centuries. Now foods are t◗ some extent first considered in their character as sources of fats starches, proteins, vitamins and minerals, although in the market food◗ are bought by individuals for their taste appeal more than for thei◗ character as sources of the diet essentials.

But never until recently has there been general appreciation of the fact that foods are something more than satisfaction of hunger in their nature as agreeable edible substances or attractive for their social aspect, and some esteemed foods actually have little nutritive value. Nothing has changed basic food habits except for a few people, all through history or even at the present time. Most of our social habits regarding food have been continued as they were established when food cultivation created human cultures, by making it clear that agriculture was a cooperative undertaking. The only changes have been by cultural exchanges and territorial extension resulting from warfare, exploration, or migration.

Strange as it may seem, there has actually been no systematized knowledge about food as the supplies for building and maintenance of the human body until the last few generations of the human race. The human ideas about food were formed and agreed upon before there was a written history, and even before there were societies and the primitive languages developed by the earliest agricultural societies. The basic human knowledge concerning foods was whether a given food was safe to eat and whether it had a pleasant taste. The pleasure found in eating it was the test of quality of any food — and this primitive assessment of a food was accepted until very recently.

It was not a good assessment. The diseases of primitive man involving his skeleton are the only ones we can state now, but he generally had bone and tooth diseases, while the apes did not have them. The same thing is true still. The apes eat whatever is edible without preparing it for eating, and therefore are adjusted to the environment. Humans have diets of choice, prepared and often denatured for eating, and at all ages may have caries, or as they grow older may have arthritis.

This idea of forced adjustment to the environment is a basic fact of life wherever it occurs. There are life forms which have adjusted to special substances rather than to a more general list of the foods of the environment, but this is a special case which emphasizes the general rule. The selective habits of mankind are in large part contrary to the general rule, and the price of our nonconformity is often a wide range of what are

Ongoing research at Nutrilite involves a product containing some protein derived from alfalfa. Here a pilot plant is processing a small batch of the protein.

Because insecticides were never used on Nutrilite's growing fields, biological insect control research was emphasized using natural methods of controlling harmful insects. In the Entomological Laboratory, one of the scientists is sorting larvae.

A pioneer in the use of Acerola Cherries as a source of Vitamin C, Nutrilite has developed this 400-acre orchard in Naguabo, Puerto Rico, where the trees are grown. Other orchards of Acerola Cherries are also being cultivated.

In the late 50's the Hemet
Farm was the location of an
experimental hydroponic
farming operation. The
Rehnborgs are standing in
front of the "Strawberry
Wall," which produced
luscious fruit.

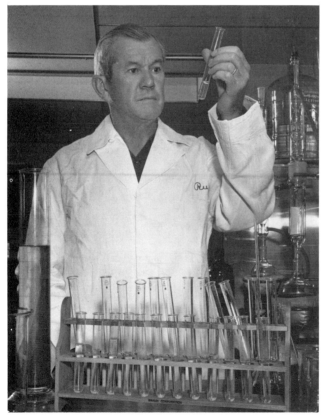

C.F. Rehnborg often
donned a lab coat
and conducted his
own experimental
work in the Research
Laboratories. His
natural curiosity and
lifelong reading of
scientific material
enabled him to keep
abreast of current
techniques and devel-
opments in the nutri-
tional research field.

called deficiency diseases, with some but not all of them recognizable as deficiencies.

This was the background against which Nutrilite Food Supplement originated. Starting with the facts, which any traveler of our modern age can confirm from observation, it is clear that diets of general use vary from district to district, and in addition are selective for reasons of custom or taste. It is equally clear that numbers of the inhabitants of any group may be subject to what are called deficiency diseases. There are exceptions, of course, but the exceptions emphasize the rules: modern diets are out of step with physiological requirements and have been since the precursors of historical man moved away from the pack life of the sub-humans into the tribal life of the earliest cultures formed by the development of agriculture. Ignorance as to the relation between the dietary habits of civilization and the emerging of deficiency ailments is nearly as general now as in pre-historical times.

This forms the background of diet supplementation. A survey shows that if the requirement for protein, carbohydrate, and fat is met, as it usually is in the miscellaneous materials of any but a starvation diet, there remains a deficiency for vitamins and minerals, and perhaps other oganic factors, which can be made up from plant sources. The survey also shows that there may be such deficiencies in an average diet. The publications of the U.S. Agricultural Department report many such deficiencies.

Man is a biological intruder into an environment existing prior to his appearance, and his appearance was itself an adjustment to the environment and not the other way around. With a few notable exceptions, man has never even suspected this fact until recent times. The modern biologist, however, accepts the basic fact of the identity of the chemical makeup of life forms with the chemical makeup of the environment. All the substances of a life form are identical with, and limited to, the chemistry of the environment. This chemistry is effectively the chemistry of the universe.

Life is integrated with, and a part of, the universe as a unit. Man is beginning to accept the fact that he is an integrated part of the universe and subject to its laws, a concession which now makes it possible to examine his relation to those laws.

The design of man, and any other living form, is a design for health and competence in the environment which shaped him. The contrasting fact is that he is less than healthy because he has not until now been ready to accept his obligation to obey the laws of the environment, and even now it is necessary to spell out the laws for him, because his customs have complicated the environment.

His primary endowment of life itself is a chemical process. He shares this endowment with all living things, but he can make decisions not open to lesser creatures by adjusting his local environment to his specific needs, and this adjustment is as simple as to insure that he eats in his diet, or adds to his diet, the chemical substances which are the factors in the life process. Put into ordinary commercial words of his total environment, this means that he as trader offers to himself as customer the food substances — or the food supplements — which add up to the total dietary requirements. These, in combination with other basic requirements such as exercise, clean air and water among them, will add up to the optimum health of his body and its capacity to function according to design.

The first plan to offer Nutrilite (although not then by that name) was a plan to offer a concentrate from plant sources. It was assumed that protein, fats, and carbohydrates were adequately supplied by an ordinary diet, as is reasonably true, and that a concentrate from green plants would supply substantially everything else that might be required. It was planned that whatever the individual deficiency, one could assume that it was adequate with the addition of enough of the known vitamins and minerals to fill the need for any deficiency in those two categories. This was not the same as trying to meet one by one the problems of the various areas.

The variation between areas could be what caused deficiencies to occur, but to correct for deficiencies it was proper to correct for any deficiency. The exact requirements were not at that time known, but it was known that the missing vitamin factors were the ones which were most generally found in the plants of any area, while what generally caused deficiencies to occur were the narrow, limited diets — for example, potatoes and meat among country folk, and salt pork and biscuits among sailors.

This then-new idea of a diet supplement in the form of a concentrate from plant sources had to be presented to an almost completely unready public. Even the U.S. Food and Drug Administration was neither ready nor in agreement. It is now better known, and then only guessed, that diets can be inadequate and often are. The Agricultural Department has issued many brochures concerning diet deficiencies, pointing out that they occur regularly, even in the United States where we have the best-fed population in the world. What then should have been preliminary work should now be done, because the basic thought that a supplementary diet from plant sources could correct possible deficiencies both had and has merit.

I would like to go back now with you to the beginnings of the Nutrilite idea, preparing concentrates as they were originally made. The notion that diet deficiencies were of factors other than proteins, fats, and carbohydrates, and that these factors, some known and some then unidentified, could be secured from green plants, was very earnestly opposed by the Food and Drug Administration. It still seems to me, however, that such a simple way to correct diets for possible deficiencies is a valid approach; and that a great many ailments (except those caused by accidents or infections by disease-producing organisms) are matters of deficiencies in the diet — usually for the vitamin-like factors and the minerals.

It is probable that our vitamin-mineral products, as presently offered, should be expanded to include more in the low-medium price range. More people now than ever before fully believe in the idea of a diet-supplement approach to less-than-optimum health. I remain convinced the idea is correct and sound. Certainly I would like to give the XX idea another workout; first doing additional work for evidence of the soundness of the idea, including (1) research for evidence of deficiency having its beginning in soil deficiency, (2) evidence for the occurrence of all the diet factors in a natural diet, (3) the connection between diets and health, and (4) the evidence that natural foods may correct all diet deficiencies.

This would be a long and extensive research project. It would be an inquiry into the idea of food supplementation itself, and a check on the ideas and earlier research we followed to determine their correctness. We were the first to connect the idea of a definite correlation between deficiency and food supplementation, and personally I am still waving a flag I would like to see justified.

Measurements of Time and Space

The following was written by C.F. Rehnborg on July 9, 1957 to his son, Sam, who at the time was struggling with some basic concepts of time and space in a Physics class at Stanford.

This is a speculative question which I am obliged to ask in non-mathematical language for the reason that I am not a mathematician. The question concerns a speculation regarding the apparently discontinuous nature of the entities of the physical universe.

I assume that matter and energy are considered to be differing aspects of one ultimate "reality," and that this matter/energy can be regarded as electromagnetic fields of force, although its "final" nature is not known. I assume that such a question as, "Where is the orbiting electron between quantum jumps?" cannot be answered. I assume that time can be considered a spatial dimension, and that it is we who arbitrarily decide that there are only three spatial dimensions, and that time, while it is a dimension, is a dimension of another character.

If, however, time is in fact a spatial dimension, as is indicated by its use mathematically, then just as a point has no dimension in space, and a moving point creates a plane in two dimensions, and a moving plane creates a solid in three dimensions, so in turn a "moving" solid in the time dimension constitutes an event.

Any specific event, such as a sun or a table, has a duration extending from integration until disintegration; but the specific object or event is merely a bundle of the durations of ultimate particles and not itself anything but a more or less temporary collection, just as a cloud is a collection of water particles and not an entity in itself.

The ultimate "particles of matter" in the events are the atoms, which, except for transitions between matter and energy, may be considered to have infinite duration and identity. In turn, while the atoms are the final particles, they are not the specific and final entities of the material universe. These entities are the nucleons, the mesons, the pions, and a long list of other similar positive and negative particles which are listed in our technical language as separate entities; but which may be, for philosophical considerations, not themselves final entities, but probably all of some fundamental character similar in final nature to one another — probably the electromagnetic fields of force already mentioned.

Even the concept of time itself is an abstraction for a continuous process of being, but this abstraction indicates both a sequence of being and a direction of the sequence of being. On this time sequence or axis, the physical measurements wc make are made in the "present," in what is effectively a plane surface marking the dimensionless instant between the future and the past. While these measurements take an interval of time to make, they are nevertheless all made (including the measurements which show the quantum effect) in this plane surface of three dimensions on the time axis, and as if they were made simultaneously. To complicate the matter further, it is not possible to measure actual simultaneity of event in the four-dimensional space-time continuum, but there must nevertheless be a simultaneity of events in time, whether or not the characteristics of the universe permit the measurements to be made.

It is fair to assume that the fact that measurements can be made, of which the essential components exist in the timeless instant of a dimensionless present on the time axis, indicates also the existence of a "reality" extending both backward and forward from the three-dimensional plane continuum in which the measurements were made. In fact, if the "substance" (whatever that may be) of the entities which are measured did not extend in both directions from the three-dimensional plane of the "present," there would be nothing whatever to measure. Therefore, it seems to me to be indicated that our successful use of the measurement of time as a dimension of an event demonstrates that the event of which the three-dimensional aspect is measured has extension in time as well as in the three dimensions of space — that what we call the physical qualities of an object or an event, measured in three dimensions, is merely an expression in our limited language of some reality which has extension beyond three dimensions — not merely theoretically, but actually.

It seems to be generally understood and accepted that the final nature of "reality" may never be deciphered. Nevertheless, there are and have been successive steps toward such understanding. The concepts of relativity and of quantum physics substantially invalidated the classical view of the physical universe which had prevailed up to that time. It is therefore possible for yet another step to be taken of equal import, and it seems to me that I am getting a faint glimpse of something which lies beyond what we now consider to be a reasonably complete picture of the physical universe. It may be that this idea has been considered fully, but at least I have not seen it discussed. I have, however, seen the statement that the multiplicity of entities which we observe in our three dimensions results in too much complexity, and seems to be differing aspects of something more fundamental.

It is not philosophically possible to accept a discontinuous universe as a final fact. The universe may be in fact discontinuous, and dissatisfaction with this picture may be a subjective human conclusion. Nevertheless, it seems as if something is required to fill in the gaps in a discontinuous universe, so that while this requirement may be only in the mind of a human being, it is also possible that it indicates an actual necessity. It may be true, even, that matter and space, with positive and negative "states of energy," may somehow be interdependent concepts.

If it is assumed that all measurements we can make in three dimensions lack at least one more dimension to be complete, and if the "permitted orbit" of an orbiting electron is a three-dimensional measurement of a real four-dimensional orbit, we would have a sort of explanation of the fact that the electron, for example, is observed only in a permitted orbit when actually it may be following a helical path in four dimensions from one permitted orbit to another. And it would follow that we could subject this to proof if we could refine our measurements, and that lack of refinement in our measurements is the only reason we have not observed this transition.

As an analogy, a true three-dimensional representation of a forked stick in three dimensions would, in cross-sections in two dimensions, show merely two ovals which approached or receded from one another as the stick was moved, and we would thereupon explain the movement as attraction and repulsion between the ovals when in fact it would be something else altogether.

Question: Is it possible that discontinuity represents a three-dimensional observation of a four-dimensional effect, or of an n-dimensional effect? If this question is not altogether mistaken it should be useful to examine it.

Developing Tourism in the South Seas

After having made several trips to Hawaii and Tahiti, and other
nesian islands in the South Seas, C.F. Rehnborg began to envision
rge-scale hotel project to encourage the development of tourism in
beautiful but remote part of the world. He purchased Les Tropiques
el in Papeete, Tahiti, as a first step, and acquired acreage with a
te sand beach on the island of Moorea, ten miles from Tahiti, as a
nd possible hotel site. This was done under the aegis of a subsidiary
oration, South Seas Enterprises, Ltd., and he sought additional
estment capital in order to develop the project on a large scale
ughout the entire area. Following are selected excerpts from the
th Seas Enterprises, Ltd. Prospectus and Addendum to the
spectus, written in 1957-1958, showing the scope and details of his
ns. Unfortunately the expanded project never materialized due to the
k of agreement between American investors and the French govern-
ntal agencies involved. It was, however, an exciting period for every-
e involved in the negotiations.

Prospectus of South Seas Enterprises, Ltd.

troduction

The area known as the South Seas Islands, reaching from Noumea in
ench New Caledonia in the west, eastward through Fiji, Western
moa, Aitutaki, Tahiti, and the Tuamotus, to the Marquesas
chipelago in the east, a distance of perhaps four thousand miles,
presents an area that holds much enchantment for those who have
ard about it, but have not yet seen it. This frontier is unique in its
velopment potential — economically as well as culturally — and is, as
t, unspoiled by western civilization.

This presentation is a plan for developing that area by means of
cquainting western interests in its economic and cultural aspects. To
ake this possible, the first step would be to develop the tourist industry
the South Seas which, as yet, is of a somewhat rudimentary character.
t this time, the tourist industry of the South Seas is about to expand into
large-scale operation. This expansion will occur by stages, but the
tages will follow one another rapidly. Signs are already evident that it
s beginning to happen.

It is planned to develop the tourist industry in step with its pending growth, and to make South Seas Enterprises, Ltd. the dominant enterprise in the area before other similar projects are developed. At the same time, it is planned to organize and operate such related business interests as may logically and successfully emerge from contact with the economy of the area.

Development of tourist trade in the South Seas is quite inevitable. It is believed this corporation can be a potent influence in assuring that this development is in accord with both the legitimate desires of tourists and the maintenance of charm in the areas it serves.

* * * * * * * * *

Addendum to the Prospectus for South Seas Enterprises, Ltd. July, 1958

The prospectus for South Seas Enterprises, Ltd. is a customary and necessary document for consideration by prospective investors. It contains facts and figures and an outline of plans. Nevertheless, as those who have visited the South Seas can appreciate, by its very character as a business document the prospectus misses the sense and feel of the scenery and the people of the area, and it is these that both the investor and the visitor and client of South Seas Enterprises will find of primary interest, and will see and meet. These constitute the charm of the area, and of the South Seas.

The project which has now taken form as South Seas Enterprises, Ltd. began with a vacation and inspection trip in 1956. Interest in the South Seas as a vacation area has been growing slowly but steadily for a long time, and some development has occurred. It was apparent that this interest was, and is, about to reach a peak. The interest of the world in Tahiti and the South Seas as an idyllic and beautiful area to visit as a tourist is fully justified. It will be the next great area of expansion for tourist trade, and it is the last one left in any way comparable in beauty and interest.

The main business interest of the Western world in the South Seas has up to the present been in the products which could be secured there for the markets of the rest of the world, such as pearls and pearl shell, copra, vanilla and other spices, minerals, and such specialties as beche-de-mer (or dried sea-slugs) for the Chinese. Such hotels as have developed have been incidental as accommodation. The major interest was in the area and in its products. Very little interest was devoted to the natives, except on the part of governments, which regarded them as producers; and on the part of missionaries, who regarded them as possible converts. Neither of these interests was by any means an unmixed blessing. The islands and the natives were exploited by foreign governments for trade, and by missionaries to build churches. Until recently, the tourists who got there were truly adventurers. Some of them have written books, beginning with the original explorers, and these books have always had a tremendous appeal.

Tourist trade in the South Seas has only begun, but it is well begun. The development, however, does not include really first class accommodations to be used when the tourists are there. In tourist accommodations, the general idea seems to be that since this is at the end of the world, one has no right to expect standard accommodations, but should be very glad to accept what is offered. Fiji has been more westernized than the other areas. Fiji claimed last year to have received approximately one hundred thousand tourists, mostly Australians and New Zealanders. Tahiti, which a very few years ago had perhaps a hundred new tourist visitors a year, now has many hundreds a month, mostly just going through on tourist steamers. But tourists will not come to stay in Tahiti until there are accommodations for them. The accommodations will have to exist before the tourists come. At present, the tourists who stay for a period of time in Tahiti do not come on tourist steamers. They come by plane, on occasional flights of TEAL seaplanes (Tasman Empire Air Lines) from Fiji.

The Nature of the Venture

The prospectus describes a venture and an adventure in development of outstandingly the best — and one of the last — native areas of the world suitable and ready for tourism.

This is a venture with both business and social justification. As a business it has the potential which it would have had, say, if it were to result in the development of Hawaii a hundred years ago; except that at the new pace of the modern world, with its communications and its pressures of population, the pace will not be so slow, nor the factors so easily managed. Tourist and commercial development of the South Seas, particularly at the remote location of Tahiti, has been delayed by lack of immediate prospective profit for commercial ventures, as well as by the isolation of the area and by the world's preoccupation with wars and unrest. Now there are tourist sailings to Tahiti on almost a monthly schedule, and two airlines are about to begin weekly service within the coming six to twelve months. Tourists will be poured into the area at an accelerating rate. Its rapid development is certain, and we are merely moving at a time just before the flood starts, with completed plans for development and a foothold already secured.

As a social influence, this venture can help the economic status of the area and hinder unfavorable developments. The area is occupied by native people of Polynesian stock, with an ancient culture modified somewhat by the impact of the western world. If these people are not to be destroyed as a kind of people — and it may be assumed that they should not be destroyed as were the Hawaiians and the Maoris — then the unfavorable changes should be opposed. I think we can contribute to the delay in change. What the people of the South Seas need is economic help as a group to hold their own in the western world. What they do not need, or want, is a change in their basic social customs or in their living habits. These are both their identity as people and their charm to the visitor.

Because this is to be a venture adhering firmly to the proposition that a business can be most successfully run if its motives and its performance are undeviatingly honest and cooperative, and that it can be frank and truthful about these, it already has the trust and confidence of the governments of the area. These governments, so far as they can, have expressed their intention to work closely with us.

I have personally promoted the development of this venture. I am not a professional promoter; however, I have seen in this venture an opportunity to coordinate the inevitable development of the South Seas area as a tourist heaven — a development that is already beginning to move forward — in such a manner as to benefit the investors I can persuade to share the venture with me, and also to benefit the people of the areas involved, as well as to control the flow of tourist traffic in such a way that it will not change the area itself.

Rather than to detail at length the information concerning the various areas involved — Tahiti, Samoa, Tonga, Fiji, and New Caledonia — I will use Tahiti as an example.

Tahiti

Tahiti is a French colonial possession and part of French Oceania, which stretches from the Tahitian group eastward through the Tuamotus, or low islands, to the Marquesas Islands. This is an aggregate of many hundreds of separate islands, extending over a distance of perhaps 2500 miles east and west, and several hundred miles north and south. Tahiti itself is the largest island of a group which is mountainous and relatively larger than most of the other islands of the possessions; and it is approximately circular except for a group of mountains connected by an isthmus to the main island at its southeast edge. Tahiti is only about 25 miles across. The Tahitian group lies at about the fifteenth to the seventeenth parallel of latitude south of the equator, and about 2700 miles south and a little east of Honolulu.

All the habitable parts of the island of Tahiti are in areas around the shore. The central part of the island is a mass of mountains, the remains of ancient volcanic craters, which rise to a height of about 7800 feet. This mountainous area is all on end, so that there are no level valleys in which settlement could take place. At places around the island these mountains come down all the way to the sea, but in other areas there are fairly wide shelves between the mountains and the seashore.

Because of the relative coolness of the surrounding ocean and the smallness of the islands, and the prevalent trade winds, the climate in the Tahitian group is incredibly lovely — clear and usually cool and relatively dry, with a temperature almost steadily in the low 80's, and from five to eight degrees cooler at night. Tahiti lies in a tradewind belt, and the high mountains of the interior of the island condense immense amounts of water from the tradewinds. Papeete lies on what is called the dry side of the island, that is, generally to the lee side of the trades; but although it is much drier, and the rainfall much less frequent, it has a tremendous supply of water from the streams running out of the valleys in the interior. Only one of these streams supplies water for the whole area continguous to Papeete, with an excess of an equal amount going down the river valley to the sea. There is a paved road completely around the island, built largely with Point 4 funds, and a number of villages line this road. There is, however, only one city in the island or the archipelago, and that is the city of Papeete, which has a population of about 26,000 — rather more than half of the people living on the island of Tahiti.

Lying at a distance of about ten miles directly west of Papeete is the island of Moorea. This island is the greatly eroded and fantastically shaped remnant of an enormous volcanic formation, of which the caldera burst out to the north in two places, creating deep and long bays of extraordinary beauty.

The economy of Tahiti is a poor economy. This is of no great concern to the natives. As has always been true, the native wakes in the morning without care or apprehension. Available for food and at hand are coconuts, taro, breadfruit, yams, red bananas from the mountains, and other vegetables. His pigs and chickens run half wild around the villages; and the sea is full of fish and shellfish. He wears clothes because the missionaries have required him to do so; and he likes French bread, salmon, and bully beef, which are not especially good for him. He may want a radio, or a tin roof for his house, as much more fetching than a grass roof, and he also gives rather liberally to his church, which he calls "the himine house." To this extent, then, he feels compelled to work, but he works sporadically.

Most of the retail business of Tahiti is done by the Chinese, of whom the city of Papeete alone contains about 6000, and there are besides a few hundred French who have official connection with the government, a number of "foreign" traders in the products of the island, and the importers of foreign merchandise. Tahitians are not represented in this business community, with but few exceptions.

Part of the expense of the French official family is paid from Paris; but part is paid for in the form of high duties on imports and exports at Tahiti, high charges for mail and for public services, and high business taxes and government fees on legal transactions. The main products of the islands are copra, pearl shell, and vanilla, which are gathered by trading ships and schooners throughout the islands of the archipelago, and shipped into international trade from Papeete — but not to the world market. Instead, they are shipped to France on controlled price arrangements, although there are exceptions by which some art objects and woven goods, especially baskets, are shipped to other countries.

Until very recently, Tahiti has been definitely out at the end of the line, very difficult to reach because of poor communications, and with no particular urge, either on the part of the officials or of the populace, toward what we are pleased to call progress. A substantial part of the population, and all of the official group, have been steadfastly opposed to any change in the status quo. Tahiti now has radio, but it still does not have any newspaper. Formerly, there was no news except the "coconut telegraph," which still functions efficiently if not accurately, and even now all the news is disseminated in French over the radio, and nine-tenths of this news concerns France and French possessions and not the world at large. It is these very characteristics which give Tahiti its tremendous charm, especially to visitors from the crowded and commercially developed countries of Europe and America.

The general Tahitian attitude, from a sharp disinterest in such a thing as tourist trade, has now softened somewhat. This is partly because transportation has been pushing its way in, and partly because the enormous growth of world tourism in the past few years gives the French the spectacle of many countries drawing large sums from this trade, while the Tahitian group and French Oceania get practically none of it.

Tahiti as a tourist area is incomparably beautiful. There is very little rain on the dry side of the island, and then only showers. The sunshine is brilliant, and the sky is so clear that one can see the tops of cumulus clouds below the horizon, with no effect of haze near the horizon; and I have never seen anywhere such brilliant stars at night, or in such number. I think in Tahiti one can literally see all of the stars large enough to be visible at any one time to the unaided eye.

The scenic beauty of such an island as Moorea is unsurpassed, and any visitor to Tahiti will spend as much of his time in Moorea as he conveniently can. The water of this whole area is so amazingly clear that one can see the finest detail of the bottom at depths in excess of 30 feet. It would to some people be worth the trip to Tahiti to see the underwater life in the lagoons. The use of snorkels and aqualungs, and of a glass-ported boat, should be part of the equipment of any establishment designed to divert its guests. Such things are not available now. There is no developed tourist area anywhere, I am certain, which affords so much beautiful and interesting scenery and diversion as this undeveloped area of the Tahiti group.

No one can say whether the tourist influx can be definitely or permanently controlled. Economic factors will for some time control it automatically, because the price of transportation to and from Tahiti is a large figure to begin with, and the necessity for spending a considerable period of time at considerable cost per day on the trip will very sharply restrict the classification of those who can afford to use Tahiti as a tourist destination, and of those who will so use it. Long-range, this restriction will tend to operate less and less positively, and great numbers of tourists will visit Tahiti. With the coming of the steamship companies and the airport, the number of tourists visiting Tahiti will, provided there is accommodation on the island for them, multiply the annual influx several times over the figure of tourists who have visited Tahiti each year in previous years. The present attitude of the government and of the population, and of the shopkeepers who will benefit in a business way, is one of increasing friendliness to the idea of initiating the tourist trade and permitting it to grow. This change of attitude has been perceptibly progressive.

The Handling of Tourists and of the Tourist Trade

There are, to begin with, two types of South Seas tourists: first, those who come through the area on ship tours, who merely stop over while the ship is in port, and whom we do not count on; and, second, those who come into the area by plane for the purpose of spending their available time at the destination. These are the tourists who will be our hotel guests.

All of these tourists entering the South Seas area, with very few exceptions, will land in the South Seas initially either at Nandi Airport in Fiji or at the airport on Bora Bora in the Tahitian group, which is 2500 miles east of Fiji and 2700 miles south of Hawaii. The tourists arriving at Bora Bora are to be transferred by seaplane to the city of Papeete. These two points, Nandi and Papeete, are therefore the foci of our operation with respect to tourists. The airport hotel at Nandi airport on Fiji, and Les Tropiques at Papeete, are the distribution points from which our tourist guests are transferred to other locations. These two are therefore essential factors as our "railway hotels."

The tourists coming into the area are not in the same case as tourists would be, for example, who go to Europe, and meet there the same general social customs as at home. Our tourists are in a new world. It is therefore desirable that we take charge of them from the moment they arrive at Nandi and at Tahiti. This means that we should have a voice in the management of their movements through an interest in the tourist agencies concerned.

Les Tropiques

Les Tropiques at Papeete is our primary consideration for hotel development at the outset, for the reason that it is one property which we have already acquired and which is in operation. I will therefore use it in this explanation as a typical location.

Throughout this venture, it is accepted as an axiom that tourist accommodations must exist, and exist where they are to be used, prior to the coming of the tourists who are to occupy the accommodations. Nevertheless, while this accommodation must exist, it is to be kept in step with the actual growth of the tourist trade. There will be, ordinarily, no sudden spurt of building elaborate accommodations for tourists who will not arrive for a long time to come. At all times, however, all of our accommodations must be adequate, not merely to accept and house the tourists who are scheduled to arrive, but to allow for increase in volume of the tourist business, and for the housing of tourists who do not fall within the control of our own tourist agencies. In the case of Les Tropiques itself, it is necessary to embark on considerable improvement and expansion because the incoming planes will, within this coming twelve months, be bringing an average of 100 tourists per week to the Tahitian group, and we will have to be ready to accommodate them.

The present tourist accommodation at Les Tropiques consists of fourteen very old cabins, and three new ones. There should be accommodation for very many more, and the plans for this accommodation have been drawn in detail and lack only to be carried out. At first, this calls for the construction of additional new cabins and of several multiple-unit buildings of ten units each; the complete refurbishing of the present old cabins; and alterations to the present public building.

At longer range, we will build a new public building on land to be filled in, and convert the present public building and dining terrace into an atelier for shops and for the use of local artists and such artisans as wood carvers and shell carvers. At all times, in this or in any other location, we expect to keep step with the increase in tourist flow and to anticipate this flow to some extent but not too greatly; and to develop this same sort of tourist accommodations and tourist diversions. We will have to be competent to handle any increase in tourist flow, and to keep in step with it or ahead of it, and we will have to be able to extend our accommodations and our activities at all points at the same pace, to anticipate developments and to prevent our leaving any vacuum into which other enterprises could move.

The land of the hotel runs (from the main road around the island) 750 feet to the point of the land on the inner reef, and from the point a planked path is built out, supported by drums filled with concrete, to an artificial island 450 feet from the point of land at the very edge of the deep lagoon. The hotel building stands on the point of land, and consists of a dance floor and dining area set under the trees and mostly under the sky, with the building itself containing a part of the dining room and the bar facilities and a lobby and the relative service areas, such as kitchen and public wash rooms. The setting of the hotel is most beautiful — the grounds covered with several hundred coconut trees up to 100 feet in height, with a view of Papeete harbor and city at a distance of two miles to the east, and the island of Moorea in full view to the west, and a view of the reefs and of the sea directly in front of the hotel, which faces a little west of south.

Les Tropiques is on the west coast of the island of Tahiti about two miles south of the town of Papeete, located on about 8.3 acres of land on a point built out partly over the shore reef. It should be understood that, at most Pacific tropical locations with a reef, there is a shore reef which is covered with a few inches of water at low tide and about a foot and a half of water at high tide, and which extends various distances from the shore. At Les Tropiques this distance is about 600 feet. Further out, about three-quarters of a mile from the shore, there is the outer reef, on which the combers break and surge across to the inner edge of the outer reef, which may be anything from 50 to 500 feet from the outer edge; and at the outer edge the face of the reef falls away precipitately to a depth of thousands of feet. Between the inner and the outer reef is a deep lagoon, protected from the sea and therefore calm, and there are breaks in the outer reef wherever a river empties from the land into the lagoon, because the fresh water admixture makes conditions unfavorable for the growth of the coral polyps. There are no lunar tides at Tahiti, which is at a tidal node, and the solar tide results in a rise and fall of approximately one foot, with high tide at noon and midnight and low tide at 6 a.m. and 6 p.m.

Diversions to be Offered to Guests

The nature of the diversions to be offered to guests should be built around their use of the area itself, rather than to put undue emphasis on the usual things found in a resort hotel. It will of course be true that there will be dance music and entertainment, and we will have an orchestra attached to the hotel as part of the staff, and a dance team made up of local girls, but this is where the usual resort hotel ends and where we think ours should begin.

When a tourist, or a tourist and his wife, comes to the South Seas, it is a venture in the dark so far as his real knowledge of what he is to meet is concerned, but definitely something on which he has extremely clear ideas. He has heard of the South Seas. He has read books about the South Seas, and he has a private imagination of what life on a coral island is like. He will not find any of these things under present conditions. He will not have anything but ordinary poor hotel accommodation at any point one can name throughout the South Seas. If he were going to Honolulu this would not matter greatly, because there are a number of things organized for the entertainment of the tourist. He can go to various restaurants; he can go to the movies or to night spots; he can go deep sea fishing; he can go on one of the glass-bottom boats; or he can hire a car and drive for himself. In the South Seas he could do some of these things after a fashion, but at present unless he wants to sit on the lanai or the terrace of the hotel he is occupying he will be hard-put to find things to do, and none of the things he finds to do will actually represent what he came to see, or thought he came to see. However, what he wants to see and do is perfectly possible of achievement.

Guests sitting on the dining terrace at Les Tropiques will look out at the reef, perhaps a half mile away, and ask "Why can't we go out on the reef?" We have already met that question by acquiring pirogues and engaging native fishermen to accompany the guests on their excursions to the reef. They go at night carrying a Coleman lantern, and find the reef a most fascinating experience. But other guests sit and look at the island of Moorea, ten miles due west from the terrace and in plain view, and ask "How do I go to Moorea?" The way to go to Moorea at the present time is to go downtown to the harbor and find a fishing boat which happens to be going to Moorea. After arriving at Moorea, one may be able to find a fishing boat that is coming back a day or two or three days later, or much later. There is no certainty. If guests ask how they can go to the Tuamotus, stretching for a thousand miles east of Tahiti, where there are natives but no Western civilization, the answer is that perhaps they can get one of the copra schooners to take them on its regular trip of one month, during which they will stop at two or three of the coral islands and at the Marquesas, for a few hours in each case.

The guests, however, did not come to Tahiti to sit on the dining terrace of The Tropics. They came to see the native South Seas, which is one step more, and a step they are not now able to take. Guests cannot even conveniently go fishing (and the deep sea fishing at Tahiti is excellent) because there are no regular sport fishing boats.

Marine Department

Over some range of time, and only a little in advance of the growth of tourist flow, we will set up a Marine Department in connection with the Tahiti locations. We will have a 65-foot cruiser to convey our guests to and from our location in Moorea and for other local trips by water; a 126-foot twin-diesel yacht accommodating 20 passengers for transport of guests to the other islands of the group and on other similar cruises on which the yacht can supply overnight accommodations as a sort of floating hotel; a sailing yacht available for day sails or on charter; one or more fishing boats, specifically built as fishing boats, on scheduled trips or on charter for deep-sea fishing; and a fleet of pirogues of various sizes, from those holding two or three passengers to those which are large enough for ten, powered by outboard motors in the larger sizes, for hire by the hour or for arranged trips by night to the reef or on other trips in the lagoon inside the outer reef, for fishing or for sightseeig.

We have an application from the Sous-Marine Club, made up of local devotees of skin diving and of aqualung diving, to assign them clubhouse premises within the hotel grounds, preferably on our reef, for the purpose of giving our guests the opportunity to take out short-term memberships with this group, so that they can follow these sports in company with men familiar with the local waters. It is also planned that we give a similar right of use of a portion of the premises to the local Yacht Club, which exists but which does not have any headquarters, so that our yachting guests can use their exchange privileges to enjoy the hospitality of other yachtsmen.

"Outpost" Facilities

Over and above these facilities for use of the area, we will follow out another step which will completely differentiate our tourist facilities, and our services to our guests, from any other similar enterprise, in a manner completely in harmony with the character of the South Seas and the natives of the South Seas.

Nearly all visitors to the South Seas have an imagined picture that to be in the South Seas means to be in a grass shack on a coral beach on an island on an atoll. If they came to the South Seas and found nothing else, they would be annoyed with the lack of conveniences, and bored with the monotony of actually living forever on an atoll with nothing to do except exist, however lovely the atmosphere or the view. Nevertheless, a very substantial portion of the guests in the South Seas would regard a chance to sample this sort of living as a complete fulfillment of what they expected to find, without too far removing them from contact with civilization and its comforts. If we put such a visitor down on an island on an atoll, and let him live a life of camping it out with relatively primitive accommodations for a few days, or even, for the enthusiast, for several weeks, in company with kindly, friendly, clean natives who live there quite uninhibited and unsophisticated, because they are in their natural habitat and not merely placed there to furnish atmosphere, he will treasure the experience for the rest of his life. It would be both a fulfillment of his South Seas dream and of "going native" and living in contact directly with natural things, that every man attempts to achieve in "going camping," but without any struggle with nature such as would be entailed in actually leaving the comforts of civilization for primitive living.

We will establish, at first at a few choice locations, and eventually at a large number of locations, "outpost" facilities in completely native areas, otherwise to be reached only at great expense and with considerable difficulty.

These facilities will consist of shelters which are actually replicas of the natives' own houses, built by natives and completely native in style, material, and design. We will put into these shelters the minimum conveniences for comfortable camping. There will be modern spring beds, but cold water shower facilities, hand basins for lavatory, and a chemical toilet rather than modern plumbing. There will be central dining facilities and natives as servants. The Polynesian native does not consider that to be your servant either degrades him or elevates you. He is completely without any sense of comparative social values. He will, in this case, be aware only of the fact that you are his guest and he must look after you.

The guest will be fed native dishes of the area, or from cans of food if that is his preference. He will wear his oldest clothes, or perhaps imitate the natives' dress and wear only a pareu, and he will spend his time achieving relaxation to a degree he cannot have imagined before he experiences it. He will be in a climate neither hot nor cold, in air of a clarity which cannot be described, surrounded by friendly folk, on an island in a sea of sapphire blue so clear that one can see 50 and 60 feet down through the water, and on a lagoon with all shades from blue through green to yellow in the varying depths of the lagoon water, filled with tropical fish and marine growths of the most astounding beauty, where he can swim or float with a snorkel and observe the underwater wonderland for a day at a time if he wishes.

Summary

This constitutes a summarization of the project coordinated by the Canadian holding company, South Seas Enterprises, Ltd. It ranges from established and definite items, such as Les Tropiques in Tahiti, through projects which have been advanced to various degrees, and down to projects which yet remain to be elaborated and tied into the picture. All of the elements of the project, however, are compatible with one another, and ready for action, and readily pushed into shape as soon as the organization which is to handle them can proceed on a definite basis. It is this definite basis which the sale of its shares will accomplish.

The project, as has been stated, is a long-term investment project. The anticipated flow of increasing numbers of tourists into the area is a certainty limited only by the possibility of world events outside the control of any individual, and which would influence and affect all other investment projects equally. This pending tourist flow will resemble a stream of water which will either flood the area or which will be channeled into services designed to control it. What happens when uncontrolled flow of people into an area occurs has been demonstrated many times in history, but specifically, with reference to the South Seas, has been pointedly demonstrated by what has happened in Hawaii and New Zealand. In both of these areas the native population has been absorbed and has disappeared, and with the disappearance of the native population the local customs have also disappeared, and much of the native charm of the areas has been replaced by Western varieties of government, commercial enterprises, and social habits as incongruous in the setting as would be a Cape Cod house in Central Africa.

The South Seas area around which this project is built is now substantially as it has always been, and constitutes a tremendous attraction for visitors, and even has the philosophical impact of a living object lesson in more natural attitudes toward life and living, and in the relation between people as individuals. It is the last great area of native culture, of absorbing interest alike to the anthropologist and to the tourist. If it is changed it will be lost forever. The governments of these peoples do not want it changed, and if we help in the ways we can to prevent change, the area will remain for a very long time as a refuge from stress and artificiality into a simpler concept of living, and a very much greater joy in living.

Part III
WORLD POPULATION AND FOOD SUPPLY:
conservation of natural resources

Foundation for American
Resource Management
Written Approximately 1954

Ecological concerns were very important to C.F. Rehnborg, and he expended much personal effort, time, and money in attempting to establish ways of remedying the damage to lands and watersheds wrought by over-use, exploitation of natural resources, and pollution. He also enlisted the aid of other men in cooperative groups to achieve his objectives.

The Foundation for American Resource Management was such an organization, a non-profit foundation funded and spearheaded by Rehnborg at first, and later joined by the heads of other companies with like concerns and ideas. It was FARM's basic purpose to preserve and manage wilderness areas "in such a manner as to make these resources continuing entities for the use and benefit of the human population of the whole world." FARM was incorporated May 13, 1955, and funded several projects, among them the acquiring of tracts of giant redwood trees which were turned over to the federal or state park systems, and a lengthy study involving the reforestation of cut-over areas in northern California where lumbering activities had destroyed both trees and watersheds.

Although FARM was discontinued in late 1965 for lack of funding and support on a broad basis, it did accomplish many of its goals and proved that men of like mind, working together, could make a difference. The following is taken from the original FARM organizational outline. Also included is a Field Visit Report written in connection with FARM's activities in reforestation practices.

BASIC PHILOSOPHY

The Foundation for American Resource Management is primarily interested in conservation of America's renewable natural resources as a segment of the problem of the renewable natural resources of the whole world. We take it that the meaning of the word "conservation" should in this connection signify management of natural resources in such a manner as to make these resources continuing entities for the use and benefit of the human population of the world. This is a necessary definition because mankind faces the clear alternative of properly conserving its resources or of eventually terminating its existence as a species. The Foundation asserts that conservation is a solvable problem, but that there are basic considerations in any effort toward achieving the goal of proper conservation that must take into account the relationship of all natural resources to all other factors in a civilized economy.

The dictionary says "conserve" means to preserve from change or destruction; to maintain an existing condition. It says that "conservation" means, among other similar ideas, a keeping in a safe or entire state. This is not what the words should mean when applied to natural resources, but these mistaken ideas carry over into our use of the word "conservation" when it is applied to the guarding of our natural resources. At the extremes, the advocates of the use of natural resources sponsor a degree of use which will tend in time to destroy the resources, while the extreme conservationists want everything in nature to remain in its "natural" state. As usual, the middle ground is the golden mean: the idea that renewable natural resources should be used; but that they should be used in such a manner as to insure their continued existence as entities in the natural complex; and used continuously as economic assets over very long periods of time. It is granted that there are inevitably certain areas which should be retained as a wilderness for the esthetic values they have, and that certain superlative growths, particularly as they relate to the giant redwoods of California and others, should be preserved in their natural state. Yet these segregated areas, as well as primitive wilderness areas, should be relatively small in size in relationship to the natural resources of our country which have value in use, and which should be used, but never destroyed.

It is a recognized fact that renewable resources are interrelated and interdependent, and that man himself is now an inextricable part of this living complex. These relationships become increasingly significant with the inevitable increase in population and industrialization and the greater time available for leisure and recreation. Such population growth intensifies and varies the demand for products and services derived directly and indirectly from natural resources, thus placing an added strain on the presently remaining resources.

Man has ended the era of "natural" balances in nature. By his power to reason and to invent, and so to devise means for modifying his "natural" environment, and by his great increase in numbers and the consequent increase in the quantity of food and other natural supplies needed for his "civilized" economy, he has profoundly changed the character of the landscape and the native or natural balances between living organisms and their environment over most of the areas of the world. He has thus basically changed the "natural" conditions for both plants and animals for each geographical area; he has altered the relation between the ground and its natural cover; he has altered the plant and animal population of each area; and he has altered the productive capacity of the soil.

Plant and animal forms of life could take over any environment as readily as man can. The progeny of a single pair of houseflies, breeding unchecked, would in a short time cover the land surfaces of the earth. A single pair of herring would just as quickly fill the oceans with herring. There could be as many elephants as there are men if the elephant could control his environment. But in nature there are restraints on unchecked multiplication. Simply, it was in the power of man to modify these restraints as they applied to himself. He did not at once make these modifications, and for endless centuries after man had appeared as a species his numbers did not increase except very slowly. The recent rapid increase in numbers of human beings, in which man's census has grown from a few thousands to a few billions during perhaps ten thousand years, and has doubled in less than the last century, has resulted from his increasing control over his environment and over the checks that restrained his multiplication. He still perishes in unnecessary numbers from disease and pestilence and from accidents, and he still dies in his endless internecine wars in great numbers, or so mismanages his resource development that millions die from starvation and malnutrition; but these have merely somewhat slowed down the process by which his numbers now threaten him with mass extinction resulting from inadequate capacity of the earth to feed, house, and clothe an excess population on a limited earth.

But man's increase in numbers also threatens his continued existence in another way for which he is himself responsible: reduction in food-producing capacity of the available food-growing areas and reduction in gross quantity of all available natural resources. It may be assumed that, because they must, men will in time control the present uncontrolled growth of populations. These problems, however, are problems of government; they require unified action by nations and can be studied but not solved by smaller units of organization. The problems of management of resources, on the other hand, have to be solved by education which creates in the public mind an awareness of mankind's integrated relationship to the environment. Government can implement and aid this awareness, but it cannot create it. It is the awareness which moves government to codify the methods and to assist in carrying them out; but it is nevertheless men, singly and in groups, who mine and log and cultivate the land, and it is each man's individual relation to his own small segment of the environment which cumulatively determines whether or not that relation is established on a continuing basis and without eventual destruction of the resources on which man's own life depends.

The problem of continuous use of natural resources has complex roots. Man does not merely have to decide whether he shall plow or not plow, or whether he shall plow along contours and not across them, or what crops he is to grow in what rotation and with what fertilizers. These are small segments of the problem, but they are not its roots.

The roots lie in the whole relationship of life to its environment since life first began. Man may change the terms of the relationship, as by wheels he has changed his own relation to locomotion, but the changes must be in the eventual terms of the total of natural laws of universal character which apply to the earth's surface and its seas.

The summation of these laws as they apply to life in an environment is called "ecology." This refers to all the factors of natural environmental control over a complex of plants and animals in an area. It applies as a whole to the total range of plant and animal life over the whole world; but it may be subdivided for analysis and study into continental areas, and into even smaller areas of a given region or often of only a few square miles, depending on the extent to which one area influences another, or is relatively free from such influence. It may never be forgotten, however, that some of the elements of influence may not be subdivided because they are not merely regional.

There is neither need nor space to consider here the whole subject of ecology as a study, but we may examine this last statement as an example. Meteorology, as the total of climate and weather, is a worldwide consideration even in the study of the ecology of a limited area; and yet meteorological phenomena are sometimes influenced in turn by the events of a relatively small area, and in these events man himself may have a strongly determining part.

The amount of water draining from any land mass is approximately equivalent to the amount of water evaporated from the surface of the sea and precipitated on the land area (disregarding for the moment the incorporation of water into organic and inorganic structures), and over a long range of time is exactly equivalent. If this were not true, then, by automatic balancing of natural forces, the level of the sea would be lowered by evaporation until it was true. We may assume, then, that the present level of the sea represents such a balance. But the total of rainfall on the land is a number of times as great as the total runoff to the sea, therefore the greater part of the total rainfall on the land represents evaporation from the land area itself. We now know this to be true, and also know that while part of this land evaporation is from damp or wet surfaces of the ground, and from lakes and rivers, a much greater part is due to transpiration: the circulation of water through plants, from roots to leaves and thence into the air. We also know that the precipitation of rainfall, from the air to the ground again, depends on cooling of saturated warm air to the point of supersaturation at a lower temperature, whereupon usually from condensed clouds at the higher and cooler levels, droplets increase in size until they are large and heavy enough to fall to the ground as rain. We also know that there is a critical level of total water contained in air, which was just referred to as saturation at a given temperature, below which the water will not condense out into clouds, and another level at which the cloud droplets cannot grow by addition of more condensed water to fall as rain. An air mass which contains such potential rain carries the contained water to another area when it moves, and usually this transfer is from an already dry area to an area which can contribute more evaporated water dissolved in air to bring about precipitation, and which therefore receives the rainfall.

In the general distribution of prevailing winds, ocean currents, and temperature zones, there are of course wide variations from any average of water from the sea and water from land evaporation and transpiration. On Kauai in the Hawaiian Islands, for example, the 600 inches a year of rain on the central mountain mass is nearly all ocean evaporation, and in the Pacific Northwest by far the greater part of the total rainfall is ocean water. Also, there are variations over the world in the "natural" totals of rainfall for an area. For any given area, however, the general meteorological conditions produce what we refer to statistically as its "average rainfall."

But of the yearly total of water vapor passing over a given area most will be found to depend in substantial part on the total of vegetation which is to contribute transpired water vapor to the air mass over that area. It is not only possible but it has happened a number of times during history that man can change the transpiration total sufficiently to trip a change into a vicious cycle of less and less water as rainfall for a given area, until as has happened in the Near East and North Africa in historical times, a green land can be transformed into a desert. The progression is now being repeated in a number of civilized areas, notably China and Manchuria, and it seems to be happening in the United States as well.

Man brings about these changes by seemingly unrelated acts. For example, he moves into a heavily forested area. He clears forest for agricultural land. He develops increasingly numerous uses for forest products, first firewood and charcoal, and then structures, drawing these supplies from what seems an inexhaustible source of supply. At some juncture he finds that the source was not inexhaustible, and then he turns to other structural materials and other fuels. In the Near East clay, bricks, and stone have been used increasingly during all of historical times, fuel has been more and more charcoal transported over increasing distances or made from brush and saplings, and for many centuries fuel has been more and more made up of straw and grass and buffalo chips. Rarely has there been any concurrent notion among the inhabitants of an area that they themselves made the changes, or that burning straw and manure was depriving land of natural organic compost and making their land, already too dry, less and less fertile.

In the area where man has despoiled the renewable natural resources, other and more important changes occurred. The clearing of the forests, the natural hill cover and water conserver, reduced the water transpiration area, totaling in innumerable leaf surfaces many times the land area. The denuded hills shed the rainfall, being eroded in the process, so that clays and sands were washed down over the arable valley lands. The runoff of water to the ocean became periodic and torrential and occurred more quickly, shortening the transpiration times of the remaining vegetation and changing its character to more drought-resistant types with less value, and the floods eroded the farmlands. The

wamps and lakes dried up. More and more unsaturated air carried more
and more potential rainfall to other areas, and the tendency to aridity
increased progressively with time. There was not time from one
generation to another of the resident population to note these changes in
the current language of daily living, but they occurred inexorably
nevertheless.

There are areas of the earth where the ocean currents, the prevailing
winds, the mountain ranges, or a combination of these, produce natural
deserts as a result of insufficient rainfall. The southwest section of the
United States, the Gobi Desert, the interior of Australia, and the Sahara,
are examples of these areas becoming naturally unproductive because of
long-range geological and meteorological conditions. These naturally
arid complexes obscure for mankind the related conditions man himself
causes, so that there is nothing odd in the fact that men have been slow
to see that they themselves have caused similar conditions in other
areas, usually by the simple step of removing watershed covers, and
usually by the removal of forests on the hills. Man has totally failed to
see that removal of watershed cover, even in areas of adequate rainfall,
has also produced ruin, because there was no natural analogy for what
followed when the runoff at the stream-heads increased the runoff to the
sea, and the accompanying floods washed away top-soil.

In a semi-arid area such as the Near East and the southwest United
States, the balance between the forests on the hills and the productivity
of the lowlands below the hills is a delicate one. Palestine, for example,
was part of the "Fertile Crescent" of ancient history and Biblical times;
and there is record of the clearing of forests on the Palestine hills, where
there are now no trees, to make room for the grazing of sheep and other
cattle, and of the heavy use of the forests of Lebanon. Forests have
similarly been cleared away from the hills and mountains of great areas
of California.

These were all preponderantly conifer forests. It is a characteristic
of conifers that they can sweep the clouds, producing a steady drip by
condensation from the fine droplets of the clouds to produce what is
effectively rain, even when the amount of water in the air is not great
enough for precipitation. The forest cover of the semi-arid hills above the
lower cloud-line, where the forests still stand or second growth has
established itself, shows the cumulative effect of this raking of the
clouds. The hills are bare of trees below the cloud-line. When the trees

have been harvested and are gone, so also is the light but steady addition of drip water to the total precipitation of the area. Most of California was grassland when the Yankees first came there a hundred years ago. It is not now, and the natural forests of conifers on the hills are almost half gone. The connection is obvious, but it is not obvious until it is cognized; and most of us never ask the question or want the answer.

It follows then that, generally speaking, the problem the world faces in the field of renewable natural resources deals with natural balances and a natural ecology in a natural world with a civilized economy.

This problem of natural balances and a natural ecology in a natural world is first of all an attempt to solve the question of water supply.

THE AMERICAN FORESTRY ASSOCIATION

IN RECOGNITION OF NOTABLE AID RENDERED IN FURTHERING THE CAUSE OF FOREST CONSERVATION IN BEHALF OF THIS AND FUTURE GENERATIONS OF AMERICANS HEREBY DESIGNATES

C. F. Rehnborg

A LIFE MEMBER

AND IT DECLARES THAT THIS HONOR IS CONFERRED UPON ONLY SUCH PERSONS AS HAVE GIVEN DISTINGUISHED ASSISTANCE TO THE ASSOCIATION & THROUGH IT TO THEIR COUNTRY.

In witness whereof we have attached our hand and seal, at Washington in the District of Columbia this 7th day of September in the year 1950.

EXECUTIVE DIRECTOR   PRESIDENT

In recognition of his work in furthering the cause of forest conservation, C.F. Rehnborg was made a Life Member of the American Forestry Association in 1950.

Water, to repeat an already familiar truism, is the basis of all life, including all renewable natural resources. Some well established figures supporting this are that it takes nearly 4,000 gallons of water for a steer and the grass on which he feeds to produce one pound of beef; 4,000 gallons of water are required to raise one bushel of wheat; one slice of bread uses 37 gallons of water in all stages of its production. In industry 40,000 gallons of water are used to "finish the woolens" of a three piece suit; 65,000 gallons of water are needed to make one ton of steel; 15,000 gallons to make one automobile; 23 gallons to refine one gallon of gasoline; 15 gallons to supply the paper used in an average newspaper; 600,000 gallons are needed to produce one ton of synthetic rubber. For domestic and industrial use, the United States uses 200 billion gallons of water per day, or the equivalent of 1 to 1.5 inches of rainfall spread evenly on every square foot of the United States. Therefore, before we can use renewable natural resources on a continuing basis, thus to sustain life and our industrial health, we have first to decide how we will renew the water supply on a continuing basis.

This question has one paramount answer: the ever continuing and increasing use of forests as the natural cover of watersheds; for the forests are not only wood, they are water for the land served by the watershed.

OBJECTIVES OF FARM

The objectives of the Foundation for American Resource Management are primarily directed to intelligent management of America's remaining renewable natural resources, and by every means to increase their total.

It is recognized that there are now many specialized researches and educational efforts in progress which deal with segments of the problem either from the viewpoint of the extreme conservationist, who maintains that all resources should be reserved for posterity, or from the point of view of those whose primary interest is in the use of the natural resources. The Foundation therefore takes the position of recognizing an attainable balance of renewable resources for the use of humanity, and of creating a permanency of productivity that will also assure a substantial quantity of these resources for generations to come; and that the forest industry should be the chief agency in making the first and greatest progress.

IMPLEMENTATION

In order to carry out the philosophy of this Foundation through intelligent resource management, the immediate plans of the Foundation call for basic research in the field of forest management and forest restoration. The Redwood region in the State of California lends itself to such initial basic research, primarily because of the number of problems yet unsolved with reference to this unusual type of forest land, and the soils and watersheds involved, and the great value of forest products and their importance in industry and to the American public. Through the cooperation of forest landowners and of the State Board of Forestry, lands in the Redwood region have already been made available to the Foundation on a lease basis for the types of research and experimentation that its Board of Trustees will determine to be of primary importance.

Projects will be set up in an order of priority based on their importance and feasibility, and their relation to 1) the management of existing forests for increased and continued productivity, for the preservation of site factors and for improved conservation of water on the land surface; 2) the rehabilitation of cutover lands, with emphasis on the methods of natural seeding and of fertility of the land for maximum growth; 3) the management of young growths, with emphasis on methods of assuring maximum growth both in relationship to soil conditions and in control of brush and other competing growth; 4) the possible increase of forest land acreage, even if not to its original total; and 5) management of water precipitated as rainfall.

In order that the Foundation may have some basic information and materials as reference for further project development, as FARM's initial project an exhaustive bibliography is now being compiled for use by researchers.

FARM will also activate a study of the areas in the Redwood region where selective cutting has been done under a variety of conditions. This study will result in an accumulation of facts that will give basic data concerning the effect on regeneration, growth rates of the residual trees, fire hazards, and other information helpful for more intensive basic research and experimentation, and for guiding the management of commercial forests.

A detailed list of possible research problems will be submitted to the Board of Trustees for their consideration. These projects will point out the importance of each problem and its effect on an attainable balance of renewable resources for use in the economy. Emphasis will be on a permanency of productivity which will assure a substantial quantity of these resources, permanent use, and permanent balance of a natural ecology adjusted to the modern world of civilization.

Mrs. Edith Rehnborg stands by plaque bearing her name, commemorating the donation of a tract of giant redwoods as part of the Prairie Creek Redwoods State Park in California.

FARM Field Trip Visit
August 27, 1955

The representative of the large logging company located at Klamath showed us three phases of operation in their experimental cutting, all of which were intended to leave standing trees for seed and shade, and all of them are great improvements over the old system of cleaning the land entirely of all growth. Each of the three phases represents improvements in their own methods as well.

In the first phase, demonstrated by one of the cut-over areas, those trees were cut which would "carry themselves" economically; that is, it paid to cut them as part of the total product coming out of the sawmill. This, as the gentleman showed us, left the stumps, snags, and deformed trees, as well as a substantial amount of young growth, because the trees were cut only above a certain diameter. But, as he explained, and as was apparent, this left snags which would be Roman candles in the event of a future fire, and also left a considerable amount of debris on the ground. All this, plus the deformed trees, constituted a drain on the nutrients and water in the soil at the expense of the young and thrifty growth left there for later cutting.

In an intermediate phase, some of these bad practices were corrected, and it was decided not to leave so many large-diameter trees. But it was not until they reached the third phase of their operation that they worked out the sound final practices, and this is the method they use at present.

In the third phase, of which he showed us a cut-over sample as well as a grove which was going to be cut in the same way, he explained that he had considered each individual tree as a personality, so to speak, each deserving treatment which befitted the situation of the tree or snag.

In this method, the decision was not made on the basis of the economic worth of the tree cut, although that was part of the consideration. Instead, the long-range effect of each tree on the site situation was considered. Snags were completely removed and salvaged for whatever could be cut out of them, regardless of whether this was a paying deal or not. The deformed trees were likewise taken out and paid at least a dividend on the cost of removing them. All the slash was cleared off the ground, and what could be salvaged was salvaged.

The remaining stand of trees was then made up of trees at a limit of a certain diameter — around 50 inches and smaller. The 50-inch trees thus represented the crop which would be harvested at the next cutting from 30 to 50 years hence, and the younger trees would be the future crops. The result was an area covered entirely by thrifty growth, with ample shade for seedlings to grow under, and yet with plenty of room for saplings to grow up into. Even the trees of the future crop would immediately have a better supply of water and nutrients, and better exposure to light so that they would begin at once to have accelerated growth. The overall scenic effect was very pleasing as well, because the slopes did not look bare, and they did not look trashy.

This picture is so definitely a part of what we should advocate through FARM as correct procedure that I think we should urge Mr. T. to write a monograph on his findings, which the Foundation could make part of its literature for distribution.

We saw virgin forest in process of being cut, and witnessed the felling of a tree of about 24,000 board feet. We looked at one already felled which was measured at approximately 80,000 board feet and which, from the ring structure, was estimated to be in excess of 1,500 years old. Both these trees had extensive areas, especially in the upper sections, which were routed — and it was easy to see that in an untouched forest where no use is being made of the products, one may have an impressive sight but a most unimpressive economic asset.

It was also easy to see that a forest containing trees of a maximum age of 150 years, being cut serially as they have passed through their peak of rapid growth, constituted actually a more beautiful spectacle than the virgin forest of mixed-age trees so crowded that growth was practically at a standstill — and with trees dying out of the stand at the age of one or two hundred years simply because they could not get their share of light to continue growing. In such a forest, a thousand original seedlings to the acre would culminate as only 30 to 40 mature trees per acre. The cumulative wastage in fiber and timber, through the process of competition and mortality of the trees below the cover, would mean that more fiber had been grown than was finally used, by three or four times, if the only cutting was to be done in these virgin groves.

On the other hand, the sustained rate of growth in the scientifically cut forest would produce both effective cover for the land and a continuous high-level rate of growth of fiber to be used; so that finally the managed forest would be more beautiful than the virgin forest, providing one could forget the unique characteristics of the very old trees. These old trees, after all, are being preserved to a high enough total of specimens in the redwood forests of the Parks System which have been set aside and are not to be cut.

From the standpoint of esthetics, the untouched groves are incomparably beautiful, but from the standpoint of conservation — in the sense of the use of products grown and better condition of the slopes on which they are grown over any long period of time — the spectacle of managed forests on the hill slopes and crowns is both esthetically and commercially more satisfying. With fiber being grown at a good rate and the undercover far less susceptible to forest fires, and with limited age groups covering the ground effectively with mature and semi-mature trees, saplings, and seedlings, the managed forest presents a much better long-range prospect than does the natural, undisturbed forest.

The only drawback is that the larger companies which can do this sort of controlled growing do not, taken together, hold a sufficiently large proportion of the total forest. The Simpson, Pacific, and Union lumber companies, as well as Zellerbach and Weyerhaeuser, which have all organized their cutting and growing on a sustained-yield basis, together hold only a minor fraction of even the present woodlands. The problem for any foundation, or group of foundations seeking to present answers to the problems of conservation, is to devise the practical means for inculcating and enforcing the idea that the ground under forest growth has to be cut over in accordance with the ideal of sustained yield and preservation of these forests as continuing entities. No one can say at this moment whether this is to be done purely by education, or whether long-range it will have to be done by education plus enforcement — which implies legislative action to require conformity in use to a pattern of permitted use.

It is probably a reasonable estimate that of the amount of wood fiber growing in a virgin forest (or even in a managed forest), something not much greater than 50 percent comes out of the forest and goes to the mill; and that of the amount which goes to the mill a substantial proportion, perhaps as high as 15 percent, represents waste. It is probable that, even though much destructive cutting has been done in the redwood area and much land removed from forest production, something better than 50 percent of the original stands in northwest California are still under forest.

Still it is a characteristic of human beings that when they make use of a resource which is present at the site in enormous quantities, it is handled prodigally and wastefully. Conservation is an idea we pick up when the supply begins to dwindle. This is so definitely a fact that there is no use moralizing or getting indignant about it. It is simply instinctive animal wastefulness, whether the resource is fish or minerals or forests. In the face of enormous supplies of fish, half the take is wasted and much more is used for such plebian purposes as fertilizer. If there is a surplus or a tremendous amount of a mineral resource, only the best ores are mined and the others are cast into tailing heaps to be reclaimed later.

In just the same way, when men cut the forest and it is producing staggering totals of wood fiber per acre, half the available value is left as waste on the ground without a qualm. Trees are felled, and sometimes a thousand years of growth is left on the ground because the tree shattered in falling. Young trees are destroyed as the mature cut timbers are dragged out of the forest. Bulldozers tear down minor growth as they build the slideways for the cut timbers. The slideways themselves are cut straight up and down hills, and later rainfall erodes the ground. Snags are left where they stand, and dead wood lies where it falls. Culls and trimmings are added to the trash on the floor of the forest. Sometimes in clearing the hill of workable timber, nothing is left standing and almost nothing is left green.

Finally, it has been the practice to burn off the slash, sometimes totalling hundreds of thousands of board feet of material an acre, merely to get rid of it and to leave the hill clear — and at times this has been considered a proper and advantageous procedure. But all of the fiber growth is usable, provided either that an economical and profitable means can be found for using it, or that the holder of the land has such long-range vision that he clears up his land, even if he does not more than break even economically on his salvage operations.

There are present processes for utilizing forest waste which simply are not being used because the forest operators are dealing with such prodigious quantities of raw material that they have not yet brought themselves to consider the problem of disposing of the waste they create as one of great seriousness. The area behind a cutting is a shambles. The waste in a sawmill is staggering. Every sawmill has a burner where many thousands of board feet or fiber are burned each twenty-four hours.

Yet at the present time in our chemical economy, there actually exist many uses for the waste products of the forest operations. Simply, it has not yet been proved to be economically sound, in the sense of this year's profits, to dispose of the waste in any other way than to leave it on the ground or to burn it. Waste wood can be reduced to pulp and sold as pulp. It can be distilled, and both the byproducts of the distillation and the end product, charcoal, are usable and salable. It is morally and ethically wrong, and probably economically wrong as well, to waste 50 percent of a crop because it is considered a waste of time to do anything else, and simply because there is so much of the supply that no one thinks of conserving it.

Some of the major projects of FARM should relate to the economic use of forest and lumber mill waste. As tentative ideas, it is feasible to run the slash from the sawmill into digester vats from which it can be dredged as pulp. It is feasible to run the conveyor belts from the sawmill operation into charcoal producers instead of slash burners, and it is possible in this connection to include equipment for by-products recovery as crudes for refining elsewhere. Furthermore, these steps of salvage are profitable in themselves. Pilot plant proof of these facts should be urged as reasons to impell forest operators to undertake more and better salvage operations.

This is not a matter of personal prejudice against individuals who operate sawmill and other woods operations. Simply, the pattern for the last hundred years has been one of waste, and it is inertia — not intent — that causes the pattern to continue to be used as a model for operations. No individual timber operator faced with the question put into words, as to why there is so much waste, will say anything but that there should not be so much waste, but that "under present economic conditions" it cannot be prevented — which is a statement, but not a statement of fact. To aver that the waste fiber from a sawmill operation has to be burned as the only way to dispose of it, is a slur on human intelligence. It may be a habit, but it definitely is not a necessity; and it is morally wrong to waste a resource — and this is a waste of a resource.

Preserving and Protecting Our Environment

Written Approximately 1962

Wherever Man lives, he makes most of the natural conditions of that area vanish forever. He clears away the forest, and with it all the things which constituted the ecology of the forest — the trees, the undergrowth of bushes and grasses, the large and small animals of the forest both surface and underground, the birds, the insects and crawling creatures, the springs and streams — everything.

As he destroys the ecology, he does not even know the name for the natural balances, the reciprocal relationships between life and its environment, which he is destroying. He covets things in other areas where he does not yet live, and his hunters destroy these also unless the governments of those areas wake up to the danger before the destruction is completed. His cattle graze out the wildlife of other forests. He sees that egrets grow plumes as their uniform for mating and that the plumes can be used for ladies' hats, and the winter furs of animals can be used for decorative coats. Animals like the sea otter are destroyed, and others have to be saved in preserves. Alligators are poached from the swamps of the world as leather for shoes and bags, and everywhere birds die when man kills them with poisons spread for the insects he regards as pests, but which kill beneficial insects as well. Near all our cities evergreen trees are prodigally cut and used for one day only, and then gotten out of the way as trash.

Increasingly Man widens the barren area he makes around the places where he has settled. He does not note the destructive changes he has brought about, or even recognize that he himself has made anything change. A short while ago lightning struck a seven-acre reservoir of crude oil, which caught fire and burned many days, sending up a great column of dense black smoke from which a rain of sooty droplets fell on the great city's buildings and streets and people and cars and gardens. Much damage was done which was seen as costly and annoying and inconvenient, but which perhaps was not generally seen for what it was: an irretrievable loss of natural resources. In an event of a year ago, forgotten just a few weeks after it happened, a huge oil tanker, the largest of its kind, was carelessly run onto a reef and its cargo of crude oil spilled into the sea. Most of the shores of the channel between France and Great Britain were fouled in a floating lake of black oil. It destroyed birds by coating their feathers, and smothered the local planktonic life of the sea surface which is the base of the sea life of any ocean area, and it left a persistent mess.

Ocean liners pump the dregs of their bilges into the ocean as they near their ports and fueling depots. Everywhere in heavily settled areas, incompletely burned furnace oils and car fuels make a stinking, unhealthy atmosphere of smog.

We do not notice or protest in any effective way the pollution caused day by day, or sense that we will inevitably reach — or may already have reached — the critical point at which we will consume more oxygen from the total atmosphere than our constantly more sparse cover of green plants on the land can regenerate for us, and thereafter move towards a rendezvous with death for the human race.

We do not even see that we constantly create more uses for our atmospheric oxygen in addition to the increasing population of the land, and steadily put under asphalt and cement millions of acres of ground on which no green plant will hereafter grow — the green plants which alone can use the carbon of carbon dioxide for plant tissues and release the oxygen for use by living beings, including ourselves.

Later, if we have not meanwhile died in nuclear warfare or for lack of enough food, there will be an increasing excess of carbon dioxide in our air all over the world, which will create a greenhouse effect and warm up the whole world. The polar icecaps will melt, during the warmer seasons, more ice than forms in the colder seasons, slowly at first, but then increasingly faster, and the level of the sea will rise to cover more and more land. We will have to adjust to living with less and less oxygen in the air, and fewer children will be born alive — a very sad way to control population numbers. There will be more human and industrial waste in the sea, and more oxygen will be used as the garbage decomposes and disintegrates, and the life in the sea will die for lack of oxygen and add its bulk to the garbage. Meanwhile, an expanding population will have caught up with the world's capacity to produce food, and we will have more problems to deal with than we can manage.

For the first time in human history we will now begin to study our environment instead of taking it for granted and thinking of it as able to supply our every careless whim forever. Maybe we are already too late in getting ready to begin our study. Time will tell, but this looks like a very good time to start worrying — right now, not a few decades in the future.

Perhaps as individuals we will consider stopping foolish habits, such as idling engines instead of stopping and later restarting them; such as cutting down a tree for one day's casual use and then discarding and burning it as trash; such as putting good food into the garbage disposal; such as running cars with only one passenger.

Let's hope we can find the answers in time, and that we can soon stop destructive demonstrations and even wars, and take a most studious look at our Earth and what each of us now needs to do with the brains Nature has helped us to develop. We have nothing left to lose, and we may have a chance for a future.

The Law of Malthus

Written Approximately 1960

In 1798, when he was thirty-two years old, Thomas Robert Malthus, an English economist, published an essay on "The Principle of Population" in which he advanced the idea that unchecked population growth obeys a universal tendency to outrun the means of subsistence because population grows by geometrical ratio, doubling again and again after a period of time, while food supply can only grow by arithmetical ratio as agricultural areas are added.

His thesis was bitterly attacked then and has been attacked many times since, but no one has ever won the argument with Malthus. The attacks usually were assertions that the matter could not be so simply stated — that the curve of population growth would decline as numbers of people began to press on food supply; that agriculture constantly improved and land produced more food per area; and so on. But the irresistible fact is that no area of land and no advance of agriculture can produce more than some finite amount of food, which is not enough because over any long enough time the increase in numbers of people will produce more mouths than can be fed. The curve of population grows constantly steeper and it has no limit. Steadily and inexorably the number of people increases, and nothing has yet been done to stop the increase or even to limit it. Malthus, in stating the problem, could only suggest voluntary continence as a remedy. Actually birth control on a scientific basis and on a world-wide scale is the only solution humanly possible to consider.

Meanwhile our forests melt away, and our forests are our water supply. Our suburban and other housing developments cover ever more agricultural land, and our freeways and expressways cut swaths through fields and forests and cities. Everywhere massive land moving machines cut into our hills. Industrial developments pollute our streams, and sewage and waste pour into them. A human living a long life can see any given area become more and more changed in some undesirable and permanent way. And all the while the human race proliferates and multiplies. We are told our numbers have doubled in the past half century and will double again by the year 2000.

You can perform a household experiment to typify what is happening. Take a drinking glass of ditch water. Drop into it a few leaves of alfalfa or grass. Look daily at a drop of this water with a microscope magnifying perhaps a hundred diameters. In a few days the water swarms with paramecia, or slipper animalcules. You can watch the captive population increase by leaps and bounds. Suddenly they all die, having exhausted their food resources and poisoned their environment with their wastes. You have witnessed the world in miniature and compressed human multiplication into a few days, but the lesson is there in stark simplicity. More human beings are being born each year than die out of the population, and the excess increases by geometric progression. After a certain period of time the world's population doubles, and the periods have grown shorter and shorter, until the next double will occur in about forty years. Nothing has been done by any race or people to change the birth rate, and nothing else thinkable can affect the rate of increase.

Man not being a paramecium, the production of food has been increased as the population has grown. But the production of food can only proceed to increase up to the capacity of the limited land area to bear crops, and we are now close to that limit. The seas can produce crops as well, of fish and other sea foods, but already we are beginning to press our fishing grounds past their capacity and are overfishing nearly everywhere. We can produce protein foods from plankton, taking over from the whales. But nothing we can do will produce a limitless amount of food, and the progression of increase in the numbers of people has no limit unless we impose one, which we have yet to do.

Some day we will reach the limit of our capacity to produce more food, and there will not be enough to feed the next increase in population. This will not happen gradually but suddenly, and there will not be at that time any further margin of time for preparation for the emergency. The last scrap of edible substance, including the seed corn, will go down the hungry mouths of the population. What comes after that may be envisaged by each of us as he pleases, except that there is no room for pleasant speculation, and the progress from now until the day of cataclysm is quite inevitable unless we meanwhile find a rational answer.

Report Concerning The World Crisis of Population and Food

In 1960 C.F. Rehnborg was asked to submit a Position Paper on the above subject to then-President Richard Nixon, through the agency of Charles S. Rhyne who was National Chairman of Citizens for Nixon-Lodge in the 1960 political campaign. Although the report is too long to reprint in its entirety, following are Rehnborg's covering memo and excerpts from the report which indicate his analysis of the situation.

* * * * * * * * *

I am delighted that this subject of conservation is going to be the material of a Position Paper, because certainly this indicates that it is not only going to get attention but is to be the basis of action.

I said before that it would be a remarkable and a magnificent thing if the United States could again do for the first time at the national level something never done before in history, in the form of a long range and scientific approach to the problem of conservation, which is finally the problem of water, which in turn will be the overruling problem of the future. The problem of securing food supplies for an exploding population may be solved by development of the inexhaustible sea as a food resource, but nothing whatever except just possibly distillation by atomic power will ever take the place of rainfall, and even atomic power cannot ever achieve the volumes of water involved in the necessary supply for a land population any larger than the present one.

But I am not satisfied long range even with the idea that the United States will move massively on the conservation problem for the continental area we live in. I think that the next step is automatically indicated as concerted action all over the world, probably through the United Nations, and that this action may well be dominated and led by the United States.

There is no possibility of making the argument that any plan with reference to world resources and watershed cover is too large. There is no problem so great, or of equal importance, and it is a problem which has to be solved, but not even secondary to the problem of population control. There is no possibility of sustaining the greater population and its necessary services unless the water supply is adequate. It may finally be true that no river can be permitted to discharge its fresh water into the ocean unused, but all the volume of all the available rivers in the areas which will carry the increased population will yet not provide the necessary volume of water if the watershed cover has deteriorated.

The overriding problem for the world government will be, as it is now for the United States, the maintenance of watershed cover and the freedom from pollution or from mud of the runoff from the watershed.

The program of conservation for the United States itself will have to be initiated and given direction within the time area of one or two individuals in the office of President, but however great the accomplishments of that President, they will never be any more than the preliminary moves, for the reason that the program itself ideally extends over a minimum of centuries and a maximum of the endurance of the human race. Therefore, the step of initiation, of which the first element is the Position Paper, should result in legislation which sets the ground rules for all subsequent developments.

The ground rules can be modified by later executive or legislative action, but they cannot be changed in principle, and as originally set up they will have to provide safeguards against pressure action due to special interest groups. It will not be possible, for example, either at once or ever, to permit the lumbering industry or the mining industry or the livestock industry to divert the principles of overall watershed control by any form of destruction of the watershed cover itself. The cattle men, for example, should never be permitted the use of the watershed cover for grazing purposes. The mining industry should never be free to clear land for a proposed real or fictitious mining operation. The lumbering industry cannot have the right to harvest timber except on a scientific basis.

At the present moment in the lumbering industry, for example, an individual lumbering company, no matter how enlightened, cannot treat its forest scientifically as a source of wood and fiber for the reason that the company which observed the scientific rules would be at an economic disadvantage as compared to those companies which did not. On the other hand, if the ground rules for forest development and use were so set that there was only one way to harvest timber, or poles, or fiber, by selective harvest, and the full maintenance of the forest cover were required, all companies would be on the same basis and obedience of the ground rules by one company would not place it at a disadvantage. Nevertheless, all of the special interest groups would combat this move, and therefore the ground rules will have to be set up by a Congress dedicated to the principle and uninfluenced by pressure groups.

This, I think, would mean that the Position Paper should be very comprehensive and very convincing.

The subject is vital, and of complete and compelling interest to all humanity. We are at the edge of a possible total destruction of our land surfaces. History records many instances where it has occurred, and we can look at the deserts which were the end result. The progressive signs of still new creation of new desert areas are there to be read by men of the sort who should be made interested in this tremendous project, beginning with the Position Paper. I am hoping that in the preparation of the Position Paper these men will be the ones who choose the language in which the problem is presented, and that they are to receive the assurance that what they do will be treated with respect and given suitable attention.

* * * * * * * * * *

FOLLOWING IS AN APPRAISAL of the future of the world in an extension of the immediate crisis of the present. The world is about to go through the crisis of adjusting population now and for the future to the capacity of the earth to feed its inhabitants and preserve its character. This memo is made in a belief that the crisis can be solved and that the best way to solve it is by concerted action of the world's present leaders: the USA and the USSR.

THE PROBLEM HUMANITY FACES, for the one who tries to outline it, is like trying to write a report on a fire while the building is being destroyed by flames. A few observers of the present threat to the existence of our society are shouting warnings to one another while the great body of Western society is made up of much calmer people conducting the daily affairs of the Earth as if there were many threats to social order but none directly threatening society itself. The reading of current journals of the many branches of the sciences is an exercise in frustration. Each science talks of its current affairs as if time stretched forward endlessly for them to study long-range effects without hurry. In newspapers and news magazines it is duly noted that some wild-eyed Jeremiahs are prophesying population explosions and pollution of the

Earth as an environment, but it seems to be generally felt that no real problems threaten us in the near future, and there is definitely no worldwide political program for dealing with population numbers as an immediate international concern for international action.

Yet the forward view is definitely alarming. Population of the Earth, which we have seen as a fulfillment of ancient destiny, deals now with increases comparable to the existing population of now-living human beings on the Earth in a matter of a generation in time. We are beings who suddenly must deal with a new order of events. We have seen the population of the Earth grow in ever shorter periods of years, and now suddenly, so to speak without proper warning, the Earth's population of all kinds of dissimilar types of men is to double in about thirty years. In about thirty years we are permanently to see two persons where now we see one person, and this unbelievable rate of increase is itself to increase by doubling three times in a century, to seven billion, to fourteen billion, to twenty-eight billion. Clearly, we cannot increase production of food for these new billions in anything like the rate of production of the billions of mankind who will now have to be fed. What is going to happen to our hitherto reasonably comfortable and rational world?

Well, immediately, the race of men is going to have to increase its production of day-units of food at the same pace at which it produces new humans to eat the food, or if we fail to do so, face the virtual certainty that the world society of human beings will dissolve into battle and become chaos and anarchy. All over the world, now, even before we give credit to the new information that we are already participants in a populational explosion, millions of individual human beings are dying of starvation (mostly in China, India, and central Africa). It has been correctly observed that if all the food now in the world were equally distributed among all the people now living in the world, everyone now in the world would be rather hungry. This state of things is like peace and plenty in comparison with what is coming to us. There exists a food shortage which very soon, say by the year 1975, will become a critical shortage in some areas. It is a race which we have already lost. We can never again, counting from today, produce food in greater quantity than we require it, UNLESS:

1) we develop new sources of virtually unlimited food, or

2) we cut the rate of new births of human beings to as low as, or

lower than, the rate of human deaths from all causes.

Flatly, we must never again allow the rate of human births to exceed the rate of deaths.

There is not any human means at the present moment, whether by human custom or by political power resting in the hands of the world's rulers, either to cull the human crop to a lower figure by weeding out the misfits and the afflicted as potential parents, or to persuade the human population of the world to lower the rate at which new births occur. It is one of the truisms that any form of life which has a lower birth rate than its death rate is in danger of becoming extinct, and that a form of life which has a higher birth rate than its death rate is in the way of increasing its numbers and of surviving in the unceasing struggle for existence. The human race is merely in the position of having made its world so safe for itself — by lessening natural hazards and natural enemies and making human contacts peaceful for culture and trade, by improving public health and lowering susceptibility and exposure to disease, and by making the individual survival rate at birth much greater — that the rate of sustained increase of the human world population is now greater than it has ever been before.

Add to this an extension of the child-bearing period and a lowering of the age of mating, and you make it rational as a fact that for some centuries there has been an increase in the net growth of populations. There has also been a medical lessening of deaths by warfare and pestilence. These have all now combined to produce an upward surge in the total numbers of regional populations. The upward surge in numbers has gotten out of control and could be fatal to the human race itself if allowed to continue unchecked.

It has become a sort of happy insanity. No political government of any world area has moved at all to control the birth rate, and yet it is the birth rate which must be controlled. There is, simply and finally, no way out of our dilemma except through the control, worldwide, of the human birth rate.

* * * * * * * * * *

Our human society, in an environment humanity has made quite favorable to itself, has abruptly reached the point of doubling its numbers more rapidly than ever before. There are now on the earth about three and a half billion human beings. In 2000 AD it is estimated there will be seven billion, and thereafter population will potentially double every third of a century so long as the capacity of the earth to supply food for its population is not exceeded.

Some time in the relatively near future, however, there will not be enough food. The earth's capacity and human ingenuity will fall short of producing enough; there will be mass starvation; and the human social order will perhaps collapse. There is in any case an interregnum during which anything can happen, and probably will — food riots, wars and the use of stored atom bombs, anarchy, epidemics, pestilences — the whole gamut.

This runaway increase of population has been foretold as a fact of natural law, most notably by the Reverend Thomas Malthus in 1798, who almost accidentally stumbled onto the law, and whose suggested remedy was restriction of the birth rate, achieved (so far as he knew) by sexual abstinence. Malthus said that food supplies could only be increased arithmetically, by increases in area of farm lands, improvements in plant species, increases in crop production, and so on, while population would increase geometrically, doubling its numbers again and again during some lapse of time, whatever the duration of time involved. Other things such as pollution of the habitat become in growing degree yet other limiting factors on population increase, but finally all humanity would have to face the stark fact that only control of the human birth rate provides any final answer.

* * * * * * * * * *

The active and present danger of overpopulation of the Earth and of resulting starvation and death of that population is a recurring concern which has been studied many times. If this subject were regarded as being important as it is in fact, it would overshadow everything else in the news, but only a fraction of the human race is even worried or concerned — not many enough to get action or to get it quickly enough.

Now people like Andrei Sakharov of Russia and Lord C.P. Snow of Great Britain have spoken out on the imminent danger and they propose immediate action. It is time for our government to look carefully at the problem, because it is even more specific and immediate than these two great scientists have said it is, and the conditions have become politically more favorable for the necessary talks and action between the USSR and the USA.

The present situation cannot be trifled with. It calls for radical steps at the very highest level. When the Reverend Thomas Malthus first published his essay on the Principle of Population (1798), concerning the eventual danger that mankind would breed and increase in numbers until food supplies would be less than adequate, all the educated men of the societies of the Earth gave attention, but only for a while. As the numbers of people increased, great progress was made in technology. The area under cultivation was increased as more and more land came under cultivation in hitherto undeveloped areas of the Earth's surface; more and more machines were used in agriculture; improved strains of seeds and improved species of plants were developed; and the control of insect pests became more effective.

At the same time, natural checks to population and longevity and wars and pestilences (for example the Black Death, which at one point killed a quarter of the population of Europe) were rendered less and less important as the science of medicine made the birth rate exceed the death rate all over the Earth, and the time that women everywhere lived and bore children was extended.

Time and again mankind became interested and momentarily exercised about the Malthus prediction, but time after time nothing ominous seemed to happen. Gradually, the people of the West began to forget the problems of overpopulation and to find them applicable only to the Eastern half of the Earth, and the run of men began to find the Malthus prediction only a tiresome joke.

Meanwhile, the prediction moved gradually towards fulfillment, with only the calendar date of the timetable out of step and moved forward. There seemed nothing imminent in the prophesy, so it very easily could be disregarded — and it was. Let us look again at what Malthus had predicted so many years earlier.

He said that under civilization the numbers of people on the Earth increased by a geometrical progression, doubling again and again in 'some period of time,' while the food supply could only increase arithmetically as agriculture was improved and more land surface was brought into cultivation and production.

The prediction of Malthus has never, in all the years since Malthus made it, been suspended or invalidated. The very presence on the Earth of any species of life depends on the accuracy of the principle, with the addition of one fact for man which does not hold in the wild animal kingdom — the developing of procedures for promoting the welfare of mankind. Among animals the rule of increase holds, but animals cannot protect themselves against the environment as man does. The rate of attrition of animal numbers by (1) being hunted as food by a predator, by (2) being unable to find enough of its own food, or (3) by falling victim to some sort of fatal accident or disease, determines whether the animal survives as a species or does not survive. If there is one more elephant on Earth now than there were any length of time ago, it means that the species can progressively increase its numbers enough eventually to cover the Earth. One less daily of any animal species than there were yesterday means that the species finally becomes extinct. Thousands of species — mammals, birds, reptiles, fish — have become extinct. Nothing dramatic; merely the environment for some reason did not let the species increase its numbers. Never before has any species but man increased in numbers until there was not enough food for sustenance, but in a few tens of years man can, and will, accomplish this feat, unless (and very soon) he takes the steps necessary to control his numbers — or better, to reduce them somewhat.

In other words, there is the simple and inevitable sequence: either man controls his increase in numbers or he does not. If he does not, the time during which his race may live on the Earth (or anywhere) extends only to the point at which his supply of food runs out or becomes inadequate and no longer.

Now look at the figures for population numbers. The total numbers of human beings on the Earth has doubled several times since the beginning of recorded history. At first the numbers of human beings alive at one time doubled in thousands of years, then in a few centuries, and there were a few times when the numbers seemed to move towards man's disappearance. More recently, the doubling of numbers has come to occur much more quickly. Today, at last, numbers will double three times in a century or even more swiftly.

As of this calendar date, the population of the Earth increases each day by 200,000 new human beings — something of the order of 73 million each year — and this rate itself increases. This does not mean that such a number of people has dropped in as visitors to share a meal or two, but that the daily population of the Earth, on a permanent basis, for the duration of an average human life, has been increased by 200,000 human entities.

It will be additionally increased by the same number of new beings who will join us in the imminent struggle for food, from now on, during every day of 24 hours which passes, until, as a whole world, we have forced an adjustment of the birth rate which will keep it permanently equal to (or lower than) the rate at which human beings already on the Earth come to the end of living and die.

No one earth or any hundred planets of the same kind and size can, or could, provide food for such a volume of continuing increase in population. It is a steady, irresistible pressure. Whatever other things we may do individually or as nations in the business of living, the overhanging fact is that we and our fellow world inhabitants face each successive day the ever-nearer end of our accustomed and comfortable world — a collective apprehension that becomes more nearly hopeless day by day, with no agreement reached among the nations of the world as to how we shall meet — and permanently correct — the situation which now faces us. The world population is already too large for the world as we have known it, with areas not yet put to the uses which serve civilization.

The complete and final answer is as simple as to lower the world's rate of births to a figure which is in balance with the death rate — the same number of human beings this year, next year, and forever (or, if we soberly reach the conclusion in our world congress), a population of smaller size, but of physically and mentally superior types, on the average, than the present population of our Earth.

Try to see what these numbers mean. There are now on the Earth about three and a half billions of human beings. Doubling means as many more additional human beings — one for one — to be fed and clothed and sheltered, to be supplied with cars and fuel and with roads on which to run the cars, with radio sets, and with the many things which we consider a normal part of living and being schooled and doing the things that the state of civilization calls for — more things even than at present. Society as we know it may well break down in the coming third of a century as it tries to adjust to the population increase — by doing things which man has never done before. These include not just things we may do if we can persuade ourselves, but things we must do to survive at all in moving into the time left to us to use our beautiful Earth for living — to become the masters of human destiny and the exploiters of our human possibilities during coming centuries and millenia, during millions and even billions of years that our Earth can endure in the future.

Wo muot we absolutely must — do in One World the things that can turn humanity from a more and more desperate mob into a permanently organized society on our Earth managed scientifically. This requires political unity which only the USA and Russia can create and maintain.

* * * * * * * * *

The making of one world would be the climactic event of human history. Severely simple and logical in principle, it would permanently end the making of war, stop the making and use of lethal weapons by individuals and nations, establish and maintain world peace, organize and promote our scientific future. By abolishing world armaments and canceling out our military establishments — except for a world police force — it would add a doubling of our international product of usable goods. World unity would emasculate patriotism, which would be a complete anomaly in a scientific One World, and subtitute for it a more worthy devotion to the welfare of humanity. The arts and sciences are now aboil with plans for the greatest advances in history, which could immediately become improvements in the machinery of the social order.

Changes for the better would come in our concepts of labor, wages, profit, and taxes, giving us instead creativeness in one's 'own thing' and advances in social activity. Amazing changes would occur as some of our honored institutions were seen as really nothing more than contrived supports for an accepted order which was less valuable than was thought in our present world society. Science would move carefully in new directions, studying heredity and other means for improving the quality of human kind in human society; restoring the balance between humanity and its ecology; limiting the numbers of the segments of society and improving the heredity in human beings; stopping the wastage of natural resources; reversing the degradation of parts of the world's surface and preserving increasing areas as 'wild' and natural refuges; trimming the numbers of human beings to balance with the Earth's land and air; and strictly maintaining such balances as (to use a single example) the regeneration by vegetation of the oxygen balance in the world's atmosphere.

The oceans could become humanity's mine for minerals. Nothing but very small traces of the light gases ever leaves the Earth's gravitational field, and everything is used over and over again. Even oxygen, locked up as oxides, is replaced by the plants using the chlorophyll process — and will only fail if we continue to use more oxygen than plant life returns to the environment. In fact, if we control the birth rate for human beings we could last as long as the Earth lasts — billions of years.

* * * * * * * * *

We have always done our historical thinking in terms of a few thousand years in the past, which we call 'ancient history,' and our individual thinking in the period of our own individual span of living. In dealing with the human race as an evolutionary whole, however, we deal with a time scale which is many times longer than the whole of the recorded or even the legendary history of mankind. There has been life on the Earth for something like three billion years; anthropoid life for something like a hundred million years; and humanoid life for ten million years. Our ancestors have lived in primitive cultures for a very long time, and, after the gradual development of agriculture, in varying degrees of civilization for perhaps fifty thousand years of prehistory before the invention of writing began our truly written history. But all this can be only a prelude to the time span during which we have the chance to develop the possibility inherent in humanity.

During the period in which our sun will continue as now to 'burn' its supply of hydrogen by conversion into helium and to expend the resulting floods of energy, very much a continuance of the present status of the sun and its planetary system in the space of the Universe, something like five billion years will elapse during which, barring cosmic accident, humanity can continue to live on the Earth very much as it is now, for a million times as long as all our recorded histories and cultures. The proviso is that now, quickly, we mend our ways — that we control our number of births at something very much less than the present runaway figure; that we disavow war and live permanently at peace; that we discontinue forever our pollution of our living space on the miraculous Earth; and that we put ourselves under some type of rule or control which has the power to stop any misuse of our only possible home — a political change for which we already have the obsolescent United Nations as a logical framework which we need only to remodel.

The United Nations (UN) was set up to control and solve our

international problems, including the causes of war. In the world it was strongly felt that the world leaders must solve the world's problems. But the leaders compromised. They always have. They set up the United Nations in a beautiful new setting and sent delegates to it, but they gave it no power to enforce its judgments. It became instead a debating society which served a purpose in causing international problems to be dissipated in words. Now, however, there is a new crisis which words alone cannot solve, in which the UN could be the intermediary, but for which it lacks the right to use enabling power. It is a situation in which the use of enabling power should have been planned even before the urgency of the situation had been recognized, because such a situation of crisis was certain to arise some time.

The Sea As A Food Source

Written Approximately 1966

All life on the earth originated in the sea. The living forms which inhabit the dry land are able to do so only because they have made a compromise with the new environment, but even at that, the compromise is in terms related to life in the sea.

A man, specifically, is a bit of the ancestral sea enclosed in an armor. Some form of skin or mucous membrane covers the exterior and interior surfaces of his body, enclosing and protecting the fluids of the body; and barring accident, there is nowhere any chink or aperture in this armor. Within the armor the trillions of cells of the body, no longer floating free but grouped into specialized organs, are bathed in this fluid, effecting by water solutions all the intricate chemical exchanges which are the life process. Some of the fluid, circulating through conduits called arteries and veins as a sort of motile organ called blood, carries food to the individual cells and transports waste materials, maintains proper salinity and alkalinity of the microcosmic sea, and percolates through the channel walls in exchanges with the intercellular fluid.

This organization was effected while life still existed exclusively in the sea. Some fishes developed gills and fins adapted to crawling on the mud of the shore. These in time gave rise to the amphibians, which in turn gave rise to the reptiles, and from the reptiles the mammals and birds developed. Some plants invaded muddy shores, becoming less and less dependent on marshy wetness about their roots, and more able to draw necessary moisture from sand grains wetted by rain.

Nevertheless, in all these adaptations for leaving the sea, nowhere has life separated itself from dependence on water. Even forms adapted to desiccation, such as lichens and spores, suspend the life processes when they are dry and resume them only when they are wet again. In all cases the sequences of reactions which are life must be carried out in solutions in water. The oxygen of energy exchanges must be carried and used in solution, and of the waste products of combustion of organic materials — carbon dioxide and water — the carbon dioxide is carried away and disposed of in solution.

This is because life, originating in the sea, remains adapted primarily to the sea, and merely compromised with a dry environment by special mechanisms. On the land, plants and animals contend successfully with differences in climate, wet and dry areas, good and poor soil, and atmospheric pressures, including relative abundance of oxygen and carbon dioxide. In the sea none of these special hazards exist, other than differences in temperature, or differences in pressure, which require relatively simple adjustments on the part of any specific life forms. Life in the sea is suspended in its food, and life teems to a limit set by some special limiting factor of supply, which generally is the element phosphorus.

Human beings and their precursors on the dry land have lived for some hundreds of millions of years in terms of the special adaptation of dissolving oxygen into the liquids of the body through membranes in the lungs, and of making up deficiencies in water content by absorbing the water of foods in digestion and by drinking water. Some animal forms are so adapted to dry areas as to require very little water supplementation except through the foods eaten.

As a result of this simple fact, our developed faculty of thinking has been in terms of the dry land. We have killed meat and gathered fruits and nuts and seeds, and drunk water from lakes and streams, and multiplied in numbers with scarcity of these factors as our limiting boundary. By the inventions of husbandry and agriculture we have increased the food potential of our environment and permitted greater increase in numbers. The sea we have seen always merely as water — useful for bathing and drinking, and by floating on a carrier of some sort, as a road on which to travel between pieces of land. It is true men accepted the existence of fish as a gratuitous addition to the sources of food supply, but in the same manner as manna was accepted from heaven.

Now, however, the race between numbers of the human population, which is a geometric progression, and potential food sources, which is an arithmetical progression, has come near enough to a climax to become an immediate problem requiring solution — and for the first time men generically have begun to study the sea.

The sea is several things we have not heretofore considered. It is spread over three-quarters of the surface of the earth. It is rich in life; an average acre of sea produces twenty or more tons of foods annually. Its limiting factor is phosphorus, and there are uncounted trillions of tons of phosphorus in the seas. The present 'limit on population' still permits staggering totals of tons of life to swarm the seas, and phosphorus is a circulating resource.

As contrasted to land areas, which can become mineral-poor by leaching and land use, the sea is the final end of all soluble mineral supplies. Phosphorus taken ashore in fish forms, for example, returns finally to the sea, and the leaching of primary rocks exposed to weathering on the land continues to add to the stock of the element in the seas.

Next, the cycles of life in the sea which produce the fish forms we eat as food are technically wasteful if we are to use the sea as a source of food. The microscopic vegetables of the sea, the diatoms, are the primary food source. Diatoms support several sequences of exchange of organic material in planktonic forms, plankton becomes copepods or krill, these become sardines, sardines are eaten by fish. Each of these steps uses five to ten pounds of one form to produce one pound of another, so that finally it requires from 5^5 to 10^5 pounds of diatoms, at the least, to produce one pound of fish for a man to eat. If the diatoms or plankton were fed as sources of food to land animals, the potential of the sea could be increased by a factor of perhaps a hundred as food for mankind. Even as fish, the sea could add to the food potential of the earth quite as much as is now produced in land crops and herds. Finally, the food sources of the sea, if not decimated or destroyed as specific forms by overharvesting, are potentially eternally renewable.

There is more. If, unlike the forms of life on land, the life of the sea lives and has always lived in a balanced environment, then the food from the sea will include the factors protein, fats, carbohydrates, vitamins, and minerals, required by land forms of life — and will supply these factors in balance. Land plants and land animals may be deficient forms of food, but sea forms may be complete and balanced.

The sea is not, however, the complete answer to the problems of the near future. The growth in numbers of people is still a geometric progression, and unless some form of control of growth in numbers is established, the problem of crisis in food supply is only deferred to a later date, not solved, by the recognition of a vast supplemental source of food in the seas.

It sums up that at the very moment the peoples of the world have become aware that the problem of survival is imminent, the human race has been given a breathing space in which to find the solutions which will permit it to continue on the earth for hundreds and thousands and millions of years, instead of starving to death or undergoing such a

complete relapse of civilization that only a relatively small group wil
struggle up through the long advances from savagery all over again. The
evolution of man has reached a heartening position of advance. It will not
stop as a progression, but while the progression may be downward as well
as not, our position and its potential rate a chance. Man can become many
things he has not yet become, but he will not do it by going back to
savagery.

Part IV
COMMENTARY ON POLITICAL AND SOCIAL ISSUES

The Right to Vote

Written in 1960

The right to vote in free elections is a right which was won by brave men with blood and sacrifice. It is a right which can be lost by the cowardly, and even by the indifferent, because it is not a natural but an acquired right, and a right to be kept only by continuing to merit it and to guard and defend it. In the natural order the stronger rule over the weaker, whether in a herd or a family or a tribe or a nation; and in a natural order, the strong do not believe that the weak have any right to a vote or to a voice in government. Their only right is to hear the voice of the rulers and to obey the edicts of the rulers. Any student of history knows these facts, and no one knew them better than the men who conceived and created the United States of America, and paid for it with their lives when they had to.

In the beginning of what was to be the modern political world, in the Magna Carta at Runnymede, men upset what was then called the divine right of kings to rule by edict, and gave life to the ideal of government of the people, by the people, and for the people. Until then, and since then, the struggle to achieve this ideal has cost centuries of effort and millions of lives. Yet you and I receive the full fruit of this ideal, the right to vote in free elections as a peer and equal of every other man, without struggle and without sacrifice, simply through the fortunate chance of being born in a country which has been for a hundred and fifty years the shining ideal of the rest of the world because these rights and this ideal exist here and are a part of the pattern of life for every citizen — and sometimes, even often, we do not take the small trouble to use our right to vote.

To have the right to vote and not to use it is a treachery to the nation and to the human race. It is the tragedy, and it might well be the doom of our modern America, that only a fraction of its citizens fulfill this duty, just through plain laziness and indifference. So long as this is true we are fair prey for those powers who do not believe in the system of government by the consent of the governed, or in free elections.

We are today in a struggle, in a cold war which may well become a hot war, with a ruthless dictatorship which is organized and disciplined and strong, and which seeks to end the dream of freedom which we represent and to destroy us. They typify the savages who in the end have always overwhelmed civilizations which had grown soft and slack and heedless, and in which the citizens held their civic duty lightly.

Those who acquire citizenship in America know and have considered what our system of freedom means. They chose our system in contrast to another. They have gone through a term of apprenticeship to qualify as citizens. They have read and they understand the words and the motives of the Declaration of Independence and of the Constitution of the United States — and they use and treasure their franchise to vote in free elections. So should you now in turn read these two documents, which very likely you have never yet read, and register to vote, and vote in the coming election, and in every election for which the polls are open to you.

In justice, if not in law, the punishment for not voting should be severe enough to drive home the lesson that the vote and what it stands for are the most important facts, and the franchise the most important duty, for every man and woman who is a citizen. If the duty is not exercised, you may well by your neglect have assured that your children or your children's children will some day not have the privilege or the chance to discharge the duty, but will live under a system which is not freedom.

Advice for the Expert
A Layman's View of Law for the World Community

This essay was written by C.F. Rehnborg in February, 1960, and released by the Special Committee on World Peace Through Law, of the American Bar Association, headquartered in Washington, D.C.

In a sense, international law is so far an idea rather than a concrete thing. It is so far principally a system of provisional understandings and treaties between individual nations concerning a limited number of legal questions they will submit to a court; and the court they use, also established by treaty, is the International Court at the Hague in Holland. This is analogous to two individual citizens of a country agreeing that they will submit certain classes of disputes between them to a court, but will take into their own hands the settlement of other classes of disputes by any method they choose, including force.

But, although it is not yet universally acknowledged among nations, the nations are nevertheless in turn the citizens of a world community, and have no more inherent right than the individuals of a national community to make their own laws without regard to others. Either this, or there is no meaning to the human belief that there is a spiritual value in human existence. The significance of all human history, however, is that these values exist. Beginning with single human families, then clans, then tribes, then nations, the idea of law and order (of allegiance to the concept that the whole group has rights to which the rights of the individual are subordinate) can be seen, historically, to have received progressively increasing adherence from humanity. Also it has grown in meaning from obedience to father or chief, into obedience to the concept of the collective rights of the group as expressed in a body of law.

The next step, equally as necessary and right and inevitable as the other progressive steps, is acceptance of the concept (not new) that the whole world of men is only a larger community than one nation, and that all the nations are the individual members of the community. I believe that the individual men of the world community are quite ready to accept this idea. The individual nations are not — or not yet.

The problem of bringing about acceptance by the nations, as nations, to the concept which men everywhere, as individual men, are ready to accept, is complicated by the fact that nations, as nations, are not truly expressive of the collection of human individuals of whom each is composed, but are in fact governed at the national level by individual men who are basically fallible human entities and only incidentally the voice of the nation; so that their human frailties, including prejudice and suspicion and self-interest, stand in the way of decisions which follow a logical progress.

The nations have, however, already taken a great and logical step of creating the United Nations, which is actually the mechanism for the attainment of international law and order, and in the United Nations so many men represent so many nations that individual idiosyncrasies are averaged out, and there is a chance for the voices of the individuals of the human race to come through; so that the problem is now to build the sequence by which the next steps come naturally to be taken in the United Nations which will progress into the final result of the rule of law throughout the world.

What is needed next is agreement between many nations, and not two by two, that a body of international law, codified and accepted by them all, constitutes the rules which will bind them in their relations with one another; and a court — possibly and probably the existing court at the Hague — to which they are obliged to submit their international problems, and also obliged to accept and obey the decisions of the court.

Even this is not more than a first step, since it is still necessary merely to expect the individual nations to accept the court's rulings voluntarily. What there must be eventually is an Authority which can if necessary enforce the decisions of the court, just as within a nation there is authority to enforce the decisions of the national courts. If, for example, a decision is made awarding damages, the national government's police power can oblige the loser to pay the damages, and is in fact obligated to do so.

In the same way, the decisions of the International Court must be enforceable. This probably means that the individual nations must, so to speak, deed to the United Nations (of which the court is an agency) the part of their independence and "national sovereignty" which relates to the rights of the rest of the world community beyond their own borders, and therefore to international law, permanently and without recourse. This may be a difficult step to achieve, but the present existence of the United Nations is itself the result of such concessions already made. Merely, the United Nations has not been given authority, and it is authority which it must have. With the authority conceded, the United Nations could thereupon form a World Police Force with authority to enforce the decisions of the International Court, if necessary.

By the same token, no member nation could then proceed against another nation in any manner except through the International Court, under penalty of itself becoming subject to the United Nations police powers.

Also, at this point, the United Nations becomes itself the expression of world opinion and of dedication to world law and order; and thereafter any non-member nation becomes outlaw when it proceeds against this world will, and can be dealt with accordingly. It is interesting to project, at this point, that although the United Nations would have armed force as well as police power (and probably the only such organized force in the world), yet it is highly probable that the weapon used against outlaw nations would usually be sanctions and not force.

The world has dreamed of, and even tried, this idea of world order before. Alexander had the dream, Rome almost achieved it, and Ghengis Khan tried to achieve it. But these were concepts of imposition of one nation's control on all other nations. It is only now that the concept has every chance to succeed, because now there is also the established concept in the world of today of equality of rights and of agreement by concensus.

The Qualities of Leadership

August 1, 1960

There have been many periods in history when the times called for a leader and none arose — or perhaps they were there in the mass of mankind, as they always are in embryo, but the spark did not touch them and they did not take fire. But in times of great crisis the sparks are everywhere and no man is oblivious or immune to them, and then the man of destiny appears — at first not quite recognizing himself for what he is, but recognizing the call and moving towards it.

When he does recognize the relationship between events, and between himself and the call, he is, if he is an egomaniac, without any hesitations or misgivings like an Alexander or a Caesar or a Napoleon, and he is then usually a military genius rising to command and to conquest. But when a destined leader of the spirits of men arises, he is at first overwhelmed with his own inadequacy, which history will not see or remember, and he moves at first with much agony of spirit and much soul-searching within himself.

Yet every man of special genius, like all other men everywhere, puts on his pants one leg at a time, and eats and sleeps and answers the calls of nature, and is full of drive and then exhausted, and has moments of doubt and depression, and does nearly every trivial thing that all other men do. It is what other men do not possess so well, or have not awakened in time to know that they have it, that marks the one man for his destiny. There is first of all for him the sense of destiny, and then the knowledge that he himself is uniquely fitted for what is to be done.

Primarily, as a special quality, he sees things whole and senses the key facts in any set of facts. He accurately analyzes his own capabilities and the capabilities of others he will use, and he imbues these others with his own vision.

He knows without overrating himself the true scope of his capabilities. He recognizes that his intimates will fail to see what first the rest of the world and then history will see in him and in what he does, but he sees this himself without undue concern that others do not see it.

He expands his figure to fit the mold but not to exceed it, because the man cannot tailor the events of destiny to himself, but must shape himself to fit the role events have given him. When he has done this, his human and inescapable inadequacies become limiting factors properly assayed, and he works around them as one does around the limitations of any instrument, but he no longer dwells on them or excuses them even to himself, because they are conditions and not faults. He will know also that perhaps other men are living at the same time with himself who could do all he will do, but they did not answer the call and he did, and that is the essential fact. He cannot now wait for them to do what he must do. On this one thing he cannot look back or even speculate: forces greater than he cast the die.

A man of destiny must stand unique. He is not merely a product of a family but of a time. In the mechanics of genes the family is the vehicle of heredity, but the man himself is an anomaly only physically related to his family. His love for his human family and his friends has responsive approval from all men, but the man himself has to see, without any vainglory, that an accident of destiny has given him special equipment and obligation which overrate his ordinary human rights to an ordinary human life. He belongs to the human group and not to himself. This only happens at rare intervals, but when it happens the one man is under compulsion from the controlling force of the universe to forego the goals and the satisfactions that belong to the run of men, and to become a vehicle for the genius or spirit of the human race.

Abraham Lincoln was as humble as he was great, and his reasons for his acts transcended always any purely personal consideration. This was because Lincoln saw, not himself as a heroic figure, but the greater things that he could share with all human beings, his fellow citizens — that the great and inspiring feature of the human mind (or soul) was the setting of ideals, even though these were impossible of attainment. He saw absolute justice and absolute love and absolute principle as the proper goals for human aspiration, and he could think of the good life as the struggle to attain them.

Men who serve ideals are instruments, and instruments are used. The user is greater than the instrument and may be, in such a case as this, the genius or spirit of the human group, which is incomparably greater than any individual, no matter how great that individual may be. One man alone, without contact with others of his kind, would never give birth to the concept of ideals and of human service. It is only in the social group which has lifted itself to the place where the ideals have meaning that these ideals can arise from the genius or spirit of the race or the group, because in the units of this group the spirit of each man feeds upon what is given to that one man by other men, and the accretion of ideas finally takes form through the minds of certain exceptional individuals as the true concept of a principle or an ideal. These ideals, when they are enunciated, are intelligible in the common language, even though their meaning extends beyond the boundaries of the language, and they are comprehended in that language by any type of mind. In fact, it has many times been said that they are best comprehended by the uncomplicated mind, such as the mind of a child, so that even the human adult who opens his mind to the reception of a principle or ideal has to lay aside the cynicism of experience to adopt the element of truth which is an idea.

Should College Sports Be Subsidized?

November 13, 1953

The question is: Should athletes be subsidized by colleges?

The quite plain and unequivocal answer is: They should not.

The reason-for-being of a college or university is education, which is a word of extremely broad meaning, but which generally signifies, or should signify, the acquiring of knowledge which fits a man to cope with the problems of mankind in its environment the universe, and to produce new knowledge to be added to humanity's store of knowledge. Education would include as a segment of knowledge the problems of man's health and fitness as an animal, and a segment of this segment would embrace group athletics as a means of physical development and as tending to health and fitness.

Group athletics in college, including competitive games, should thus be not ends in themselves but a means to an end, completely amateur, completely honorable, and without the faintest flavor of commercialism or of gladiatorial combats for the public entertainment of spectators. Competitive sports have always had, and should have, an element of the keenest interest for both the participants and the spectators, but the essence of collegiate sports is not that they are a business, but that they are simple and clean sports, played honestly and fairly for their own value and interest, and not for the profit they are to produce in terms of money.

Under the system of subsidizing athletes (mostly by secret deals in tacit acknowledgment that the system is both dishonest and dishonorable, and in fact largely because athletes are being subsidized, college athletics has become simply a business, directed by individuals called coaches whose status should be volunteer or else paid subordinate instructors in physical education, but who have assumed an artificial importance which commands larger money salaries than those paid to professors of the sciences.

Under this system parents produce sons, whom presumably and probably they love, who are sent to colleges for education (the parents think) to fit them to take proper places in the social order and to serve the ends of mankind; only for the parents to find instead that they are, often without their consent and quite contrary to their intent, supplying free raw material to a group of athletic coaches with which the coaches are to acquire vicarious glory as the winners of great public contests and regional championships.

The fact that some of the young men who form the bulk material will be injured, sometimes irreparably and permanently, is to the coaches merely an annoyance resulting in the temporary or permanent loss of good but expendable sports material; but to the parents a matter for helpless dismay. The atmosphere of the modern college is fogged with the belief that it is an honor to die for dear old alma mater and the glory of the coach, when the notion is actually the most stupid and false emphasis on the wrong value. The fact that a particular young man required to execute a particular maneuver in a particular game will for the rest of his life nurse a trick knee is of no real concern to a coach; but it is of very real concern to the parents and should be of concern to the school authorities. The primary and proper function of sports in a school is to build the sound bodies in which the famed sound minds are to reside; but college sports have become a not-too-clean form of big business, and the present renown of many colleges is not in their academic standards and the quality of the men they turn out, but in the sports standing of their athletic teams; and those teams include men who did not come to college to learn any of the accumulated knowledge of the human race, but were subsidized or paid to come there to make the coach, and perhaps the college, more famous as a sports center.

To ask the question whether college athletes should be subsidized is not asking whether the system is clean. The system is well known to be not clean, but a dishonest approach to a problem which should not exist. The question posed actually implies instead quite another question: Is the reputation of a college for conducting successful gladiatorial combats so important to the particular college that the college can and should make shady deals to increase its reputation as a sports center? Should not the question be instead: Are we talking of colleges or of professional sports promotion?

The Purpose of The Boys' Club

August 3, 1960

C.F. Rehnborg believed that an individual had an obligation to give back to the community in which one lived and worked, something of value, whether it was in material things or time or services. He therefore established an organization called "Buena Park Kids" in 1949. Initially funded by the Rehnborgs, Buena Park Kids became the Boys' Club of Buena Park in 1952, and the funding was shared by the Andersen Trust, an endowment program for Boys Clubs in the Southern California area.

As an active supporter of the Boys Club movement in Buena Park until his death in 1973, C.F. Rehnborg not only donated funds but also donated the Club's first building on Whitaker Avenue in Buena Park, as well as its present location on Knott Avenue, which was dedicated in 1961. Mrs. Rehnborg has carried on her husband's support as a member of the Board of Directors since 1973, serving as both President and Chairman of the Board, the position she now holds. The Boys' Club budget has grown from $26,000 to over $300,000 annually, with funds raised through public and corporate donations, endowment interest, and the United Way.

The problem for boys is to find things to do. They can always find things of some sort to do because they boil with energy and curiosity and the sense of adventure. But at this stage the problem begins to concern the adults of the community. An explosive and unpredictable energy is loose in the home or the community. On the other hand, the potential of energy on the loose which is a boy cannot be simply caged, for a number of reasons, of which the most important is the fact that this exploring energy is in the process of developing as an adult entity, and control and not restraint is the only solution which will not stultify this development.

When the community was a simpler organization than in modern times, the adult group did not see any problem with any requirement for action by the adults of the group. Boys, like kittens or puppies or wild animals, got social instruction from the family group and school, but adjusted to the terms of life by experimenting with the environment, alone or in groups. When the groups picked up rogue habits, they were called gangs, and it was gangs with a somewhat vicious group spirit which made communities begin to pay attention to the problem, and in fact to recognize there was a problem.

Starting with recognition that boys, like adults, prefer group activity, and strongly tend to conform to the mores and standards of the group — the universal human tendency — organizations, of which the Boy Scouts is an outstanding example, began to systematize the outdoor activities of boys — and later, of girls. But two reasons why this is not enough are, first, that the Boy Scout activity is not a daily but an occasional activity, and second, that the whole problem of youth direction is very much more complex than this, and is a community and not a group responsibility.

It is as much a public responsibility to give direction to the development of boys in their activities outside of school, as it is to organize their school activities and to instruct and train them at home, and the nature of this wise control and direction is just as truly a charge on the whole community and the whole nation, as our schools and home training. This is increasingly true as society becomes more complex.

The answer is a natural one — boys' clubs. Every spontaneous formation of a neighborhood group — something boys have always done of their own volition — is a boys' club. The difference is, that if the community organizes the club for all the boys of the community, the boys can have their own club facilities, rather than some packing cases or a tree house or a cave dug in a bank, and they can have scientific organization of their natural curiosity and energy under direction of a trained youth worker. The activities also, rather than games of "cops and robbers" and of mischief, like breaking windows in any abandoned building, can comprise not only organized games, but constructive activities such as working assignments and field trips — and the quite wonderful experience, for a boy, of well-equipped premises of their own for games and work and social life quite separated from parents and parental fault-finding.

Boys' clubs are such a natural answer that the idea has already gained strong impetus, and many communities have boys' clubs now, and even more communities are acquiring them.

Only — and this is important — these clubs now have to be organized and supplied by individuals in almost all cases. Only rarely does a community accept the need for a boys' club as a community charge, and at once and willingly organize a club and adequately support it.

Fortunately, there are individuals and foundations which will undertake this initial task of organization. A notable example is the Andersen Trust. Its method is to undertake the construction, and at first the whole expense, of the boys' club activities, and then gradually to withdraw support by stages and to expect the community to pick up the difference as a community obligation. In this way, the club becomes in time community-supported wholly, instead of in part, and not the charge of an individual or a foundation.

This thinking, and the example of the Andersen Trust, impelled Mrs. Rehnborg and myself, acting through Nutrilite Foundation, to build a boys' club at Buena Park. Buena Park was a rapidly growing community with no facilities whatever to occupy the young population.

We constructed the club at first as a youth club, to include both boys and girls, but the parents neither took any part in the construction or maintenance of the club, nor did they permit such mingling of the boys and girls of the community. We therefore turned to the Andersen Trust, and to the idea of a boys' club exclusively. We built the club facilities and presented them to the club, and for the first few years paid the expenses of operation, including the professional staff. Then, when the Andersen Trust joined us, they shared these expenses, and together both organizations began to withdraw their full support and to expect and encourage the community to pick up the charge as a community enterprise. No proper feeling of pride and responsibility could possibly be the community sentiment, unless its Boys' Club is recognized by the community as a community enterprise, and not under obligation to individuals or other organizations. In the case of Buena Park, the community has increasingly accepted the club as a community responsibility. At this time, Nutrilite Foundation and the Andersen Trust supply not more than twenty-five percent of the maintenance and equipment expense of the Boys' Club of Buena Park, and we expect confidently that within a short time the club will be a community enterprise entirely, and that the Foundations will become merely two of its yearly contributors for their due share of the community responsibility.

From a modest beginning as Buena Park Kids in 1949, the Boys' Club of Buena Park was affiliated with the Boys' Clubs of America in 1952. It is now located in its own building at 7758 Knott Avenue in Buena Park, and serves the youth of the community, girls as well as boys.

The club itself, so far as the boys are concerned, has been a complete success, both in the interest which the boys have in it, and the degree to which it has washed out the problem of mischievous activities, or what the elders feel fond of calling "juvenile delinquency," which is a modern name for what they themselves did at the same age.

Such an enterprise as a boys' club pays dividends far beyond any expense it occasions for the community, notably in the character and point of view of the participating boys. It is our hope, and that of the Andersen Trust, that the Buena Park Boys' Club will presently serve as

From left, P.D. Wingate of the national Boys' Clubs of America is presenting the E.L. McKenzie Award for the Prevention of Juvenile Delinquency for 1982 to Mrs. Edith Rehnborg, with Buena Park Boys' Club Executive Director, Paul Marsh, looking on.

an outstanding example of full acceptance of a community of responsibility for its youth, because the interest now among the parents is as strong and as effective as we hoped it would be when the enterprise was initiated.

Some of the youngsters who were in the club at the beginning are now the present generation of young men in the town, and they believe, as we do, that the club meant something definite and helpful in their development as citizens.

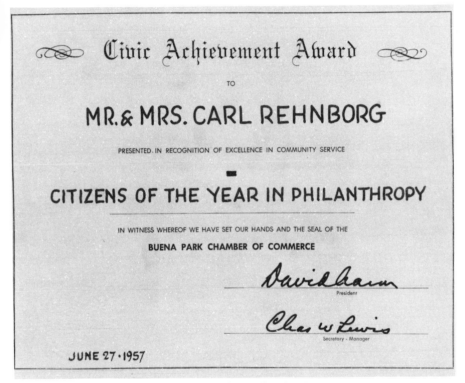

This award was presented to the Rehnborgs by the City of Buena Park in appreciation for their many helpful activities in the City's behalf.

The Meaning of Profit Sharing

Written Approximately 1954

C.F. Rehnborg was one of the early adherents to the principle of profit sharing for business and industry. In cooperation with a large group of other business leaders, he helped to organize the Council of Profit Sharing Industries, a non-profit organization formed to promote that principle. At one point he served on a Committee within the Council, and wrote the following report in connection with his Committee's work.

Any executive who initiates profit sharing in his organization does so to give substance to an ideal. He is not, as an end in itself, setting out only to increase the money returns to the stockholders of his company, but to create in his organization a voluntary association of self-respecting men and women working to a common end, by making them sharers in the product of their common effort. If this is not his primary purpose, neither he nor his shareholders have any proper place in the Council of Profit Sharing Industries.

The Purpose of the Council of Profit Sharing Industries

It is stated, and presumably it is true, that the purpose of the Council of Profit Sharing Industries is to spread the philosophy of profit sharing. It was also stated by nearly all the speakers at the Convention just closed that the virtue of the philosophy was to preserve the free enterprise system, which is a matter of barking up an imaginary tree as well as constituting a sort of emphasis on economic benefit as the major objective. Actually, what is meant is preservation of freedom and of innate individual and collective human rights.

Assuming, however, that the purpose of the Council is to spread the philosophy of profit sharing with all its connotations of individual freedom, and of work as a rewarding human experience, and of ideals of quality and service in the work done and in the things produced for the benefit of all concerned, then certainly membership in the Council is not selfish, but unselfish and philanthropic (in the sense of love of men). Further, it is evident that to give encouragement to the principles of the Council is to advance the greatest movement in the modern industrial world. "Profit sharing" is as good a name as any, because profit sharing is the mechanism by which the ideal is made operative — but it is the ideal and not the mechanism which is the objective.

The result of profit sharing is the integration of the working individual, the objective of all the philosophers of humanism through all of history. Men cease to be the chattels of an employer, hired for gain to the employer and considered to be expendable as are other mechanisms, and instead become self-respecting, free individuals cooperatively associated to achieve a common end.

Moreover, work becomes, not an exchange of unwilling and enforced labor for an equivalent in food and shelter, but a rewarding and ennobling experience as a logical and necessary part of the whole of living. The "survival of the fittest," an ignoble explanation for success, becomes a competition to give quality of service for adequate reward, which even the materialists are beginning to see is a consequence of the nature of the universe.

In summary, it is presumably proper to say that the objective of the Council of Profit Sharing Industries is to extend to the other workers of our country, employers and employed alike, the benefits which those now in the Council consider are to be achieved by the philosophy.

The Principle of Profit Sharing

We read in the daily press at the time this report is written, and at all other times, of strikes by labor against industry, giving at various times the demands made by the strikers, and the settlements made by the struck organizations (or by organizations threatened by a strike to avert a strike).

It is pertinent to the considerations governing the organization of the Council to analyze the meaning of strikes. Strikes are in fact an attempt by the workers to force business organizations to recognize the principle of profit sharing. In the hands of labor leaders the presentation and securing of this result, by the agency of strikes or of threatened strikes, increases the power of the labor leaders and of their unions as a force in the economy, simply because *industry evades the problem and labor does not.*

If industry met the problem by recognizing the basic fact that the people comprising a working organization do in fact have a normal right to share in the product of their combined labor in the organization, the motive for strikes would disappear. When a strike is called for the purpose of securing an additional share of the profits of the organization for the individual workers in the organization, to grant the labor demands made through their union is in effect to admit the contention, but illogically to permit the union organization to anticipate the future profits indicated by the past history of profit making, which in the independent opinion of the labor union justifies the demand for an increased participation.

If the industry affected met this question positively and not negatively, and of its own volition made a continuous and equitable distribution of the distributable profits realized from the operation, two results would follow. First, the reason for the initiation of strike procedures would not be present and the strike would not be called; and second, the sound social and moral obligation discharged in the practice of profit sharing would guarantee each worker his due proportion of the net results achieved by the common effort of all individuals in the organization. Further, the distribution would itself be equitable to all concerned. While a demand by a union for profit participation in the form of increased wages penalizes only the company in the future event the profits fail to materialize in the operation, the actual periodic distribution of actual profits automatically balances itself to any level, even of no profit. It is not legitimate to argue that in this case the entrepreneur or the individuals who supply the capital for the operation are taking the only chance on losses. The suppliers of capital initiated the business because of the prospect that it would produce profit, and all the individuals in the business have a stake; and whether or not the profits are improperly anticipated by strike demand, or actually distributed under profit sharing methods, any company must make a consistent profit or else cease to exist.

In today's world there is a conflict between the concept of a profit economy and of communism. The theory, if not the practice, of communism is defense of the innate rights of the common man. Because this is also the theoretical motive of organized labor unions, it follows that, whether or not they are conscious allies, communism and unionism have the same stated objective. We are aware that communism does not consistently practice, or even ever practice, the principles of its philosophy; but it is the philosophy, and not the later acts of communistic governments, which is making it possible for communism to advance and to capture new ground. It is the philosophy with which they convert and subvert new areas. The experience with nonfulfillment of its promises follows the taking over by communists of government procedures, when it is too late for the subverted people to reverse their course. Study of the literature emanating from countries now being subverted will make it clear that it is the claimed advantages of communism, based on promises to advance the interests of the common man, which makes the fact of subversion possible.

The making of a profit for rendering a service (as the reason for organizing and conducting any business or service) is the only motive, basically, that business has ever had for organization during all of human history. If the record of businesses so conducted had also throughout history been a record of recognition of the rights of those who do the work, then Marx and Engels and Lenin would have had nothing to write about.

The record of business, however, is an ages-long record of exploitation of the rank and file of labor by the entrepreneurs of businesses, and more recently the development of a procedure by which the representatives of that same labor have become increasingly unreasonable with the increase in their power. Now the tendency is toward oppression of the entrepreneurs by labor. Neither of these developments was inevitable, and neither was in accord with fact.

If, now, American businesses, making a common and accepted working philosophy of the principles for which the Council is supposed to stand, were with profit sharing to take the bold and final step of making the practices of business consonant in all respects with the rights of the human bodies involved, and this move were to be made in general by the majority of American businesses, and not by only a few, thereupon America could become the exponent and the most powerful advocate imaginable in the world (as it is at present divided) of a working philosophy based on ideals which are entirely practical and at the same time expressive of the highest ideals of all the teachings of the human race throughout its history. The principles for which communism stands would be permanently on the defensive, with no chance whatever of resuming or maintaining the advantage. All the workers in the world, outside the orbit of communist power, would instinctively recognize the obvious fact that this is not merely an answer to the communist ideology, but an active and positive expression of a better and truer philosophy — a philosophy in no way, and at no point, out of joint with the basic fundamentals of business procedures. For it must be recognized that business procedures based on economic fact, such as the profit motive and its corollary, competition, are necessary to effect the exchanges of goods and services upon which the existence itself of large and stable populations depend, and that neither Statism nor Communism are logical answers to the problems inherent in such exchanges.

For these reasons, among many others, the whole emphasis of the Council of Profit Sharing Industries in its pronouncements and other public explanations should be placed where it belongs: on the philosophy involved. It does not damage this philosophy, but enhances it, that the results of the use of the philosophy increase the efficiency and the earning capacity of the company using it, at the same time that it dignifies and frees the individuals it affects. This ennoblement and freedom involves all the separate components of the business form: the entrepreneur, the executive staff, the workers, the products and services, and the public served by their joint effort. In its consistent form profit sharing has sound and useful merits and no demerits. Failures of the form are failures to apply its complete philosophy. It cannot be used simply for the purpose of increasing profits, for then the elements which would do more than increase the profits have been left out. It can only be used as the enlightened application of a practical and rational concept embodying the highest elements of idealism and humanitarianism. It is both good, and good business, but its *reasons* precede the good business, for it is the *reasons* for the installation of profit sharing as an element of any business which must precede any anticipation of economic benefit. If its conditions are satisfied, the economic benefit is inevitable, but the economic benefit is a result of the procedure and not the first reason for initiating it.

Profit sharing is exactly what the term implies: a sharing among all the members of the organization of the distributable profits of operation. It is not wages and it is not an incentive payment. Profit sharing applies to all individuals of the group, on a group basis, as a division of group profit. It is usually necessary to develop a formula based on net pay rates and length of service to determine the relative amounts of individual shares, but the individual shares are not related either to individual efficiency or to group efficiency. Profit shares are based on the simple fact of membership in the organization. Incentive pay, however generous, is not profit sharing. Incentive pay is used to better profit and to lower price for quality, which it usually does, but it does not ordinarily lead to, or include, sharing of the group profit on operations. When it does, it is no longer "incentive pay" but "profit sharing." The philosophy can take almost as many separate forms as there are separate businesses; but the philosophy itself must be the ruling principle in determining the form or in assaying it.

To formulate an explanation of profit sharing as a principle we should begin consideration of the concept at a point very much further back than the point at which it is applied to the operations of a company. Rather than the specific application we should consider the underlying philosophical and human fundamentals of the concept.

All the mores and ideals of a human society are the sum of the beliefs of the individual members of the society. The existing social beliefs influence and formulate the beliefs of the individual as he develops into an adult, but the total of belief is not static. The individual makes contributions from his own thinking, and exceptional individuals make sizable contributions and even cause basic alterations in the thinking of the society. In general these additions move the social concepts to a progressively higher plane; but it is always true in the end that the ideals of the society reflect the ideals of a substantial majority of the members of the society, whether the level of the social ideal is high or low. Laws, for example, are generally observed only if it is the opinion of a very great majority of the society that they should be observed.

But laws are a system of prohibitions, negative in character. On the positive side, in the realm of ideals, there likewise must be substantial agreement of the majority in the rightness of the ideals. In our society a system of ideals related to the teaching of the humanist philosophers over the period of recorded history has received a degree of acceptance not previously known in so large a group; and our society has accepted also the fact that the basic principles so far accepted have proved in practice not to be impractical, as they have been represented to be, but entirely practical and productive of much good to individuals and community alike.

The basis for the philosophy is humanism: the search for the best forms of relationship of man to man in the complex which is a culture or a civilization. The segment of these relationships which has application as profit sharing relates only to business procedures; but the basic motivations of all segments of the philosophy can be assumed to be identical.

Profit sharing is not for the purpose of combating unionism, or merely of increasing employee productivity, or of reducing labor turnover.

The primary purpose of profit sharing is to give effect to the humanitarian ideal that the joint effort of employer and employee, together, to produce products or services at a profit, should logically be followed by some sort of sharing by employer and employee, together, of the proceeds of the effort. The beneficial effects of low labor turnover, higher product quality, increased productivity, good employee and public relations, and of tranquility, cooperation, and efficiency within the organization, are side effects. The side effects are inevitable, but they in turn are merely confirmation of the opinion of all the teachers of the human race that the highest standard in ethics is also the most practical course of procedure possible for an individual or a business. It has been said over and over again, and proved to the hilt, that any other type of behavior defeats itself.

The primary purpose of membership in the Council of Profit Sharing Industries is not to increase the individual profits of the participating companies. The primary purpose is to extend the benefits experienced by the people operating in companies under profit sharing to yet other companies, simply and only to enhance the dignity and human value of the people working under such procedures. This being true, it is an effort which should be supported adequately, or not at all.

We are a nation of people who, almost as greatly as do our cousins, the British, dislike exposing ourselves to the danger that our sentiment will show up as sentimentality to our fellows; so we consistently pretend that we are not sentimental. Nevertheless, if we are to consider the idea of profit sharing, we are going to have to face up to the fact that actually we are dealing with love of our fellow men under circumstances which merely permit us to pretend that we are being very practical and not sentimental at all. We will be following the precepts of Jesus of Nazareth, and of Hillel before him, who reduced all the principles of human intercourse to two basic laws: love of God and love of fellow men. Hillel added, "All else but this is commentary." Jesus said, "On these hang all the Law and the Prophets."

We cannot produce any consistent reason why we should be afraid to admit the fact. We are all pragmatists, concerning ourselves with the

practical or matter-of-fact-application of principles and concepts, and ou
distrust of sentimentality is quite sound; but Jesus and all other grea
teachers of the human race have insisted that love, as the principle o
outgoing and outgiving desire to do what is right and good, is the mos
practical type of behavior possible — in fact, have insisted that any othe
type of behavior is altogether impractical, leading inevitably and always
to all the social ills we observe and deplore in civilized complexes. Any
amount of consideration of this matter will always bring us to the same
conclusion. Justice, fair play, cooperation, consideration of the rights of
others, and all other "noble" human characteristics, are the fruits of
motivations having their source in the sort of love of which Jesus spoke;
and all their opposites are the fruit of varying types of selfishness, or hate,
or fear.

Very few businesses start on a large scale. Most businesses begin as
an idea held by one man, which grows and expands if its goods or
services warrant confidence in the users of the goods or services. As it
expands it requires more "hands," who are actually extensions of the
physical and mental capacity of the first man, the entrepreneur.

Let us say the business, as an extreme example, starts with a capital
of a hundred dollars and grows into a business worth a hundred million.
Obviously, all the increments of value were built collectively by the group
of the entrepreneur and his "hands," whatever the relative value of the
individual services. The incresed sales and profits, the increases in
capital and reserves, the increase in physical plant, the value of goodwill,
were all brought into being by the collective group. In the old-style type of
business, however, it is the custom that the "owner" alone receives the
increment. He holds the "shares" which represent the total value of
increment, and the profits accruing year by year are paid to him as
dividends on these "shares" of stock. The workers, his "hands," receive
their "wages" as current payment for their "labor," and in settlement of
any possible claim they might have to the increment resulting from the
collective effort.

Obviously, this does not represent an equitable arrangement,
however honored in time and usage. As a result, the "union" has an
argument, and gives it effect by demanding more "wages" as settlement
for the postulated claims on increment of value in the business. In
addition, since the "union" is human and as unreasonable as the
"capital" against which it makes the claim, its claims have only the

oosest relation to any facts concerning the existence or nonexistence of any increment from which to pay the claim.

Profit sharing is a practical and simple way of bringing about the simple, logical and just notion that all members of the group called a company are to be participants in the fruits of their joint effort. This can take almost any form: an actual percentage division of that portion of the company's net earnings which are available for distribution, or any other method by which it is effectively brought about that in addition to their "wages" the workers of all classes shall receive a payment which is not wages but a distribution of increment. It cannot, however, take the form of incentive pay and nothing else. Clearly, the final effort is not to bring about divisions of wages alone by a system of "norms" used as they are used in Russia, but effectively to bring about the division of increment. Ineffective workers do not belong in the group, but there is no implied intent to create a class of "Stakhalanites" among the workers permitted to remain in the group. Norm-exceeders do not represent normality, and profit sharing refers to normal people.

The "typical employee" is as much a fiction as the "average man," but he represents a composite picture. This typical employee leaves his schooling and starts work for a company, works until retirement age, and then retires. Without any provision made by the employer for the employee's years of retirement, only the rare individual will himself have made any such provision. Social security provisoins made by the government, from contributions made by the employee and his employers, are a partial attempt to correct this combination of social injustice and individual lack of foresight.

But the facts are really quite simple. The employee has given the cream of his productive life to the service of the employer. The employer has bought the whole man, and should pay for him, since the man is human and not a machine, and moral issues are involved. Profit sharing is a reasoned attempt to meet this obligation. If it is cash profit sharing, it is assumed the individual will make his own old-age provision from the money received above his rate of pay. If it is deferred profit sharing, the employer makes the provision for the employee by putting the employee's retirement funds into a trust. In both cases profit sharing is discharge of a duty to share the proceeds of effort among those who have made the effort, and it is only incidentally generous. The generosity is an effect of comparison with those companies who do not discharge the obligation. It is "right" merely because the common rules concerning employment are "wrong."

All deviations from the rigidly simple picture of one employee and one employer effect the detail of operation of this discharge of duty, but not the principles involved. If the employee has many employers during the term of his working life, and each has made a contribution proportionately to the requirements of the term, the total result is the same: the employee is the beneficiary of provisions for his years of retirement. There is no requirement for the employer to do anything not consonant with proper business procedure, nor any requirement to contribute more than is justified by the rate of earnings made by the company. Merely the measure of success of the specific company is a measure of the extent of the provision. The employees of a company as a group are provided for in terms of the success of the group.

Actually there do not exist two such entities as "capital" and "labor." Nothing exists but men and women who work in a company or organization, as a group, to achieve a common end. Whether the individuals concerned so see it or not, the "owners" of a business are trustees for a group of human beings.

For very many logical and necessary business reasons, and legal reasons, and social reasons, the business itself must be an entity, a "fictitious person" empowered to carry on business transactions as if it were a human individual. For the same reasons, there must be centralized controls, and there must be a line of command and responsibility. For human and logical reasons, there must be a preferential standing for the individuals or groups who make the whole effort possible as the "entrepreneur." Shareholders must elect directors, and directors must elect officers, and the officers must delegate power to assistants and subordinates and conduct the business. There are logical standards for the preferential "wages" and dividends given these varieties of individuals. But all this is supplemental to the basic consideration that everyone, these groups and the workers alike, creates the business and makes it grow and yield a profit by their collective effort; and that the "workers" are not rightfully excluded from participation in the fruits of the joint effort.

The relationship of employer and employed has existed in human society for as long as there has been a system of exchange of the products of labor; and this system extends back to the most primitive human ocieties, prior to the range of recorded history. Modern business differs ot in principle but in complexity. The complexity is the result of the ndustrial revolution: the substitution of machines for human muscle.

Until recent times the employer-employee relation was usually that of master and slave or bond-servant. Businesses were either small handicrafts, or the merchandising of goods assembled by the merchant from the handicrafters and sold at a profit. Only the individual views of the master determined his treatment of his slaves or bond-servants. Some fairly large enterprises were organized under this system. Guilds developed, mostly during the past thousand years, as organizations of craftsmen; but it was not until the application of power to machines that the workers at the lowest level began to build up the old craft guilds into what we now have as labor unions.

In the broadest sense, the ancient relationship of owner and slaves has been accepted as the model of the relationship of employer and employed throughout history, with the modern difference that wages have taken the place of bonds. New ideas always grow by grafting onto old ideas. The quite modern concept of copartnership between capital and labor is only at the beginning of being accepted as valid. At the present moment, unions represent labor on the basis that there is a complete separation of interests between the owners of the business and the workers in a business; and the doctrines of communism are based on the same fallacy, seeking to establish "the dictatorship of the proletariat" as a substitute for "capitalism." To a substantial degree, this point of view is shortsightedly encouraged by the owners of business enterprise, who "bargain" with unions on the basis of the existence of two opposing interests which have to be reconciled, rather than integrated.

Labor-management conflict in the modern age is an outgrowth of the mechanization of industry, and of mass production, which permitted the development of larger one-purpose enterprises, replacing manufacture of special wares by single artisans and apprentices on a smaller scale. In essence the present conflict is a quarrel over the division of profits. The ancient idea that the entrepreneur owns all the tools of the enterprise, including the human tools (as, in fact, as slaves, he did so own them until recent times), has in larger enterprises led to the organization of workers into unions capable of the power of negotiation with the employers. This is because the ancient idea has become more clearly seen as in opposition to the newer concept (itself an outgrowth over many centuries of what is termed the Christian ideal) of the innate rights of human beings as individual entities. While it is true that men have always been divided into the two classes of rulers and ruled, and that even at the present time most of the human race is so divided, yet the prevailing belief in our time is that this division is out of line with the concept of individual integration, and has never been legitimate, except as an element of organization discipline.

The entrepreneur actually has legitimate ownership (as opposed to legal ownership) only of the idea or ideas on which the enterprise is established, and of the starting capital on hand or accumulated while he conducts the business as a lone individual. (The corporate form, of capital subscribed for shares of ownership in a joint enterprise, modifies but does not basically change this elemental fact.) All additions to capital, or net worth, are accumulated from profits: the proceeds as gain from work done by the enterprise. Therefore, if the original entrepreneur has been joined in the activity by other individuals as workers he employs, the additions to capital (tools, real estate, equipment, and reserves) have in principle been accumulated as a result of a joint effort of entrepreneur and workers as a group. This does not refer to wages, but only to profit. Wages are currently drawn by all members of the organization, in one form or another, and are for subsistence; and they constitute part of the cost of the goods or services sold by the organization.

Admittedly there is no formula for determining in an individual enterprise the record form, or legal form, of certificates of ownership in these accumulations of capital, other than the present form of interest vested in the ownership of the shares of stock or equity in the whole enterprise, which are held by the entrepreneur (as in fact a trustee for a group). Admittedly there is no reliable formula for computing the actual amounts of accumulation due to joint effort; to additions to capital from savings invested additionally by the entrepreneur or the members of a joint stock enterprise; or to additional ideas of the entrepreneur, or additional ventures initiated by the entrepreneur into the developing business. But a formula is not required. The principle of joint interest exists, and this is the reason for the concept of profit sharing. Profit sharing is a reasoned, equitable, deliberate attempt to determine a proportion of total profit, which, when distributed among the members of the group who produced the profits and the accumulations, will in some just measure make a return to the individuals concerned for their ontributions to the joint effort.

The formula for profit sharing is also not fixed. The proper formula or one business is not necessarily, or even usually, the proper formula for another business. In general, however, only those profits are distributable which remain after the business, at the discretion of the management, has set aside the correct sums for reserves, depreciation, taxes, and new plant and equipment. These are in all cases determined by the management as a part of its function. The initial determination cannot be entrusted to the whole group in business any more than it can be in any organized procedure.

The principle, nevertheless, remains always in effect, whether or not it is observed in any one specific business activity. The principle is that profits which are distributable are to be allocated both to capital and to labor, in recognition that both were instrumental in accumulating the profits. In fact, if there is no profit sharing at all in a given business, to that extent the business is being conducted on ancient presuppositions which have no basis in the facts of the modern world. The logical conclusions from the indisputable reality are that an enterprise of multiple membership is a voluntary association of a number of individual human beings; and that ownership, both of tools and of the earnings of the enterprise, is shared by all the individuals involved, without regard to the formula by which these shares of relative ownership are calculated. Any distribution, any formula, any move towards fringe benefits or profit sharing, or even any strike settlement, is a tacit admission of the truth of the principles involved. The scale or measuring stick is merely the problem for determination by each enterprise, for its own reasons.

In all this, it is recognized that there is no final answer to the fact that the entrepreneur takes a risk of loss as well as a risk of profits. There does not, however, need to be such an answer. On consideration it may be seen that while the object of a business is to render a service for a profit, if there is a loss there is no division of profits, and if the losses continue and the plant "fails in business" all the individuals in the enterprise had a stake in plant and equipment and all alike have lost that stake.

This fact of a stake may also have substantial reality. It is entirely possible, as part of a profit sharing plan, especially of the deferred type, to arrange that the employees as a group have the opportunity to invest a proportion of trust funds in the shares which represent legal ownership of the enterprise. It is also well known that individual employees are read to invest in the securities of the company for which they work.

Profit Sharing — The Categorical Imperatives

Confucius, Lao-tse, Gautama, Socrates and Plato, Zeno, Epictetus Jesus, and a host of philosophers and humanists have, for the pas twenty-five centuries, tried endlessly and vainly to introduce the concep of love into the thinking of the human race. Doubtless earlier history is filled with many others for whom the records are lost who tried with equal earnestness, and equally vainly, to convince humanity that the concept of human brotherhood was not merely a trick in the use of words. We know at least of the prophets of the Old Testament.

Humanity in the mass, however, has persisted in a basic belief that this is a universe of tooth and claw, in which fate is merciless, and love among men is foolishness, mercy and forbearance are evidence of weakness, justice is uncommon, and for each man self-interest is the rule and anything else is dangerous. In great part this is a natural result of the fact that humanity had to rise from savagery to develop cultures, bringing with them the primitive rule that life depended on self-interest and self-preservation to the exclusion of everything else, and intensifying these elements with inventions for better defense and better offense in the struggle to secure individual or collective advantage. But nature, which is in fact inexorable, is merely amoral. It is not immoral.

Jesus, who expressed the ideas better than anyone else, said that there was a God who was Love, that men had in them a touch of the divine, and that the rule of Love was basic to all human endeavor. He said also that when Love was the rule of life all inequities and injustices among men disappeared, and that all manner of good came to be — the knowledge that set men free, amity and peace, and attainment. He said the God of Love, who bore to men his children a relationship akin to that of human father and child, gave as a father all that was desired to those who in loving prepared themselves to receive it, or even, because God was Love, to those who did not so prepare themselves, just as rain fell on the just and the unjust. He said that men were "neighbors," and told the story of the good Samaritan. He said that the greatest were those who served most, and that strength was justice and forbearance, while selfishness was fear and weakness and abuse of power.

These propositions analyze into evident and demonstrable truth, but they have never been used at the national level or at the collective level. They have only been seen at the individual level, and our history is filled with great and good people who have given love to mankind in living. Perhaps our difficulty is that the principles have been made to seem specifically "Christian," and many people do not so term themselves. But the principles are not specifically Christian principles. They are basic to the business of living. They are universal fundamentals, beginning at the individual level but tending to extend themselves to every level of human organization. Jesus himself included all humanity in his pronouncements.

For some reason — perhaps the quite admirable characteristic of diffidence based on a sense of final values — men and mankind do not choose to aver that their motives are altruistic. They do not like to be called "good." This is all right. Jesus also disavowed the title of "good." But Jesus also made clear that the principles are "divine" or universal in character, and that the principles are greater than men or than manking. When we obey law — even though statutory law is merely a negative limit on acts and not a rule of living — we accept that we are not specifically good. We have merely evidenced a willingness to do what is right. So it is with the affirmative, positive statements by Jesus of the categorical imperatives of human conduct and human association.

In our times the principles stated by Jesus have begun to receive collective recognition and respect from men as groups. The concept of profit sharing is such a recognition. Perhaps, instead of stating that this concept has merely economic and social justification, we should begin at least to consider the possibility that the concept is not economic, and also not mawkish or sentimental, but a general willingness to recognize and observe the very highest category of Law: universal and fundamental Law — and Law which is affirmative and not merely negative.

If we at least admit this possibility we can perhaps permit ourselves to admit also that the principle of profit sharing does not need to be explained or apologized for, and that while it does have economic justification, at the same time it has much more. It is basically right, and because it is of itself a categorical imperative in terms of a Law of supreme sanction, it is as a modus operandi inevitably and completely successful. When it is not successful in fact in any specific instance, always it will be found that the principle was sacrificed for expediency, or was left out of the practical form used and then called profit sharing.

Part V
AN AMATEUR ASTRONOMER
SHARES HIS THOUGHTS

Speculations On How Life Began

Following are two letters written by C.F. Rehnborg to his son, Dr. Sam Rehnborg, sparked by his reading of the book, "Origin of Life" by A.I. Oparin. His lifelong interest in astronomy led to his acquiring a number of telescopes, starting with small models and culminating in a large (5-inch) Questar with a finder-scope, ensconced in its own small telescope house at the Rehnborgs' vacation home at Idyllwild in the San Jacinto Mountains. The Rehnborgs also donated a number of fine telescopes to the Astronomy Departments of some local high schools and colleges. Mr. Rehnborg took great pleasure in a weekend of 'viewing' at Idyllwild and was prone to stay up until the wee hours watching the stars, warmly dressed and usually wrapped in a blanket against the night chill of the telescope house, which was not heated. Nevertheless, his wonder and delight in watching his favorite constellations is very evident in the excerpts from his Astronomical Journal which are included in this section.

June 28, 1962

Dear Sam:

When you read "Origin of Life" by A.I. Oparin, as I hope you will be able to do soon, you will notice that he has picked up as an origin for the earth itself the cosmology of Jeans, according to which the near approach of another star to our sun drew out a long tidal filament which condensed into the planets. This thesis has been discarded in the years between 1935 and now, for one which is a revival of the much more ancient idea of Laplace — the nebular hypothesis — according to which our sun and planets condensed from an extended cloud of gas and dust.

By this revived hypothesis, the formation of a family of planets around a sun is almost an inevitable occurrence, and modern astronomers feel that all the stars which a spectrography shows to be single rather than double, and which have a long period of rotation instead of a short period, and are of spectral type F or G, are suns with families of planets. The slow rotation (for example, the period of rotation of the sun is approximately 28 days) is explained by the fact that the larger part of the moment of momentum of the total system is concentrated in the planets rather than in the main body of the sun.

According to this hypothesis the universe is homogenous, and the factors of mass, age, and temperature are the only ones which differentiate one sun from another. In turn, the only difference between the atmosphere of one planet and another is due to the mass and therefore the gravitational attraction of the individual planets. A planet of the size of the earth or of Venus can hold the gases which are in our atmosphere; a planet which is smaller cannot hold as large a number of gases or as much of any of them — and planets which are very much more massive, such as Jupiter, will have kept virtually all of the hydrogen and helium which were in the original gas cloud from which the planetary system evolved.

This change in theory does not vitiate but only extends the thesis which is the subject of Oparin's book, because by it all planetary bodies will have original atmospheres composed mainly of the reducing gases ammonia and methane, and water vapor, without any free oxygen or nitrogen. And the oxidizing reactions which are the basis of life will be based on the OH radicals of water, as he says they are on the earth.

By this hypothesis, the evolution of life will be the extensive formation of organic molecules from the reducing gases and the carbides of the rocky surface of the molten earth, and all life wherever it appears will follow a common pattern. It has already been demonstrated in the laboratory, that a mixture of $NH3\ HOH\ CH4$, for example, will spontaneously give rise to such substances as amino acids. This indicates that it is a fundamental reaction which will occur wherever the corresponding elements occur, so that life will originate wherever it can originate by the same processes in which it originated on earth.

We know that it did originate on the earth, and the thesis of this book is that it originated according to natural law and not as an accident. Therefore the extension of the possibility of planetary families to suns other than our own (and modern thought is that perhaps fifty percent of all the stars in classes F and G are accompanied by planets), means that life is a common occurrence, that it probably occurs throughout the universe, and that it is probably of a similar nature wherever it occurs.

Oparin's book, written in the '30s, is therefore of more importance now than when it was written, and his explanation of the primary or fundamental reactions of the life process is wonderful and inspiring, as it is laid out in the simplification of the life reactions which begins on page 110. I found the book tremendous from beginning to end, and singularly free of any suggestion that it left few unsolved problems, or that other suggestions concerning life origins were valueless. What it did instead was to synthesize all present knowledge and indicate the enormous range of unanswered problems, but it did dispose of the notion that we have to look for a supernatural explanation for the origin of life. If life is a supernatural event, so also is the whole of the universe. Perhaps this, after all, is the statement which resolves the conflict between religion and science, providing the religions can be persuaded to lay aside their dogma in favor of the theory of an origin for life wherever conditions are suitable for it to occur.

With love, C.F.R.

* * * * * * * * * * * *

July 6, 1962
(Dictated from Tahiti)

Dear Sam,

After a morning spent in dictation concerning the complicated details of affairs at Buena Park and here, following are some notes on your notes to me in reply to my June 28th letter.

For example, you say, "Another complementary factor is that in higher organisms the DNA is somehow condensed in chromosomes (the only time DNA is found in a free form is in bacteria, and bacteria have no chromosomes)." The virus, which is even simpler than the bacteria, is merely DNA in a small protein envelope waiting to enter a more complex living form, bacterium or higher, in order to replicate, and the virus has been called "a gene in search of a chromosome."

Either life is a miracle occurring on the surface of one satellite of one sun, or satellites are as common as suns and life is a thing which can arise on any of them if the conditions are right. The right conditions are inherent in the formation of the sun and its satellites from the gas and dust of a cosmic cloud. When the satellite is of a certain critical size to a close approximation, (and our earth is a type example of this size) it will have an atmosphere, and the atmosphere will contain water, ammonia, and methane, and — just possibly — some CO_2.

Recently the experiment was performed of putting these gases together in a closed container under sterile conditions, and the mixture was then warmed and intermittently subjected to an electrical discharge from a spark plug. After a period the contents were analyzed by vapor chromotography, and a collection of amino acids was found and identified, so that we have here a demonstration that the formation of organic substances is inherent in the atoms of carbon, hydrogen, nitrogen, and the OH radical from water. These form the organic substances which are the basis of life, under a set of suitable circumstances which probably are the most common circumstances in the universe, without the intercession of anything exterior to the system. It may even be that the CO_2 of the experiment can be eliminated, because it is more and more probable that CO_2 is a product of the life process and all oxidations occur through the agency of the OH radical of water.

It is possible and even probable that the presence of CO_2 in the atmosphere of a planet is an indication of life on the planet, and we know that the atmospheres of Venus, Earth, and Mars contain carbon dioxide — and probably water vapor. In the case of the sun, the statement can be made with a fair degree of accuracy that three of its planets carry, or have carried, or are in process of carrying, life forms similar in their essentials to the life forms on earth.

At the same time it has become more and more reasonable to consider, as I said earlier, that when a star has a slow rate of revolution on its axis, it is because its moment of momentum is largely distributed among a family of planets. Rather more than half the stars of the same general type as the sun have such a slow rate of rotation, and presumably, families of planets.

Suddenly we have a picture of a universe which is more consistent and logical than it has ever been supposed to be before. When the Chamberlain and Jeans hypothesis of the close approach of another star was assumed to be the reason for the existence of the sun's family of planets, life was a phenomenon so accidental and so rarely possible that we might have been the only examples of its occurrence in the universe. Statistically, if no other way, this would have been a very strange picture to have to believe. But when, on the basis of recent reasoning and experimentation, we can state that a high proportion of the stars in our galaxy, and presumably in other galaxies, have slow rates of rotation and presumably families of planets, we have a new and more comprehensible picture of a universe in which life is quite a usual thing nd not a rare accident, and we can stop depending on mythology to supply the missing link of a spark of life. Sparks there probably were on any planet having an atmosphere, through the agency of the electrical discharges of thunderstorms, and the nature of the collections formed from a cosmic cloud within certain ranges of size. The homogeneity of the materials of the universe is admissible as well as demonstrable by spectroscopy, and by the observed character of the atmospheres of the existing planets of the sun.

Now we get back to Oparin. Before he knew that the crucial experiment of the creation of organic molecules from gases was a possibility, or even a certainty, he had assumed that this occurred in the primitive atmosphere of the earth. Because any living thing has such a tremendous complexity, he assumed that simple organic compounds were formed, and that during the billions of years of available time these compounds in the "hot thin soup" of the primitive seas began to show more and more organization. The organization is just as inherent in these primitive molecules as the molecules were inherent in the primitive compounds from which they were formed in the primitive sea.

At first the greater organization merely meant the capacity to add numbers to a structure, and at some critical point, the separation of one droplet into more than one droplet because of the limitations of size and surface structure. No one has yet bridged the gap to suggest a method for the progression from organization to replication, but like all other great advances of modern science, this becomes something which we can reasonably suppose will be found if the search is initiated. Obviously it has occurred.

It has occurred on the earth under conditions probably general throughout the universe, and presumably it has occurred everywhere else that it could occur. Beginning with the astronomical researches of Herschel and his followers, and the growth of chemical and physical science, it has become more and more evident that we exist on the satellite of a sun which is a member of a galaxy, that there are innumerable other galaxies, that the conditions under which suns come into being are of the same sort everywhere in this universe, that the ordinary constitution of the dust clouds from which suns may condense are such that the raw materials for organic development will be present, that suns will have satellites, and that these satellites within certain ranges of size will be the homes of life.

The other point you made was in asking me the source of the energy which would be expended in the unwinding of a replicating helix. You can answer this question better than I when you have added the one thing you left out.

The organizing molecules for the present complexity of life are the living catalysts, the enzymes which sometimes speed up the rate of reactions between organic molecules by a factor of a million or more. And it gets steadily more evident that the organizing action and the enzymatic structures are matters of the operation of templates, which combine and release the atoms by means of electrical potentials. You will have to supply the explanation of the agency by which calories of energy borrowed from the sun become electrical potentials and electrical fields. I do not have the answer, but certainly over recent years it has become increasingly evident that enzymes are templates which assemble and release organic molecules, and initiate and speed reactions between these organic molecules.

No one has yet written the paper for which I tried to be the electrical spark to your latent possibilities and knowledge. But someone will write it before very long. When it is written it will leave us with a picture of a universe of which our earth is a representative sample, and the conviction and perhaps the possibility of proof that everything we know on the earth is common to the universe — and that the universe is infinite in space and endless in time, a truly living thing.

Affectionately, C.F.R.

Is There Life On Other Planets?
Written Approximately 1963

A recurring question is whether there are other planets of other suns which hold living beings, and especially sentient living beings analogous to man if not exactly like him. Recently the tendency of opinion among astronomers has been to hold that life arises wherever conditions for its survival are favorable, and that the history of the sun and its planets may be representative of many similar histories of many other stars, and not exceptional.

This change of opinion — and it is very much a change — has been due to changes in general opinion of the manner in which the sun came to acquire its family of planets. First of all, it was the vehement opposition of the various religions to any change in their 'revealed' knowledge of man's origins and nature which stood in the way of all attempts to get man out of his stationary square earth at the center of the universe. This opposition arose from the fact, apparent to anyone, that only on such a flat earth which constituted the whole of the universe could the Biblical story of the creation be true. If the stars were other suns, or otherwise stated, if our sun were only another star among those in the heavens, then either the existence of life must be due to a special creation on this one planet, or the biblical story became subject to doubt.

Copernicus did not dare publish his thesis that the earth and the other heavenly bodies revolved around the sun, rather than the sun about the earth. Bruno was burned at the stake chiefly for having made the heretical statement that there were other worlds and other life in the universe. Galileo was forced to recant his statement that the earth revolved around the sun; and his priestly inquisitors and judges would not even look through his telescope at Jupiter and its moons, and kept Galileo virtually a prisoner for the remainder of his life.

But Galileo's telescope and its successors, culminating in the 200-inch telescope on Mount Palomar, and the observations and discoveries of generations of astronomers, scooped out the foundations of the position taken by the church. Nowadays even the church sponsors astronomical observation, and long since has rationalized the conflicts between its dogmas and the flood of discovery. But at first the opposition of the church caused astronomical theory to be very timid so far as the origin of life was concerned.

Laplace produced his famous nebular hypothesis, which postulated the condensation of a gas cloud into rings, which in turn condensed into the planets, and a central residue which became the sun. This theory finally lost ground because it was held that the rotation of the mass of gas which would produce the planets would not result in the formation of a central sun, or in any case would not result in the numerical values for angular momentum which are actually observed in the case of the sun and its planets.

Later, the theory of a close passage of a star to our sun took the place of the nebular hypothesis. It was called the tidal hypothesis, and it was supposed to have created colossal tides which drew out a long plume of matter from the substance of the sun, which condensed into droplets which became the planets. The greatest attraction of this hypothesis was that statistically it would be an exceedingly rare occurrence — so rare that it might indeed have happened only once in the time during which the cosmos had existed. This rareness, in turn, enabled the church to adopt astronomy by making its inescapable facts possible to regard as consonant with dogma.

But increased knowledge of the physical universe and increased refinement of theoretical physics have brought the nebular hypothesis back to favor in a new form. It can account for the tidal formation from a primeval gas of the galaxies of stars, and in each star or star system it can account, by the principles of turbulence, for the formation of single and multiple stars and families of planets. Among the stars we can observe at relatively close range in our own galaxy, perhaps one in three is a double or multiple system. This is confirmation of calculation that stars have limits of possible size, and the existence of any double stars, much more the existence of many, goes a long way toward demonstrating modern theory that the possession of a family of planets is probably more normal for a star than for it to be isolated as a single body.

This does not appear specifically in the literature, but (a) it is now thought that relatively huge masses of gas undergo condensation into stars at one time; (b) that condensations which are to become stars can be observed in many bright gaseous nebulae, and by extension can be assumed to be present in nebulae which are dark because not yet illuminated by condensations which have begun the nuclear conversion of matter into radiant energy; (c) that the Great Nebula in Orion is such a nebula of glowing gas in which stars have recently been formed and are now continuing to be formed; and (d) that the group Praesepe (and perhaps the Pleiades) has recently become such a group of new stars, while there are many groups of stars having a common motion in the star fields near us in the galaxy. Stars, when double, are rarely of equal mass. They are usually widely different in size.

Next, there are several stars which show irregularities of proper motion without having visible companions, a fact which can be explained by assuming that these companions are below the limit of mass which could initiate the nuclear process and radiate. Finally, it is possible and even compellingly rational to suppose that the graduations in size of the components of a multiple system from the minimum mass of a luminous body range down through planetary masses of every size to planitesimals, comets, and meteors. This much has to be assumed, until refinement of the measurement of stellar proper motion irregularities, especially for near and faint stars, has statistically indicated the presence of sub-luminous companions for a larger number of stars. We can only hope that the future will bring great improvements in observational procedures, and in telescopes themselves, which will make it possible to distinguish planets around stars other than our own sun. The distances to these other stars are so very great that planets shining by reflected light cannot be separately perceived, even if for optical reasons the glare of the primary stars did not hide them completely.

Since someone should make an assertion for logical if not for good scientific reasons, and I have no scientific reputation to be shaken by errors in reasoning or logic, I assert that perhaps every visible star has a family of planets, and that many of them (at least two out of eight around the sun) present environments favorable for the development of some form of life. Further, I am sure that there exist planet-size bodies without suns, but very few suns without planets.

Even in the case of Venus, an apparent exception which may not be the carrier of life, it is possible the existing conditions are related to conditions which once existed on the earth, except that its rate of diurnal rotation is too slow and therefore would make any development of life, at least on a land surface, endure variations of temperature between its long days and nights which would be far too great not to interfere with metabolism as we know it.

We start with the fact that the materials of the universe are substantially the same in all areas, as far as present knowledge goes. If, therefore, a star condenses from a cloud of gas and has a family of planets, these planets very likely will vary their characteristics with their size just as in the family of planets about the sun. If they are as small as the earth, we may postulate that their gravitational fields will retain the same array of gases in the planet's size range. A planet as large as Jupiter or Saturn or Uranus would retain hydrogen and other light gases, while planets as small as Mercury would have no atmosphere or water vapor at all. At the beginning, it is thought that all planets include in their primary constituents the same materials from the original cloud of dust and gas. Simply, what is retained varies from preponderantly hydrogen, as in the massive central sun, to none at all of the gases or the lightest elements in the case of Mercury or an asteroid.

In a planet the size and mass of the earth, it seems reasonable to me that the conditions are set for life — chiefly because of the presence of carbon as the gas carbon dioxide and as metal carbides, and of nitrogen and hydrogen as ammonium radicals, of oxygen and hydrogen as water or water vapor, and of carbon and hydrogen as methane. When these gases were assembled in a closed system and exposed to electrical discharges, they automatically formed organic compounds, with special reference to amino acids, the basic constituents of life. In every case of a planet so placed as to receive about the same amount of radiation from its central sun, and of approximately the same size as the earth, we may conjecture that life will arise as it did here on the earth.

It may not be the same form of life. There is even the possibility that life with characteristics we do not even imagine can arise on a massive planet such as Jupiter, with totally different physical conditions and very different characteristics from life as we know it on the earth. However, the general thesis remains unchanged: that wherever in the universe the conditions for life exist, life very probably has arisen or will arise; and that life may be as common in the universe as any other of its general characteristics and attributes.

Notes On Observations

It is the evening of September 9th, 1963, at 9:15 p.m., and I am at the moment looking at M-39 in Cygnus, NGC 7092, a cluster of some 30 inches diameter at 21 hours 30.4, 48 degrees 13, and a distance of 815 light years, containing some 25 stars which the catalog calls a large open cluster of bright stars best seen with low power.

Actually, this particular cluster is too large even for the Erfle eyepiece on the 12-inch telescope, but if I were to put on a lower-power eyepiece, much of the detail would disappear because there are background stars also.

* * * * * * * * * *

I am slowly forming a number of conclusions regarding what is convenient and feasible for the amateur observer.

For example, I find it most convenient to choose a relatively small sector of the sky and then to position the telescope and the finder telescope, and the guide scope, so that I can reach this small area without once changing my position on the rotating platform; in fact, sitting still and not rotating the platform at all but maybe changing the height to the eyepiece with the three-sided stool; letting the observable sky drift over and turning the pages of my observing guide to the objects which successively drift into the area of a best or most convenient observation.

But if I were designing a telescope, or even if I were buying another, I think there are a number of changes which could be made to benefit the amateur observer. In the first place, the viewing point should be through the axis so that the observer could sit in one position regardless of the section of sky he was observing.

Next, it should be extremely convenient to change eyepieces. These things are not true of telescopes as they are presently designed. They have evolved somewhat, but the inconveniences that the early observers were obliged to put up with are kept in the current designs, somewhat like the dashboard and whipsocket on the early automobiles. The time has come for the telescope to be designed in accordance with the best of present knowledge of the possibilities. There were no early amateurs of the present type. They were all dead-serious men working hard on a small area of the sky at a time.

The modern amateur is interested in the whole sky. He is following charts and catalogs made up by the army of early serious workers, but he is enjoying a spectacle rather than seriously contributing to the store of knowledge. This is no more wrong than it is to study subjects in textbooks compiled by the experts, to acquire knowledge of a particular subject. Astronomy is merely another branch of human knowledge for which there are textbooks, but the amateur should not need to duplicate the labor of the early discoverers to taste the results of their work, wherefore as I have just said, telescopes for the amateur observer should be designed for the amateur observer — and this is not being done at the present time.

* * * * * * * * *

These are notes on observations. This is the evening of September 12th, 1963. I am looking at a star in Scutum, NGC 6705, a cluster of some 200 stars at a distance of 5675 light years at 18 hours, 48.4 minutes, 06 degrees 20. The catalog classifies this as a grand galactic cluster, semi-globular or fan-shaped, in a star cloud visible to the unaided eye in a dark sky.

This is quite adequate so far as it goes, but it is really a most gorgeous spectacle and it would be impossible to exaggerate its beauty. There is, as the catalog notes, an 8th magnitude star at the center of the cluster, undoubtedly very much nearer to us than the cluster is, but it makes the whole thing look like a jewel set in a brooch. Besides some 200 faint stars that can be resolved at 200 power in the 12 inch telescope, there is the cloudy suggestion of many more stars just too faint to be resolved. It is even a beautiful cluster in the 3 inch telescope, but in that only the central 8th magnitude star can be resolved.

I had forgotten to say that I have the telescope now set up to use the 10-power scope for wide angle focusing on brilliant objects; and the 3-inch guide telescope with a 25 mm. plain eyepiece in it, orthoscopic, and without any need for cross wires, used as a high power finder scope, and this combination is working most satisfactorily.

* * * * * * * * *

In Aquila, NGC 6709, 18 hours 49, and 10 degrees 17, there is a very pretty cluster of forty stars at a distance of 2600 light years. It is not noted as remarkable in the catalog, but it is extremely attractive in the glass. Its stars are arranged in streams, and are nearly uniform in brightness. I should record this as one of my favorites.

C.F. Rehnborg's beloved telescope was housed in a small "telescope house" at Idyllwild, California, in the San Jacinto Mountains where the air was sharp and clear. He spent many happy hours there.

Twenty-six hundred years ago, when the light from this cluster started traveling toward us, was just about the time that the first five books of the Old Testament got their final brush-up into their present form in the Temple at Jerusalem. Some 650 years later Jesus was born. I find myself unable to visualize this distance in space, let alone the much greater distances that are involved in astronomy.

* * * * * * * * *

I am now looking at the cluster NGC 7062 at 21 hours 21.5, 46 degrees 10, at a distance of 7,800 light years or almost ten times as far as the other, with a diameter of 500 feet compared to thirty, and with 30 stars included in it, as against the other group of 25. Eight hundred light years, the distance of the first cluster, is not a nothing in terms of human existence, but 7,800 light years is probably as long a time as the whole of human civilized history, certainly somewhat longer than any known writings of history. It is far more intresting to regard this grouping and its distance with the awe it calls for and which we rarely give it, than to regard figures without considering their significance. It is a sort of introduction to the staggering distances of the optics in our one galaxy, and the yet more impressive figures for the other galaxies visible on photographic plates.

A cluster like this is the result of condensation of a gaseous nebula which has proceeded to completion, but so recently, astronomically speaking, that the cluster has not been disrupted and scattered by the other nearby masses of the star vacuum, and yet this is speaking of a sequence which most likely has consumed hundreds of millions of years to reach its present stage. And we as human ants are only accidentally able within the last few years to discover its existence or to comprehend its meaning.

We do not know if any other intelligent beings elsewhere have made the same discoveries, or even greater ones, or whether hundreds of thousands of such groups have done so. Certainly no one anywhere has seen it without a telescope unless equipped with eyes equivalent to telescopes, because nothing that one can see with the eye alone suggests that such a group is there. It is only when I look through an eyepiece capable of gathering thousands of times as much light as my eyes and magnifying it to 200 times its apparent diameter, that the group is visible at all, and even then its members range downward in size to the limit of visibility of the telescope.

I want to write, of all of this, that I do not know how one can do justice to it in words without harping on one theme to the point of becoming boring.

— C.F.R.

The Illusion of the Moon's Size

Written Approximately 1960

When we look at the moon near the horizon, it appears to be much larger than it appears to be near the zenith. This illusion is treated as something of a phenomenon, but there is a plausible though unproven explanation.

When we look at the sky in the daytime, we have the impression of a vault because the color of the sky makes it seem opaque, like a fine-textured solid, against which the clouds show in relief and seem obviously nearer than the blue-textured substance of the sky. To one side and the other, clouds of steadily decreasing apparent size extend until they seem to meet the earth at the horizon, and the blue of the sky seems to do the same thing at a greater distance.

We are conscious of our possession of binocular vision, by which the separation of our eyes enables us to detect that one object is nearer to us than another. This faculty, however, does not operate at much more than a hundred feet, and beyond that point we extend the capacity to distinguish between nearness and distance by analogy with our short-range ability to judge distances.

This is the trick of perspective, in which of two objects of known size the nearer one extends over a greater angle of vision, so that an object grows visually smaller in dimension with distance. For example, a twig held in the hand becomes larger than a tree in the mid-distance, and a house at a distance seems obviously smaller in angular dimensions than one nearby. In the sky, however, looking up from the ground, there are no intermediate points of reference, such as the objects in a landscape, and we are unable to determine by the evidence of our senses alone, how far from the ground the clouds are suspended in the air, and how far beyond them is the blue of the sky.

At night the opaque daytime sky melts away, and in a midnight blue sky the stars all seem to become merged with the sky and to be all at the same distance, although we cannot determine what that distance may be. To the ancients, with only eyes as guides, that was final: the stars were set in the crystal dome of the sky.

We have another illusion in this regard, by which the full moon at the horizon seems a larger object than when it is overhead. This is because our sense of sight gives us an impression which is literally translated by our mind into an effect of perspective. To us it seems obvious that the vault of the sky, like the clouds, should be farther away at the horizon than it would be overhead, as would be true of the ceiling of an extremely large room.

Instinctively we extend the terrestrial analogy of size diminishing with distance, as in the comparison of the nearby and distant house or tree. We know that, roughly speaking, both houses and both trees are of the same size. Nothing tells our eyes that the scale of distances to the tree and to the moon are vastly different, so that the distance to the moon overhead and the moon at the horizon is virtually the same. Our eyes instinctively tell us that the moon, apparently farther away at the horizon, is larger than it seems because it must have shrunk its visual size in going away from us to the horizon. Further, the tree outlined against the moon at the horizon is much smaller than the moon, but would be large compared to the moon if it were nearby.

But this illusion of a vault for a sky is just that — an illusion. When one looks into the sky at night he is actually looking into an infinity of distance, limited only by his ability to resolve with the eye, or the eye plus a telescope, the objects which are there in the depths of space. The faint blue glow in the constellation Andromeda, which we are told is a galaxy similar to our own, means that one is actually looking at an object containing a hundred billion suns like our own, some twelve quintillions of miles away (12,000,000,000,000,000,000) and as directly regarding it as one would the house next door.

The Origin of Life

Written Approximately 1962

When we look with even a small telescope into the depths of space, we can see misty areas, such as the nebula of Orion in Orion's sword, which are actually enormous clouds of dust and gas, mainly hydrogen. Brilliant stars are in this gas, causing it to shine with a soft light, and there is much evidence that the stars are new and have been formed from the gas. The spectroscope tells us that this gas cloud includes, besides hydrogen, the ammonia radical and methane, as well as carbon dioxide.

When our sun and its family of planets were formed, it was by condensation from a similar cloud of gas, reliably thought to be some 4.6 billion years ago. As a result, the sun and its planets contain substantially the same elements. The sun envelopes more of the gases, especially hydrogen, which were held to it because of its greater size and more powerful gravitational attraction. The larger planets, notably Jupiter and Saturn, did the same thing to a lesser degree, and both of these planets have extensive atmospheres of ammonia, methane, carbon dioxide, hydrogen, and water vapor. When the earth was younger, its atmosphere contained the same gases, but no free oxygen and perhaps no nitrogen, because these gases are the result of the life process.

For a long time it has been common opinion among scientists that life was a rare statistical accident, very possibly occurring only on the earth. But it seems to me a commonsense conclusion that, like the general occurrence of the same elements throughout the universe, the life process may be a common occurrence as well.

Better acquaintance with chemistry, especially of the life process, has changed the supposition that life must be rare, or at least changed speculation concerning it. Now it is known that proteins, the basis of life, are built up from the same gaseous radicals as are in the interstellar dust and gas clouds and the atmospheres of the larger planets, and less plentifully in the atmosphere of the earth. An experiment has been performed in which these gases (ammonia, methane, carbon dioxide, and liquid water) have been sealed in pure form in a glass container and shaken while electrical discharges were passed through the mixture. When the container was opened, it was found to contain a mixture of amino acids — the building blocks of protein — formed from combinations of the gases. The conclusion would be that these gases in contact with one another form components of the life process, that the gases are of universal occurrence, as are also electrical discharges, and that the amino acid components of the life process are a universal consequence wherever conditions are favorable to their formation and temporary preservation.

Now a new look has been taken of the whole matter, and our notion of what occurred on the younger earth has been modified and given a new direction. It is now postulated that life may be possible throughout the universe wherever the universal materials for its genesis find local conditions suitable — as they were on the young earth.

It may be assumed, and seems borne out by spectroscopic examination of existing dust clouds wherever they are visible in space, that all the clouds of gas and dust in space are essentially the same, and that all stars formed from these clouds are in general alike. Sizes of the stars alone determine their relative brightness and temperature. The spectroscope confirms this.

Next, we can determine mathematically that suns much larger or much smaller than our sun would be poor centers for families of planets, the larger suns being too hot and not "living" long enough for the processes of evolution and life to run their course, and the too-small ones being unable to warm the planets and support life, although "living" even longer than our sun. We can speculate also that there may be many suns of suitable size, and probably around them many planets suitable for life. In this connection there is the observation that our sun rotates slowly on its axis, as do many of the suns of suitable size, and that this is because the angular momentum in the solar system is mainly in its planets, so that by analogy the other slowly rotating stars are possessed of families of planets.

We may assume, finally, the possibility that life will occur wherever it can occur — that the appearance of life on a planet depends on its proper size and position in a zone of proper temperature near its sun, being otherwise a natural result of natural characteristics of the gaseous radicals involved, since they naturally combine as amino acids. We may further speculate that as a consequence life generally has a similarity of qualities, although not necessarily of forms.

Let us look at the sequence in more detail. In our beginning a cloud of gas, perhaps a light year or six trillion miles or so in diameter, developed turbulence or instability and separated from a larger galactic cloud. This would be a common occurrence, and is happening now in nebulae we can observe telescopically.

Our beginning or proto-sun condensed from this gas and dust by gravitation. It acquired a very slow rotary motion because there is a very slight difference in rotational speed around the galaxy of the outer edge of the cloud as compared to the inner edge. This speed of rotation slowly increased as condensation proceeded and the proto-sun grew smaller, although still immensely larger than the present solar system. Subsidiary turbulences grew and developed, so that the cloud tended to develop a larger central mass and many lesser aggregations of matter, and there was a general tendency for larger masses to capture smaller ones. Finally there were loosely aggregated bodies with large gaseous envelopes ranging in size from comets and meteorites to planets, all revolving in the same plane and in the same direction as the central proto-sun.

Finally the central mass, the proto-sun, losing less and less of the heat generated by contraction as it grew denser and more opaque, grew more and more hot until it emitted light. Finally its central regions reached the temperature at which nuclear reactions were initiated, and the higher temperature made all the solar constituents again gaseous. Now the smaller and nearer of the planets and planetesimals began to be warmed and to lose their lighter gases to space, beginning with hydrogen. The nearer and medium-sized condensations, similar in size to the earth, had relatively enormous envelopes or atmospheres of ammonia, methane, carbon dioxide, and water. As the water condensed to form oceans on the now-cooling earth, terrific thunderstorms and rain occurred on a scale never seen before or since. Volcanic activity occurred on a great scale, producing greater electrical discharges and new additions of water from the rocks, and carbon dioxide formed from the steamy air reacting with carbides in the rocks.

The primitive gases were dissolved in the water of the oceans and reacted to become amino acids, and in turn to form proteins, so that the oceans were a sort of nutritious soup. Among the constituent particles of the oceans, by the statistical laws of numbers and time, certain ones combined to form replicating molecules, the initiation of life. Before these had fed on and exhausted the store of amino acids and proteins in the soup, the process of photosynthesis occurred in early plants, or the whole process would have come to an end. Perhaps it did, many times, only to recommence the development until there were forms which could synthesize sugars from the soup by photosynthesis, and the chain of modern life could begin.

The earth is our one and only home, and we would well begin to study its resources and their conservation with much care, because they are our limiting conditions for life in the future.

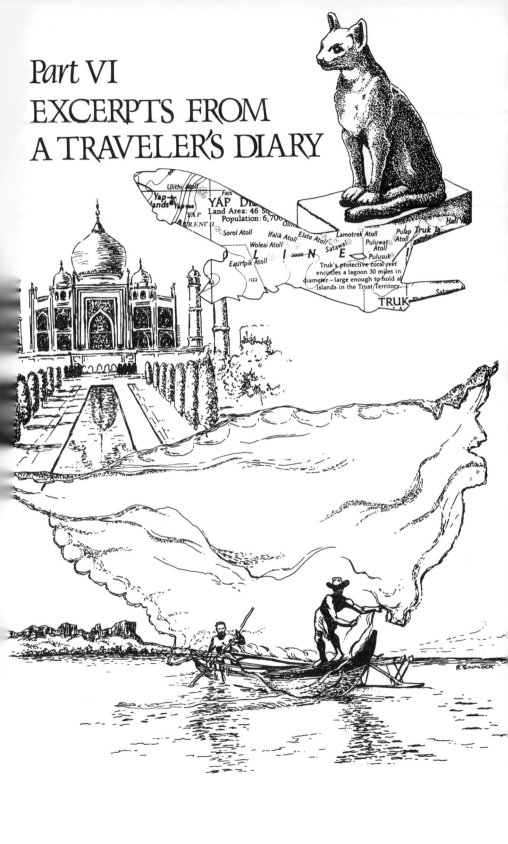

Part VI
EXCERPTS FROM
A TRAVELER'S DIARY

Ulithi Atoll
Fais
Yap
Islands Yap isa
YAP D
YAP Land Area: 46 Sq
RENCH Population: 6,70
Sorol Atoll
Ifalik Atoll Elato Atoll Lamotrek Atoll Pulap Truk Is
Woleai Atoll Satawa Puluwat Atoll Hall
Eauripik Atoll Pulusuk
Atoll
L I N E
1122 Truk's protective coral reef
encircles a lagoon 30 miles in
diameter—large enough to hold al
islands in the Trust Territory
Satawa

TRUK

R. SINNOCK

Excerpts from a Traveler's Diary

Having lived in China for approximately 12 years, C.F. Rehnborg had a well-developed taste for travel and boundless curiosity about the peoples of other countries — their cultures and the geographic features of their lands, their social and political structures, their history and their future. He was interested in how they lived, what they thought, how they earned their daily bread, and above all, how they ate — their nutritional habits and available food, and the apparent effects. In 1953 he and Mrs. Rehnborg took a well-earned holiday and traveled through England, Scotland, Norway, Sweden, Denmark, Germany, Switzerland, Italy, Egypt, Israel, and Greece, returning a second time to Italy and Switzerland, then to France and back again to England and Ireland, and finally home . . . a journey of about four and a half months. The following "trip reports" have been taken from his complete record of that journey. This was not his first trip to Europe, nor was it his last. He continued to travel both for business and for pleasure, but the island of Tahiti was his all-time favorite location, where he and Edith Rehnborg maintained a home near Papeete. We have added some essays about Tahiti and the Polynesians, as well as notes on further island explorations in the South Pacific.

Touring Norway

This is Wednesday, July 16th, 1953 and we are at the Carlton Hotel in Oslo, Norway, where we arrived day before yesterday evening, and from which we will leave for points in Sweden day after tomorrow morning.

We have had a very wonderful time so far, in spite of the fact that most of the time it has either been cloudy or raining. In England we saw only two or three clear days at Windermere, and in Norway we have seen very little blue sky except for one day at Laerdal. Edith reminds me that I wanted her to tour in the open Jaguar and it certainly would have been a mess if we had, but in this car it has been perfectly comfortable. The rain doesn't seem to matter at all, and in fact it is not steady rain, it is simply that the sky stays cloudy and every now and then it opens up with a shower.

I wrote to you from England, or rather from Scotland, so you know that we've found beautiful roads and beautiful scenery. In fact I have been using my magazines of color film at such a rate that if I had not been able to find ten more of them at Bergen and set up some sort of allocation of the magazines to the various countries, I probably would have run out of all I had by the time we got to Italy.

Norway is completely beautiful. I think it still remains true that the fiords on the western side of British Columbia and the panhandle of Alaska are more terrific than the Norway fiords, but they are also far more unfriendly than these waters. Here the fiords are used by people and wherever there is a space on the banks, there are farm houses and settlements, and the fiords themselves are used as traffic lanes and are crowded with boat traffic. There are more links by ferry between points on the fiords than there are links by road, and the various settlements have their own landings and apparently their own boats. The amount of land water is terrific. Of course, it would be terrific with such a steady type of rainfall all through the year, but literally in the western section, between the fiords and the lakes, there is just about as much water surface as land surface.

The fiords are very much over-simplified on the maps, and I think, somewhat like roads and railroads on an ordinary map, they are shown far wider than they are in fact. Actually most of them are fairly narrow, long tongues of water where glaciers have scoured out the rock in their flow to the sea in past ages. The lakes are also long and narrow and are actually either the indentations left by glaciers at points higher than sea level in the same rock valleys, which left a sort of sill of rock at the lower end, or else the result of blocking by enormous slides.

Geologically the present contours of the land are so recent that very few of these lakes have filled in at all except very slightly at the upper ends. But whatever land has filled in in this manner and come down from the sides as detritus from rock falls, has become covered by soil and is the only level ground of the area. Beyond small amounts of grain and garden truck apparently grown mostly for the use of the local inhabitants, almost all of the farming seems to revolve around animals. The farms are extended up the sides of the valley and some of the tilling is done literally at a 45 degree angle of slope of the land. Most of this farming however is grass, apparently not planted crops, but native grasses growing very luxuriously in the wet climate. In fact the climate is so wet that the hay cannot be dried on the ground. Instead it is pulled down to relatively level spots or gentle slopes and there strung on wire by hand or else built up in a vertical cock around a tall pole and allowed to dry, so to speak, suspended in the air.

Between Laerdal and Gol we came over a high pass at an altitude of about 3700 feet, which at this latitude is well above the timber line, and there we were able to observe exactly what had been described to us concerning the animal husbandry. During the summer all of the animals — sheep, goats, and cows — are driven to the higher pastures above the timber line for the summer, and the grass harvested in the lower points near the settlements is dried on the racks, and stored for winter use. Then as winter approaches the animals are driven down to lower and lower levels, until when the real winter has come they have arrived back at the settlement areas, and are from that point on through the winter fed on the hay which was cut locally and stored for them.

The farmers who take care of the animals move up to the higher reaches with them, and live for the summer in houses which are built there for that purpose, and the milk is collected, just as it is with us, in forty-quart cans at whatever point the animals are, and transported down to the lower levels. Some of it is marketed as fresh milk, but I imagine most of it goes into the making of cheeses, because there is apparently no provision made for sterilizing the carrying containers.

They are merely washed and sunned, and it isn't possible the milk can stay fresh for very long.

The roads which connect the various points are not many, and they are all fairly new, but they are splendid engineering jobs. There are no level stretches and no straight stretches in these roads. They curve constantly and are going either up or down all the time, and a tremendous part of the total of roadway is literally carved out of the living rock of the hillsides. This is not done by making a vertical cut on the side of a hill and pushing the loose rock over the edge, but by blasting out a shelf into a vertical, or nearly vertical, rock so that you drive on the road surface with an overhang above the car, and in places the overhang goes to the outer edge of the road because the rock surface is literally vertical.

These shelves are not cut very wide, but here and there along them there are wider places where cars may pass, so you are to get the picture of a shelf which ascends or descends, not level but either climbing or dropping, with some degree of curve every fifty feet, and you on the qui vive for meeting cars, with the problem each time you meet one whether you are to back up to the next wider place or the other man is to do so. The result is an average speed of something under 15 miles an hour, hour by hour through the day, so that by the time you have covered a hundred miles you have done a good day's work of driving. But the marvel is that the roads are there at all. It must have looked to the men who started the engineering work like a virtually impossible job, but they certainly did it.

These roads are not paved, except for a mile or two outside of the larger towns, and within the towns, and the last twenty miles coming into Oslo from the north. Instead the roads are made of macadam, but a very carefully laid macadam. First there is large rock, then smaller rock, and finally gravel surfaces, and these gravel surfaces are intensively worked, apparently every few days and apparently on the old New England system of having a farmer responsible for the road a certain distance each side of his holdings. They use good equipment in the form of road scrapers, but apparently the tools are passed along from section to section to men who work locally.

They are very thrilling roads, to say the least, and I hope anybody who follows me here will have the same advantage of having met people who tried to scare him by over-emphasizing the dangers of the road, with the result that the roads seemed fairly tame compared to what was expected. If you hit it cold, I think your hair would stand on end most of the way, but when some hundreds of cars use the same road each day, it finally dawns on you that it can't be quite as terrifying as it looks, because there is no evidence anywhere that anyone has any accidents. In fact, as compared to California we only saw the evidence of two accidents in England and none at all in Norway. One thing at least, there is never a dull moment while driving.

So much rain as falls here means a lot of water, and all of that water comes down these steep hillsides and precipices, and along the very steep valleys, in literally hundreds of beautiful cascades. Some of the cascades drop long distances — a matter of several thousand feet — tumbling down the hillsides in a large number of successive waterfalls, and some of these waterfalls also are very high. In fact, along the fiords, some of the waterfalls come down from lips that overhang the walls below, so that the waterfall a hundred feet down from the lip is fifty or more feet away from the cliff face. A very large one of these, in particular, had a single vertical drop of about 600 feet — the natives said 200 meters, which would be a little more than 600 feet — and in the same waterfall there were other drops, none of them quite as high, but the whole adding to about 350 feet. But it is hard to pick out one to admire because they occur just as far as you can see, and at times there will be eight, ten or more waterfalls within view.

The roads, surprisingly enough, don't get very wet, because the water goes down through that macadam surface and leaves it rather smooth and dry even when it is raining fairly hard. One does get his car splashed. The Jag has been dirty along the sides from the moment we started from Bergen. It was washed once but it was dirty again ten minutes after leaving the hotel, so we haven't washed it again, and by this time the light dusting of mud along the sides seems to be practically a part of the car. I haven't had any mishap along the road so far except once. I forgot to mention that most of the people here travel by bus rather than by private car, and the buses are of standard size, so you can imagine what it is like to meet one of them on an average narrow road. At one point, coming from Gol down to Oslo, on a particularly narrow curve, but fortunately on level ground, the road had a ditch at each side rather masked by the grass that grew in the ditch, and when I turned out to let a bus pass I turned just one inch too far and slid down one side into that ditch. No rock, however, only mud. The bus driver w what happened but he didn't stop. He kept on going, but the next venty cars that came by did stop, and all the occupants of all the venty cars piled out to help get our car back on the road. One of them as driving a Jeep and had a tow line, and he hooked onto the front and ulled us out of the ditch. And then everybody smiled and congratulated verybody else and shook hands and got back in their cars and drove ff, including us.

Touring Greece

On Thursday (Sept. 24, 1953), we left the airport at 10:00 a.m. for Athens, where we were met by the representative of American Express and taken to the Palace Athenee, a brand new hotel. As we came into the city we could see the hill of the Acropolis in the center of town, and some of the ruined temples in the valley below it, where once a river flowed through a grove of trees and Socrates started his peripatetic school.

The first evening we were there we went to the open theatre at the foot of the Acropolis, where we sat on marble benches in a semi-circle and watched a play of Euripides done after the manner of the fifth century B.C., on a bare stone stage, with a chorus in the ampitheatre under it chanting while they moved in disciplined dance figures and struck attitudes expressive of the moods of the play. The work of the chorus was very effective, because the actors could merely have declaimed their lines and let the chorus show the moods they were supposed to evoke.

The play was Hippolytus, and it was done in modern Greek. Of course the Greek meant nothing to us, but we had an English synopsis of the play, and could follow the story through the movements of the actors. What interested us was that there were no "acts." The chorus marched in, the actors appeared, the play went on from beginning to end, covering about two hours, and then everybody marched out, and it was over. I had never seen it before, and I found it very interesting, but I wouldn't have to go every evening of the week to keep entertained. I think I could get along without it for long periods of time between plays. One of the things that amused me was that when the hero was dying from very severe wounds suffered in a chariot accident, he showed so much energy and talked so loudly we were sure it would take hours or

even days for him actually to die, but he died in a few seconds when ▌
came to that point.

On Friday, Sept. 25th, our woman guide met us in the morning ar
we went to see the Acropolis and the Temple of Jupiter, and th
excavations of the old marketplace being done by what the guide calle
the American Archeological Mission, apparently a combination ◖
various American universities. It was sad to discover that the ruine
condition of the Acropolis was mostly the work of two moder
destroyers; one, the Turks who carried off the statue of Athena and thei
lost it in a fire in Constantinople, and then used the temple, which wa
practically intact, as a powder storage magazine. It exploded an◖
destroyed the temple during the fighting at the time of the war for Greel
independence in the 1820's, entirely blowing out the center of th◖
Parthenon, which has been only partially restored.

The other destroyer was Lord Elgin, the ambassador to Turke⟩
about that time, who took all the art treasures he could move away from
the Acropolis, including the friezes of the Parthenon. The British, who
have what is left of these treasures, convey the impression Lord Elgin
was a great philanthropist who preserved the treasures for posterity, but
actually he was merely a businesslike robber who was out to make
money. He took his loot to Italy, and spent nearly two years trying to
find a buyer for it, but there was no museum which would meet his price,
until finally the British Museum made him an offer. He then loaded the
stuff into two shipments on two separate ships, one of which was lost at
sea in the Mediterranean off the Italian coast, and the other one of
which reached England, and it was only the stuff which was on this ship
which now survives. The rest of it is about two or three thousand feet
down in the Mediterranean.

But the greatest destroyers of all, in Greece and elsewhere, were the
Christians. When Constantine turned them loose as the official
purveyors of religion and a new world power, they had an orgy of
destruction in all the so-called "pagan" strongholds throughout that
ancient world, and they destroyed all they could of the pagan antiquities
throughout the Roman Empire — which was pretty much the whole area
of the Mediterranean and the surrounding countries. In addition, in
Athens, as in Rome, a great part of the ancient marble found its way into
the lime kilns and became plaster for the brick and mud huts of that
time. Only a few columns stand of the great Temple of Jupiter, and the

me kilns, which in the hands of the Turks incinerated the rest, were till standing by the temple when the Greeks took over. It is amazing to think that any men, Turk or otherwise, could bring themselves to make lime out of a work of art, but that is precisely what they did.

On Sunday, the 26th, we drove 100 kilometers to Corinth and spent the day looking at the ruins of the old city there, which has been partially excavated, and the old temple at Eleusis, between Athens and Corinth. We also visited the Byzantine Temple of Daphni which the Turks practically destroyed in a crazy experiment to recover the gold of the inside decorations. The temple is in the shape of a Maltese cross, with a high dome, and the Turks used it as a furnace by building enormous fires in the center of the nave; but as the gold was incorporated in the tiles used in the mosaics, entirely covering the interior of the church, all they did was to destroy the mosaics. They didn't recover any gold. Only part of the mosaic work is left, but it includes a portrait of Jesus, in the top of the dome. This to me is the most interesting thing of its sort I have seen, because it shows Jesus frankly as a Jew, not blond but black haired — a rugged strong face of great character. I tried to make an exposure with my camera, but to insure against failure of my own picture I bought some of the illustrated postcards on sale at the church, because this picture is really terrific.

Greece is even more dry and waterless than the other Near East countries, including Palestine, and the Greeks have done much less towards reforesting the hills, although they have begun some work on that. For the record, I want to aver I do not think this near eastern Mediterranean area can ever achieve economic stability, or be able to feed its people, until it has effectively restored the watershed cover on the hills by reforestation and has cut down on the size of the grazing herds, particularly of sheep and goats. The mountainous country of Greece is quite beautiful, and the road along the shore to Corinth gave beautiful views. The water of the sea is amazingly clear and of a beautiful blue color, and at one point I took a picture from above of a fishing boat working near the shore, which looked, to the eye at least, not like a boat floating on water but like a boat floating over the rocks under it, held up by a sort of special blue air.

I was particularly interested in Eleusis. In my book I made a point of the fact that the Eleusinian mysteries were the basis of most of the ritual of the Christian church, and of some of its dogma, and you can see it all worked out at the temple. The temple and the mysteries were wound around the fable of Demeter and Persephone, her daughter, who was abducted by Pluto. Demotor, with the help of the other gods, finally worked out a compromise by which Persephone spent six months of each year with Pluto in the underworld, and six months above the ground with her mother. The temple had a cavern where Pluto seized the girl and took her down through the earth, and also the well through which she returned to the surface each year. The whole thing is based of course on the mythological difference between summer and winter, because Ceres or Demeter was the goddess of agriculture and of natural growth, and winter was explained as her period of grief when she did not allow anything to grow.

The mystery concept finally produced the idea of resurrection, symbolized by this yearly return of Persephone and the plowing of the earth each spring, and the reward of the Eleusinian initiates and believers was the promise of resurrection and eternal life. The details of the mysteries are still mysteries, because death was the penalty for their disclosure by any initiate, but all the basic elements of the Christian theology, especially concerning resurrection and eternal life, were here in the Eleusinian mysteries for many centuries before the Christian era, and are in detail like the Christian beliefs.

On Sunday, the 27th, we left Athens and flew the three and a quarter hours to Rome, arriving about 2:00 p.m.

Touring Egypt

It is September 27, 1953, Sunday, and we arrived back in Rome about an hour ago at 1:30 and are housed again in the Hotel Flora, where we will be until October 1st. It is nice to get back to the dictating machine, because I would certainly hate to write out in longhand the pages of notes I have accumulated. Before I get really started into it, there is a general observation I would like to make.

What we expect to see in the Orient and the Near East and what we actually see are two quite different things. Most of us have quite definite preconceptions about what is to be expected, and these preconceptions are based on the general reading we have done in a lifetime about the Orient and the Near East, plus the blurbs of the travel folders, and also the somewhat ecstatic accounts given by Americans who have been there and come back; so we look for teeming millions of people, without Western conveniences, and as picturesque as the pretty little picture

:ards we used to get at Sunday School which illustrated the life of Biblical times.

Instead you find the teeming millions, all right, but millions of people trying their very best not to be picturesque. So far as they can, they wear Western clothes; so far as they can manage to be so, they are sophisticated; the hotels are run to fit the tastes of the Western visitor; the shops are stocked with things that are best designed to separate the visitor from his cash; the cities have paved streets filled with motorcars; and they have electricity, telephones, trolleys and buses, and water and sewage systems. There is of course plenty that is characteristic of the country, and it is picturesque, but not in the terms you expected to find, and everywhere you have to go out of your way to find the picturesque at all.

We left Rome for Cairo on Tuesday, September 8th, and traveled picturesquely in a four-motor Constellation with one stop at Athens. We left Rome at a few minutes before six in the evening; so the trip was made in darkness, and while we saw Athens as an illuminated city on our way south, we were transients and had to stay behind the Customs barrier during the half hour of our stopover.

The plane was delayed and was very late arriving at Cairo; so we didn't get to the city and to our hotel and in bed until nearly 4:00 a.m. The Cairo airport is noted as twelve miles out of the city, but Cairo is enormous; so the outskirts came to meet us just a mile or so from the airport. Our reservations were for the Hotel Carlson, but the American Express man who met us took us to the Hotel Gizeh Palace instead. Even this was a third-rate hotel, although it was right on the Nile River and had a nice veranda for our room. But there was a funny sort of shower for our bath and no hot water, and we shared the room with quite a number of cockroaches. The next day when we went to the American Express Office, they told us when they had learned we were assigned to the Hotel Carlton they were absolutely amazed, because the Carlton is about fifth-rate, and so they sent us to the Hotel Gizeh Palace on their own responsibility, but they still didn't send us to a first-rate hotel because they supposed from the fact we had been assigned to the Carlton that we were economizing. The next morning, Wednesday, September 9th, we were up at 8:00 o'clock in spite of the fact that we had only got to bed about 4:00. Edith, who was awake first, awoke me by calling out that there was a felucca sailing up the river; so I rushed for my camera and got a picture of it.

Cairo is located where the Nile splits up into two main branches and several minor branches and runs down through the Delta some 150 miles to the Mediterranean, and it is an enormous river. When we got there it was in flood from the melting snows off the highlands of Abyssinia, where one branch of it, the Blue Nile, rises, and from heavy rains in Equatorial Africa around Lake Victoria where the other branch rises. It was a rich ochre-mud color and ran very swiftly, coming only a yard or so from the top of the parapet which lines the bank. It is, in fact, diked from some distance above Cairo all the way to the sea, and, like the Mississippi River, if it breaks the dikes it floods the country, although the dikes on the Nile are not as high as those on the Mississippi.

At a few minutes after nine, Abdel, the guide, came to start us on our conducted tour of the city. That first morning he took us to a number of mosques. I suppose, as a Mohammedan, he thought these were the most important things there were for us to see. They were, in fact, very interesting, especially the one called the Blue Mosque, due to the liberal use of blue tile in the mosaics of geometric designs adorning the interior. One cannot wear shoes in a mosque, but instead of requiring us to take our shoes off, they had special canvas gadgets which were strapped on over the shoes, and which are about half the size of snow shoes. Edith looked like a beautiful duck. I didn't see myself, but undoubtedly I was far funnier.

Each mosque, and Abdel said there were approximately 5,000 in Cairo alone, has tombs built into the corners of its interior structure. Usually the tombs are for those who financed the building of the mosque, but the thing I remember most is the priest who sat cross-legged on a carpet on the parapet at the entrance of the Blue Mosque with what I thought was a very serene and beautiful face.

Moses and Jesus are both rated by the Mohammedans as prophets of approximately equal stature; so Abdel was able to show us, in addition, the exact spot where Moses was found in the bulrushes. This, disregarding the fact that the Pharaoh whose daughter was supposed to have "found" Moses lived several hundred miles farther up the Nile. He also showed us the cave under the synagogue in the Jewish quarter where Jesus lived while in Cairo with his mother Mary.

We noted another interesting fact. Just as the churches in Rome were built by dismantling the Colosseum and various so-called pagan temples, the mosques in Cairo were made of the facing stones of the pyramids, plus the materials of several Egyptian temples.

When he had shown us the mosques and the historical spots, Abdel showed us the shops, and showing the shops is the main purpose of his life. There is an old story that it takes ten Englishmen to get the better in the bargaining with one Greek, and it takes ten Greeks to beat a Turk, and ten Turks to beat an Armenian, and ten Armenians to beat a Syrian and ten Syrians to beat an Egyptian, which is equivalent to saying it takes 100,000 Englishmen to beat one Egyptian, and believe me, that's true. Abdel made our stay in Egypt the most expensive period of an equal number of days we have spent anywhere since we have left home. Some of it, of course, was due to the fact that in the shops they showed us some things that we wanted, such as perfumes, Damascene trays, and alexandrites, a kind of gemstone which changes color. On all of the things we bought (of course in shops to which he led us directly, rather than to any other shops, because he did have an arrangement with them), Abdel naturally made commissions; but he put in his really fine touches when he took us on our camping trip to the desert, of which I will tell you a little later.

Another thing that contributed to our piling up expenses is the currency, plus the way the tips are worked. The unit of the currency is the pound — 34 Egyptian pounds to 100 United States dollars, and the pound is divided into 10 piastres. Each piastre, therefore, is worth as much as three of our cents, but the Egyptians unite in helping you to believe the piastre is in fact the equivalent of a cent. Automatically, therefore, our tips tend to be about three times too large. There is a smaller unit called the millieme, which is a tenth of a piastre so that a pound equals 1000 milliemes, but in practice the foreigner never sees the smaller coin. In addition, everyone gets into the act. You cannot give a tip which will make the one who receives it act as if it is enough. The Egyptian receives the tip in his open hand and lets it lie there, looking at it disgustedly, and then looks at you as if he were trying to understand how anybody could be so stingy, when the chances are you have tipped on a decimal dollar basis and have already given him more than three times as much as you should.

In addition, where one man in the United States moves to do what you need done, such as moving your bags, in Egypt five or more men start at the same job, and each of them expects a tip. When you leave the hotel, everyone who works there lines up for his tip, not only the ones who did things for you, but those who happen to be in the hotel at the time; and if your stay is for several days, you will find the maid goes off duty and another one comes on duty, the porter goes off duty and another one comes on duty, the waiter goes off duty and another one comes on duty, and so on forever. In other words they work shifts to double the tips. If you are wise, you will tell yourself that a ten piastre piece is actually thirty cents; and if you are wise, you will also tip, not as you go, but at the end of your stay, and then only to the person who is on duty at the time you leave. If you do this, you get exactly the same kind of service — that is, indifferently good — and you can't get better service anyway, even if you tip eighteen times too much or tip everyone who asks for a tip. But with prices and tips high, there is no doubt that staying in Egypt is expensive.

On Thursday, the 10th, we made a trip to Sakkara and Memphis. Sakkara is probably the oldest of the pyramids and is of the design called a step pyramid, and at Memphis, once a great city and the capital of Egypt, nothing remains on top of the ground except two tremendous granite statues of Ramses II, a statue of a sphinx, and the traces of the foundations of a temple, although there is a large area of mounds which probably cover other ruins, all now covered with date palm groves and mud villages. The statues now there, all quite badly damaged, were dug out of the mud by the kindness of individual donors. Both were monoliths perhaps 50 feet tall, but both now lie prone on low foundations. The interesting thing about both of them to me was that a very tiny queen, standing a little less than knee high, is carved standing behind the leg of her lord and master, her hand tenderly touching his calf.

At Sakkara about three miles farther away and up out of the lush valley, on the higher desert ground which adjoins it, there has been extensive excavation of the tombs, although there is much yet left to do. We went down into the chambers under one of the pyramids. The pyramid on the surface has been robbed of its marble facing, and the weather over the past 4000 years has greatly eroded what was left standing, but the inclined plane down into the chambers under the pyramid, and the hieroglyphs which covered all of the walls of the hamber inside, were as fresh and clean as if they had been made a week ago. All of the writings in the tombs now being excavated are being carefully studied.

I had often wondered how they found all of these buried antiquities, but it turns out that the hieroglyphs in the tomb usually mention the existence and location of earlier tombs, so by working back through successive ages the archeologist can make a fairly complete catalog of the tombs they can expect to find. Occasionally they get fooled, however. A case in point is the tomb of Tutankhamun. It is the only one so far discovered which had all its treasures intact. We went to see them in the Cairo museum, and they are terrific beyond description, with hundreds of articles made of solid gold, some of them individually weighing several hundred pounds — and Tutankhamun was not a very important king. All of the other tombs have been broken into and robbed, either by thieves who also followed the clues in the hieroglyphs, or by the priests of the temple themselves, since they knew where the burials had been made.

The burials were quite secret for the simplest of reasons. All the men concerned in carving, decorating, and furnishing the tomb, and the individuals who moved the body into the tomb, except the priests, were carefully hung up by their heels and their heads cut off. This fact of the disposition of the participants is part of the records in pictographs in each of the tombs, and we saw it in several — the rows of headless corpses hung by their heels and a neat pile of heads. Tutankhamun was a special case. Tutankhamun's father suppressed the worship of the ancient gods and declared that only one god existed. He moved his capital and made a serious effort to establish the worship of the one god as the official religion, but Tutankhamun when he succeeded his father was about 16 years old only and had none of his drive and character, so that the priests were able to persuade him to restore the old religion. When he died, still very young, he was buried in pomp and splendor, but the fact of his burial and the location of his burial place were kept entirely out of the record, so that when the tomb was found by Lord Carnarvon, it was found entirely by hunch and by accident.

On the afternoon of the tenth, at the start of our scheduled conducted tour, we went out to camp on the desert near the pyramids. This is where Abdel got in his best licks. Before we got there he kept mentioning entertainment, photographer, and stuff of that sort, and I should have taken warning, but I was simple enough to suppose these were included in the tour. Instead, we had a camel race and entertainers in the evening, and a photographer who took approximately $30.00 worth of pictures of Edith and me in queer garbs, all of which we had to pay for extra and none of which we had asked for. In other words, Abdel merely ordered for us the various things he thought we would stand for, and then when the bill came in we paid for them, but they weren't things we wanted, and as a matter of fact, the presence of so many people in the camp spoiled the trip on the desert as far as I was concerned, and Edith was mad enough to kill all the Egyptians in Egypt. But leaving out the unpleasant parts, it was definitely an experience.

Egypt lies in a valley which would be completely desert but for the fact that there is a Nile River. It has not rained except in sprinkles too light to measure for the past six years, and it is the usual thing that it does not rain for years on end. The valley itself is irrigated, and has been since the dawn of history, by water lifted out of the river into canals and

The Rehnborgs are relaxing in the dining tent of their desert encampment, with Abdel, their guide, at right.

onducted by gravity to points away from the river and farther down the river. Prior to modern times, this was only supplemental irrigation, to maintain crops after they had been planted. The great irrigation was the flooding of the whole valley by the Nile at high water, in June or July and on into August, and the yearly crop was not planted until after this flood had subsided, so that there was only time before winter to grow one crop.

In modern times, of course, there is the great dam at Aswan, and other systems of irrigation canals throughout the valley, and the delta canals are kept full by gravity intake points further up the river and by

With pyramids in the background, Carl and Edith pose in native Egyptian garb which they found cool and comfortable in the desert heat.

pumping, so the fields grow three and four crops beginning in March and ending in November. Always, formerly, only the valley has been green, after being soaked down by the Nile, but now it is continuously green by continuous irrigation, with no longer any general soaking as when the river used to flood the valley. Right at the edges of the flat river valley, where the land rises by about an average of 100 feet, the desert begins, and on the desert there is not even a trace of vegetation — no living plants of any kind, but only stony yellow ground covered in places by drifted sand. The great pyramids are on the west bank of the river valley about 15 miles from Cairo, and the pyramids and the accompanying temples and tombs are on this utterly barren ground.

We camped in a sort of valley between higher rises about 2 miles south of the pyramids, and it was a most elaborate set up, with a sleeping tent and a dining tent and a kitchen, and more servants even than we would expect to find in the China of the old days. When night fell the stars were so bright I am inclined to believe that the sixth magnitude was not the limit of vision, as it is usually. At sundown there was an infinitely thin wedge of moon following after the sun, and when Abdel saw it, he dug into his pocket for his money and stood with it in his hand while he made a wish, probably for more money, although I can't see how he can need it, judging by the amount he was able to dig out of us. We had an excellent cook, and a waiter who attentively fed us until we were like stuffed sausages, but just when I got ready after dinner to go out and look at the stars for a while, the entertainers arrived. While they did fairly well, they were utterly a bore as far as we were concerned, and they set the management back quite a chunk of money later. Finally we got to bed and slept in a world which absolutely did not have a sound in it, except occasionally a dog yapping in a native village miles away.

On the morning of Friday, the 11th, we woke early and broke camp and went to visit the Sphinx and the pyramids. So much has been told about the Sphinx and the pyramids that I don't have to add anything except the two items that interested me most.

One is the joining of the stones. The stones in the walls, especially in the walls of the temple near the Sphinx, are enormous by any standard, some of them from nine to twelve feet long and four feet square. In addition some of them are cut with mortises to fit into a stone above or below that course, or to make a right-angle turn at a corner, and finally hey are laid together without mortar, on plane surfaces so true that literally there was not even space between the stones to insert the edge of a razor blade. Effectively, they are joined almost as closely as gauge blocks, and the Egyptians themselves say they were moved into position on a film of water.

The other thing that interested me was Farouk's house. Giving himself special privileges, as I suppose he could, he built himself a house, modeled after the Temple of Luxor, at the foot of the largest pyramid on a rise overlooking Cairo, which the locals say he used for his gayest parties, but which is used by the present government to put up visiting V.I.P.'s. Incidentally, if you can believe the man in the street, 99% of the Egyptian population is solidly behind Naguib, and Farouk is finished. He doesn't even have a chance to be buried in Egypt when he dies. If you will listen, they will go on for hours telling you the things Farouk did while he was king, over and above the things which were reported in the press, such as losing or spending 30 million pounds (or about a hundred million dollars) in the course of one two-month vacation in Europe. He had a number of palaces in Cairo alone. I drove past one of them, and it was three kilometers from corner to corner along one side of the grounds of the palace.

On Saturday, the 12th, we went a little distance north of Cairo into the delta to the site of the old city of Heliopolis, of which nothing whatever remains but one monolithic obelisk. Probably the valley around that obelisk is covered with traces of ruins, but it is also covered with farms, because one of the consequences of having a valley which is flooded annually by a muddy river, is that century after century layers of mud are laid on, until now what was the ground surface at the time Heliopolis was the capital is perhaps ten feet underground.

Near Heliopolis there was a very ancient tree, of which the name as nearly as I can render it is sycamore — not a sycamore such as we know, but a tree which bears fruit similar to a fig — and this particular tree is said to have been the tree under which the Holy Family rested on their trip into Egypt. Near it there is a Roman Catholic church with pictures on its inside walls, and rather good pictures too, showing the details of the massacre of the innocents and the flight into Egypt. On the wall also is a proclamation to the effect that by the great kindness of the Pope a visit to this church at the tree is equivalent to an indulgence. The tree, incidentally, is very venerable, with an enormous trunk but only a few

Their desert trip included camel rides, entertainers, and a staff of servants with an excellent cook. Edith and Carl are at center and far right, with the entire group.

live shoots. It may or may not be 2,000 years old, but it certainly looks as if it could be, as does also the ancient olive tree we saw later in Athens, which is supposed to be one of the grove of trees which stood around the academy of Plato.

The evening of the twelfth, we went by wagon-lits to Luxor. Luxor is 450 miles up the Nile, and the trip takes eleven hours, and it is the dirtiest and dustiest trip I ever hope to take. The roadbed is of mud mixed with pebbles, and the train, from the second car after the engine, travels in a cloud of dust like the cloud that follows a motorcar going across our deserts. We had to depend for ventilation on the ventilator fan which drew air down through a ventilator in the roof, and inevitably some of the dust came in with the ventilating air. Furthermore, it was sizzling, baking hot, and we practically staggered off the train at Luxor in the morning. Our hotel at Luxor was also called Luxor Hotel, and it was built to be fairly cool although it was rather barren. As we had arrived in the morning we started at once on our sightseeing. Our dragoman this time was not quite so rapacious as our Cairo guide, Abdel. At least he got me only into one shop, where I spent $270.00 for stone-age artifacts.

Luxor and Karnak and Thebes were the three wings of one very great city, usually referred to collectively as Thebes, which, at the time most of the temples were built in the 14th century B.C., was at the peak f its greatness, and perhaps at that time was the most important and wealthiest city in the world. What is left, of course, is a collection of tragic scraps, although the scraps are terrifically impressive — the most impressive man-made things, I am quite sure, that exist in the world.

We went at once to see the temple of Amon at Karnak. It is being most carefully excavated and restored, and it is tremendous. I took rafts of pictures, which will describe it better than I can in words, but there, as elsewhere on the trip we have made, the thing that bears me down is the awful destruction later men have inflicted on these ancient monuments. They were built so massively and beautifully that if left undisturbed they would have lasted for literally tens of thousands of years, but they have been used as quarries, and later conquerors have purposefully and intentionally defaced them. Obelisks and columns have been pushed over; statues have been mutilated; and the temples have been systematically wrecked by vandals and mischief makers, and by the bigots of other religions.

There was an avenue of Sphinxes, a paved street bordered by perhaps 4,000 statues, which stretched approximately three miles north and south from Karnak to Luxor. The avenue and the Sphinxes were pretty thoroughly damaged and destroyed, and then they were covered by the mud of the Nile and by the accumulated debris of villages built over them. The villages were built of mud bricks, and the accumulation of trash and ruined buildings, on top of which later villages were erected, has resulted in mounds sometimes fifty or sixty feet above the ruins, with present day villages on top of the mounds. The government has bought out the inhabitants of these villages, and is wrecking and removing their dwellings. It is interesting to see the excavations both at Luxor and at Karnak, which have begun to work towards one another along the avenue of Sphinxes, so that the excavated portion runs straight along the old level into a cliff of mud and trash, and there disappears as if under a cloud.

When we were at Karnak, and later in the Valley of the Kings on the other side of the river, we ran into an Egyptian motion picture company which was making a movie, using the ruins and the tombs as background and working a script titled, of all things, "Scandals of the Nile." The leading man is Hamid Bey, the foremost Egyptian motion picture actor, and it was rather funny to see the way he strutted and preened himself for Edith and me to notice him; but Edith paid no

attention to him and I never even tumbled to the fact he was an actor.
only heard his identity later from the guide. The director, a rather
dapper young man, was very hammy indeed. He carried a riding crop
I suppose because he had heard that once upon a time Hollywood
directors carried riding crops, and I suppose it was the carrying of a
riding crop that marked him as a director. This motion picture company
got in our way, or rather we got in theirs, whichever sounds the more
reasonable, so that we had to go through part of the temple of Karnak
on the lope, and in the Valley of the Kings we had to miss entirely seeing
the tomb of Tutankhamun, although we did see several which were
more interesting as to decoration and splendor.

All through the various temples, both in the older cities in the lower
valley and at the city of Luxor, the statues with the name of Ramses II
appear so often you get the impression he built at least half of the things
that exist. Actually, he built an enormous number, as well as many
colossal statues of himself cut in single blocks of granite (which I don't
dare use my stock of adjectives to describe because both the concept and
the execution of them are so impressive). But Ramses II also had a little
trick of erasing the names of other predecessors and substituting his
own, so that the cartouche of Ramses II appears in many places where it
does not properly belong. But at least Ramses didn't destroy anything,
he merely relabeled the things he found especially applicable.

There were several out-and-out destroyers, however. One was the
brother of Queen Hatshepsut. Hatshepsut was in the direct line of
descent, but her half-brother was not. Yet as the descent could only be
valid and legal through the male line, Queen Hatshepsut was married to
her half-brother, and being the stronger character of the two reigned as
queen. She built lots of things, including the temple of Deir el Bahiri,
and in all these temples, as it was the custom, erected the carved tablets
which were the equivalent of motion pictures for that day, detailing the
events of her reign, in which she always pictured herself and her half-
brother husband. But when she died, and she died first, her half-brother
became Pharaoh instead of second fiddle, and he immediately set about
erasing all traces of his sister-wife; and so everywhere you find the
panels show not Hatshepsut and her brother, but her brother and a
space chipped out where Hatshepsut used to be. He did this job so
thoroughly that only in one corner of one temple did he miss a single
image of his sister-queen, so that there is one carving, and one only, to
show how the queen looked when she lived.

Another destroyer was Cambyses, who lived about six centuries after Ramses II. Ramses during his lifetime conquered Persia, among other places, and pretty thoroughly wrecked it. Six centuries later when Cambyses conquered Egypt, he wrought six-centuries-old vengeance on everything he could find that Ramses had left, particularly the statues of Ramses himself. Over on the Thebes side of the Nile there is a colossal twin statue of Ramses at the entrance to the Ramesium, a temple Ramses also built and in which he had monolithic statues of himself; and in the temple of Luxor, also, there were something like 18 statues of Ramses.

Cambyses destroyed all these statues and the temples in which they stood, except that in the temple at Luxor two or three of the statues had fallen down in the six hundred years between, and had been covered with Nile mud, so that Cambyses missed them. These have been dug out and re-erected, but all the others from Memphis for 450 miles up to Luxor lie in pieces where Cambyses left them.

Most of these statues were enormous and massive monoliths carved from a single tremendous piece of granite. Cambyses had no dynamite; so he drove wooden pegs into holes carved into them, and then poured water on the pegs, and when that didn't work at once, he built enormous fires on the statues and then poured cold water on them while they were hot. The result is that most of the statues are not only broken but badly scaled, but they are still so tremendous and impressive it staggers the imagination that they could have been made at all. They were cut out of the hills and carved into statues before there were any iron tools, and I asked many questions before I found anyone who could even suggest how they could have been cut out at all. I wondered if the Egyptians had mixed diamond dust with their bronze, but I was told diamonds were unknown to the ancient Egyptians. Finally I found someone who could tell me. There are extensive deposits of emery in the Mediterranean area, probably produced by volcanic action, and the Egyptians used their soft metal tools with emery dust, just as a moden gem cutter uses a steel wheel and diamond dust. With their soft tools and emery dust they drilled holes in the quarry and used wood blocks soaked in water to split out the blocks, and then laboriously and slowly chipped and polished the finished statues from the single block of granite — an amount of patient artistry it is almost impossible to imagine.

On Monday, the 14th, we went across the river to visit Thebes and the Golden Desert and the Valley of the Kings. There are only a few bridges on the Nile, and none at that point, so we went across in a boat The river is over a mile in width at that point, very swift and dirty and very like the Yangtse. To get to a point straight across, we were first towed several miles up the river and then rowed across, falling down with the river current until we landed at the point we wished. It was so like China I had to keep reminding myself it was Egypt. The boat was just the same sort of boat that we find on the Yangtse, dumpy shaped, caulked with pitch, but very fast and serviceable, and it had a sail — a latteen sail — but as there was no wind that didn't help any.

On the other side we were met by a car and driven over dirt roads, rather good ones at that, across the flat valley to the slope of the hills where the temples were, and up through a gorge into the Valley of the Kings. I don't suppose the Valley of the Kings looked like anything but a desert valley before it was excavated, because the tremendous amount of rock carved out of the tombs was carefully carted down the lower valley that led up to the amphitheatre, so that there was nothing at the site to show anything had ever been dug out there. But in it they have found the rock chambers of twenty-odd royal tombs, and know at least fifteen more exist. Nothing has been done there since the discovery of the Tut tomb in 1920, because the frantic digging then by a number of American institutions and other investigators was prompted by the anticipation of finding treasures to take away for the American and British museums. When the Egyptian government glommed onto the whole of the Tut collection and put it in the Cairo Museum, leaving nothing whatever to be carried away, and indicated that in the future the same course would always be followed, American money especially for excavation work stopped coming in, and all the undiscovered tombs remain undiscovered.

We went into one tomb, the tomb of Seti, three hundred feet in all down into the native limestone rock of the hill forming the side of the valley. Other tombs opened all over the place, some with entrances only a few feet away from the one we went into, so probably part of the care taken to record, within the tomb, the location of the other tombs, was to prevent tunneling into an existing tomb in the making of a new one. Long flights of stairs led down into the hill. These were new flights of stairs put in by the archeologists, because the original stairs were chipped by the priests who sealed the tomb so that it could not be reentered by the original stairs. Part of the way into the tomb there was a square vertical shaft across the passage which went down in a sheer drop for perhaps a hundred feet. This was supposed to stop or trap anyone who tried to penetrate, but just before we reached the shaft we could see a carefully chiseled plan of the whole tomb on the wall, which showed where the tomb extended beyond the shaft. The men who robbed the tomb simply dug a shaft of their own around the well and the monolithic stone blocking the passage beyond it, and carted out everything the tomb contained. Perhaps it was the priests themselves who did this.

This tomb was uncovered and explored in the early 1800's by a Frenchman who, after he had taken out what he could find, which was very little, turned the excavated tomb over to the Egyptian government. The Egyptian government placed a guard in it, but while the guards were there someone, probably the guards themselves, developed a lucrative business by cutting out the cartouches or signatures of the king from the hieroglyphs on the walls, and I suppose selling them to tourists. The cartouches were cut out by chiseling into the limestone around the oval frame of the signature, and then chiseling under it to break it loose, so that each of these cuts destroyed also several rows of the hieroglyphs on each side, and nearly all the walls inside the tomb are defaced in this manner. All the walls and reliefs and hieroglyph bands were colored, and the colors were still there after 3500 years, nearly as fresh as when they were applied.

While we were there the Egyptian movie company began to use the tomb for one of its sets. I had often wondered how the work was done in these deep tombs, with no light available other than the light of candles or torches. Since candles and torches would have sooted the walls, and as there is no soot on the paint, obviously they did not use torches. The movie company showed me how it was done, and the guide confirmed it was the method the ancient Egyptians used. The movie people set a polished metal screen at the entrance where the sun could fall on it, and a series of other screens down the stairways and passages of the tomb all the way to the bottom. The man at the entrance kept the reflected light from his screen focused on the second screen and the reflected light was diffused by the other screens the whole length of the tomb, all the way down to the innermost chamber of the tomb. It was quite interesting.

Back on the shelf of the hill, facing the river plain where Thebe
stood, we visited the Ramesium and looked at the giant broken statues o
Ramses, but the Colossi of Memnon were out on the plain on th
approaches to the temple, and this year, at this time, the plain wa.
flooded to a depth of perhaps ten feet, so we couldn't go near them. All o
the hills back of the temple are covered with tomb entrances, but man
Arabs live there, and each tomb is used as the back room of a house buil
in front of it. The tombs are cool in summer and warm in winter (that is,
by comparison with the outside air), so I can hardly find myself blaming
them. Naturally all of these tombs are now empty of everything but
Arabs and have been for the last few centuries.

Driving back to the river and our boat trip across to Luxor, the road
led along one of the irrigation canals for a distance of perhaps two miles.
That two miles I suppose is representative of any two miles of irrigation
canal in Egypt and here is what we saw: there were a number of shadufs,
a pole about twelve feet long with a crosspiece about three feet from one
end cradled in a forked stick on each side. The short end has a big mud
and straw ball built around it to act as a counterweight, and suspended
from the long end over the canal is a gasoline tin, or a basket lined with
mud to make it waterproof. The worker pulls against the counterweight
and dips the bucket in the canal, and then the counterweight helps to lift
the bucket two or three feet to the irrigation canal which runs away from
the main canal across the field. Then there were water wheels in which
an animal, either a donkey or a buffalo or a camel, went around in a
circle and ran a wood-toothed cogwheel, which turned another vertical
wheel, which lifted water in rim buckets and tipped it into the canal.
Another way of lifting water: two or three places had single-cylinder
gasoline pumps.

In the canal we saw dead dogs, dead goats, and one dead buffalo. We
also saw people bathing, people washing their faces, people drinking the
water and dipping it up to take home to cook supper with. Just like
China, as Fuzzy will remember. I took pictures both of the water wheel
and the shaduf, and the sequence in both cases was interesting. The
man stopped lifting the shaduf bucket until one of them had swum
across the canal and had got a tip. The boy driving the camel instantly
stopped it and yelled for his brother, who swam across the canal to get a
tip.

When we got back to the Luxor side I made a second visit to the emple there, this time by myself, so I could browse around without a guide to interrupt my thoughts. I boiled all over again at the unnecessary damage done (in this case especially by the Christians, who inherited the Jewish belief that a graven image was somehow sinful in itself, and therefore should be destroyed). Parts of all these temples were at times converted into Christian chapels — the guides and the local people all say by Constantine, but this is not necessarily quite exact. What happened was that when Constantine, in A.D. 325, made Christianity the official religion of the Roman Empire, it was a Roman Empire which extended to the limits of the then known world, except to the area of India beyond Persia.

The moment Christianity was made official it blossomed, or rather sprouted up like a mushroom, and the Christians, who had been the underdogs until then, suddenly became the upperdogs. Since the Christian segment of the population up to that time had been made up preponderantly of the serfs and slaves, the movement as a whole reacted as you would expect the repressed group to act anywhere in the world. They became suddenly as arrogant and intolerant as formerly they had been meek and unassertive. They did not merely move into these pagan temples and use them, they converted them. If the temple was oriented to the east and had a sanctuary wall with the image against the wall at the west end, the Christians put the altar at the east end and knocked down the image and destroyed it, removed the sanctuary wall, and knocked a hole in the west portico of the building for a new entrance. If the building had decorations on the interior the Christians either chiseled them out or covered them with whitewash and plaster. If there was an altar to the pagan deity the Christians knocked off the decorations, erased the inscriptions, and put a new inscription on the front which dedicated it as a Christian altar. On almost all these altars I have seen, the name Constantine appears somewhat in the character of a patron saint in whose name all of these changes were made. All these things were done to the south end of the temple at Luxor.

There is a curio dealer in Luxor near the hotel (whose shop is in fact part of the hotel gate) who has a remarkable collection of stuff. I went in to buy a chipped arrowhead and ended up with a collection of things. By the time I got to the stage of paying for my purchases Shalib, the guide, showed up, so he must have got the news of his commission by wireless. In what little I have read about Egypt I have not run across much discussion of the prehistoric antiquities, but the country is full of them. On the little plateau near the Sphinx, also, there is a great deal of flint and I picked up a number of worked pieces which either were very crude tools or else had been discarded before they were finished for some fault in workmanship.

To wind up the stay at Luxor we went to the home of Shalib and had tea with him and his family. Shalib had a wife, a son, and a daughter, and was obviously very fond of them and they of him. The son was an especially intelligent and attractive young man, who is doing a pre-med course at the Cairo university preparatory to becoming a doctor.

When evening came we got back on our wagons-lit for the hot eleven-hour trip back to Cairo, hotter and dustier and more uncomfortable, if anything, than the trip south from Cairo to Luxor. We were met by Abdel and taken to the Semiramis Hotel, which is a top-notch hotel, where we were given a most comfortable and attractive room on the side looking down river away from the sun and with a fully equipped bathroom. Edith immediately retired from circulation for a 24-hour rest, and in the afternoon I joined her, but as it was still early in the day I saved the rest of the morning for a call on the American Consulate.

The following morning, Wednesday, the 16th, we left at 10:30 a.m. for Cyprus — that is, the plane was scheduled to leave at 10:30, but didn't leave until 11:45, due to the kind of mishap I suppose can only occur in international air traffic. When all the passengers had cleared customs and passport inspection, and they started to assemble the plane load, one customer could not be found. That passenger had simply gone into a corner when he finished his routine and sat down to read, but the corner was in a waiting room not commonly used, and they spent an hour and a quarter trying to locate him, and meanwhile twenty other passengers waited, and all of the business at the airport and customs was tied in knots until they did find him.

We haven't seen any rain or stormy weather since we first arrived in Italy, so we had the usual smooth and uneventful trip. It was interesting to fly over the Nile delta and to see the absolutely sharp lines where the irrigated land gave way to desert. The Delta itself represents the approximately ten thousand square miles of the Mediterranean filled in by the silt from the Nile River, to an original depth of between two and four thousand feet. The silting-in extends on a gradual slope for a great distance beyond the place where the land now lies above the level of the

Mediterranean, because the change from the muddy water near the shore, where the branches of the Nile flowed in, to the deep blue of the Mediterranean, extended far up the Israel coast. Where the Mediterranean is clear, it is of the most amazing blue, almost sapphire color, and it is so very clear that one can easily see down into the water at the shore line for a depth of approximately 100 feet. I wished many times for the spare time and a traveling companion who wanted to swim, and our aqua-lungs and air tanks, because the underwater life in the Mediterranean is very rich, and I am told that there are no sharks or any dangerous fish whatever.

The Taj Mahal
November 16, 1966

To look for the first time at the Taj Mahal can be the high point of a lifetime for sensing and comprehending the glory of a complete love. The empress of the Shah Jehan, Mumtaz Mahal, bore him sons and daughters and took his heart with her when she died in 1631, three hundred years and more ago. The building of all other temples was stopped while in seventeen years hundreds of artisans built this gem-like building above her, the most beautiful mausoleum, perhaps the most beautiful building, in the world.

"Built of pure white marble, it stands on a vast marble terrace, crowned by a great dome in the center and smaller domes at each of its corners. From the angles of the terrace rise four slender minarets. Subservient and supplementary to the glory of the outline is the beauty of the ornamentation. All the spandrils of the Taj, all the angles and important details of the architecture, are heightened by being inlaid with precious stones such as agates, bloodstones, jaspers, and the like. These are combined in wreaths, scrolls, and frets as exquisite in design as they are beautiful in color and, relieved by the pure white marble in which they are inlaid, they form the most beautiful and precious style of ornament ever adopted in architecture." Thus the encyclopedia.

The surrounding low wall of the area is of red sandstone, as is also the massive and nearly unadorned entrance gateway. Both frame the white marble of the Taj Mahal unobtrusively. The visitor enters through the gateway unprepared for the view that is coming. Lines of tall young trees frame the white marble building and its image in the long reflecting pools, and the image is breathtaking. At the building itself or its great white terrace, smaller details show, especially the inlaid flowers and wreaths. Each cluster is embedded deep into the marble surface with the utmost precision. The flower shadings of color are shown by variously colored whole pieces of carnelian and agate as petals separately set into the design. There is almost too much to see. Attention is drawn from building to building, to domes and minarets, and then to the meticulous details of the structures. The beauty of the ensemble is so overpowering that it is hard to register on the mind, but one remembers forever that one has seen the Taj Mahal, and reviews the intriguing details again and again.

Directly under the central dome is the imposing tomb of the empress. The whole design is keyed to the presence of this tomb. At one side, very near but quite unrelated to the whole pattern, subordinated to the pattern and to the empress, is a smaller tomb holding the remains of the Emperor Jehan. When it came his time to die, so far as he could he rejoined his empress. Then one is told by the guide that invaders have stolen the gold sheeting which once covered the domes; that the domes shelter thousands of bats; that when the Taj had been completed, the hundreds of artisans who had constructed the shrine were blinded so that they could never do similar things again. It may all be true but perhaps is not. It makes no difference at all, except to inject the last notes of grief and despair for the end of a whole-souled love between a great man and a great woman. The Taj Mahal has become for the world the beautiful but final memorial to love by fate destroyed — a memorial done perfectly but never to be done again. It strikes all the chords of beauty and feeling, and sounds a dirge as well. It is as complete and imperishable in its meaning as it is unforgettable in its loveliness.

A Trip to the Tuamotos
July, 1962

In these modern days of all the conveniences, Tahiti has an eleven thousand foot runway which handles about a dozen planes in and out each week — jets, turboprops, DC-4's and Connies — and there are other runways at Raiatea and Bora-Bora, where the DC-4 goes each day of the week. But to go to the Tuamotos, one has to go back at least five years to the time when there was only the flying boat, which lands on the water in the lagoon at the destination. The flying boat itself was a jump from stone-age days by way of sail, and later by Diesel engine. Going to the Tuamotus therefore does not take us back to primitive days, but even so they are a lot — a good big lot — more primitive than Papeete, Tahiti.

When we got to the airport at Papeete, the flying boat lying in the lagoon about a thousand feet from shore was especially interesting to me, because it was the same one we had chartered to fly from Fiji to Tonga and on to the other islands of the Tahiti group, way back yonder in 1957. I therefore knew the worst seats on the boat — the ones in the belly of the ship, at the very bottom of the hull and opposite the toilet — and as I watched the other passengers pressing ahead into the launch which was to take us out to the flying boat, I knew we would get those seats as the very last passengers to get in place. Well, we got them, both going out to the Tuamotos and coming home two days later. "We" means Edith and myself and our friend who accompanied us, Simone Hintze, the young wife of the Les Tropiques Manager. With her we had something none of the others had — a bright gal who speaks both Tahitian and Tuamotan, as well as French and English, and who had friends at all our stops.

The office of R.A.I., the French inter-island service, had said to be on hand for departure at 7:30 a.m. We did not, however, start out to the flying boat until nearly 10:30, because we had to wait for members of a travel club to arrive from their place on Moorea. To board a flying boat one climbs down into a launch at the landing, and up into the flying boat where it is tied up at its mooring, and then the reverse procedure at the destination. Nowhere are these things on a level with one another, so two men on the plane and two men on the launch handle the passengers something like a sack of meal. Most of these sacks of meal have arms and legs to help effectively, but when I had crawled down the floor of the launch to where they could reach me, I flew through the air with the greatest of ease and through the hatch into the plane, entirely without giving any help myself.

Our seats at the bottom of the hull were too low to get to see through the portholes until we were under way. The bottom of the hull is the last to leave the water when taking off, and the first to strike it at the landing —and at high speed water is a much harder substance than one imagines. On the way out we paused only at Rangiroa to drop a few Tahitian passengers out in the lagoon, out of sight of the landing, and then flew on to Manihi where we landed in the lagoon about 1:00 p.m.

There are hundreds of islands in the Tuamotus group to be visited, but we made it to just two of them. The Tuamotus (or, literally, "low islands"), are all alike, except that some like the two we saw are larger than the average. On the larger ones, one does not see the other side of the atoll; it is below the horizon. But from the air they spread out as on a great map, a ring of coral reef which here and there has widened to an island of coral sand, covered with coconut trees. It is the coconut trees which are the basis of the economy, and have been since the islands became known to the Western world. The dried nut-meats, or "copra," are expressed for an oil which at its best is a natural cosmetic. Actually, however, it is dried in the sun, becoming in the process somewhat infested with insects, and the oil oxidizes, so that finally the copra, shipped to the western world, yields only an oil which has to be refined before being used in soapmaking and the pressed cake is useful only as cattle feed.

Darwin speculated that atolls were the ring of reef around a tropical island (Tahiti and Moorea and the rest all have them now), which grew at the same rate as the island they enclosed sank under the sea over long periods of time. At Bora-Bora one can see it better: the reef at Bora-Bora has in spots widened into islands on which coconut trees now grow; but the central island still is fairly high and obviously of volcanic origin. No better theory than that of Darwin has been advanced.

On the high islands the reef is cut by passages in the ring of coral wherever there is a fresh-water river to lower the salinity of the sea water and to prevent the growth of the coral polyps. When the islands have sunk below the sea some of these passages remain to allow the tide and the water from the waves breaking over the reef to flow back into the sea. Manihi has only one such opening, but it is very wide (perhaps two hundred feet), and deep, so deep that the bottom is much lower than one can see through the crystal-clear water. There is only a solar tide of less than two feet, but the amount of water that flows through that opening is prodigious, first into the lagoon and then out of the lagoon, at perhaps six knots speed or more. The village of all the inhabitants of the thirty-mile ring of reef and islands is on one lip of this passage to the sea.

A flock of small launches was on hand to receive our passengers, a few to each launch. The current was flowing inward, and as is usual with a swift current, there were fairly high standing waves. Altogether, the launches took us from the lagoon out through the passage and the standing waves to the concrete abutment at the village side of the channel, where we were boosted to the dock. We found the whole village assembled in costume to welcome us, and the chief made a speech to tell us the village was ours. And they nearly made it true, doing everything their limited facilities made possible. To begin with, water is very scarce. Fresh water is rain water drained from the roofs into cisterns, and there are wells where the rain water falling on the island can be pumped from the ground mixed with sea water which is more or less brackish, but can be used for washing. If neither of these suits one as drinking water, they will gather young coconuts and cut them open for drinking, and they are filled tight full with slightly sweet, absolutely pure sap which satisfies thirst very well. But the bathing facilities are outdoors. One stands under the drip from a barrel through the tip of a sprinkling can, which then drops into a tub in which one stands, because it will be used a second time to wash clothes. The bathing place is enclosed by sheet-tin walls.

Meals were served in a pavilion put up by the airline (and prepared by a good chef, although he had forgotten to bring the coffee and not much was left from the last time). We were lodged by the natives in their homes, which were clean but very primitive. Sheets hung from wall to wall multiplied the number of rooms available, but there were no mattresses on the beds. The springs themselves were the foreign luxury, and at that they were softer than the ground — but two nights on just springs covered with a spread was enough for us for a long time to come.

In the evening we were entertained by native dancers, both men and women. Each area — I suppose each island — has its own style. At the fete (annual Bastille Day celebration) in Papeete the competing teams were required to have a minimum of 20 members, and Manihi did not qualify because there were only sixteen members in the team. The kind of dance they did was the "otea," a descriptive dance done with the hands, and singing the distinctive Tuamotan songs, which are very melodious.

There were swarms of children. The South Seas generally are making the greatest contribution percentage-wise to the population explosion, and in Tahiti as elsewhere in the Pacific area something like fifty percent of the population is under the age of twenty. As soon as they are old enough, the more enterprising find their way to the big city at Papeete, but in the meantime they make their own amusements, including playing with sharks.

As part of the landing quai there is a community fish pool. The youngsters (and oldsters) fish in the deep and swift river which is the lagoon entrance, and drop their catch into the community pool which is connected to the outside water for water change, and when one wishes a fish or two for the next meal, he scoops them out of the pool. When we were there the contents of the pool included several sharks of four to six feet length, and at times the kids get down into the pool and wrestle with the sharks, apparently without the slightest fear of getting bitten, even by accident. So I asked if the sharks were toothless and was told that no, they were pets; that there were two kinds of sharks, these and the dangerous ones. One of our group, an American married to a Tahitian and living in Papeete, told me that he used to dive with a young Tahitian in Manihi who is famous even among the Tahitians. They swam in the pass opening to the sea, and when the really big sharks of the dangerous variety came near, he simply pushed them away with his hands, until one day a very small shark did not "push" but nipped a small piece out of the muscle of his shoulder. And from then on the famous pusher did like the rest of the divers: let the big fellows alone and expected them to do the same in return, as they usually do. It seems to be accepted as a rule that the shark, although not predictable, usually attacks cripples or scared and thrashing swimmers, but is indifferent to anything as large as a man if the man shows no signs of being in difficulty. All I know is, if I meet one I shall move in the direction of the exit from the water, and hope I can seem convincingly not too scared.

And again speaking of the deep and swift water of the pass: there were three dogs which quite as a matter of course swam across the pass at slack water to the uninhabited other side. When they came back they would swim upstream against the current and cut across. They seemed quite well aware that a dog is a nice bite-size for the big sharks outside the reef, and when the current was too strong they just doubled back to the other shore and much later tried again. When they finally made it, they shook themselves dry and rejoined the home pack.

The houses of the village were in general rather poor specimens. Of course they are only for shelter from the sun, and from storm and wind, but where they used to be made of native materials they are now more and more made of concrete brick with tin roofs. The tin roofs are understandable as better for collecting rain water for the cistern, but they definitely lack the charm of the coconut thatch. And most of the credit for copra is used for food in cans. There is a little shop in the village and its stock is mostly salmon, mackerel, sardines, bully beef and other canned meats. The natural island diet was fish and coconut, and it produced people with perfect health and perfect teeth. But for some strange reason which the wisest have not yet explained convincingly, white rice and white flour, the whiter the better, have been accepted with bad teeth and bad health as being very much better wherever civilization as practiced by the white man has been brought to a native population. The natives here still eat fish from the sea, but the coconut has become copra or food for the pigs, more than food for man, and a can of corned beef with a loaf of French bread is an almost ideal picnic lunch or a dinner at home.

The Tahitians are happy-go-lucky and delightful by our western standards. Their islands had no natural wealth but camphor trees and the coconut, an island covered with the fossilized guano called phosphate rock, and pearl shell in the lagoons. All these except the coconut have been taken away at a profit to the merchants and the white man, but not to the profit of the Tahitians themselves. The shell can reproduce, and is now taken under controlled conditions, and copra can be made and collected year by year, but both are still producing more profit for the white man than for the native. There is now a plan to establish an "industrial section" at Papeete, but what will be industrialized is not yet clear.

The passengers of our plane had been urged by the airline to bring gifts for the natives, who actually do not receive any special payment for their hospitality, and who in the area of their means extended very warm hospitality. Edith remembered to do this, to the delight of the many children and adults, and when we presented a special gift to our host, he in return gave us two glass floats such as cost fifteen or more dollars in Hawaii or at home; which simply illustrates once more that one cannot get ahead of the Tahitians in the matter of making gifts, except perhaps to the children who yet give very warm smiles and evident delight as a more than adequate return.

It was a most worthwhile trip, a most illuminating trip. Even at so short a range as Papeete, the outer islands had remained something of a mystery. Now they are seen as just more islands and more people, with a system of living just a bit more primitive than Tahiti's but in principle much the same. Nowhere, on the other hand, is there still the spot out of touch with the world, of which the romancers have written for the last twenty years. They have all heard of all we have, and are not too much impressed. It is still true that bluff and pretense are discounted, and that a stuffed shirt makes no impression and no progress at all. It is still true that in the general philosophy of living we can learn much from the Polynesian. Life should be simple and simply lived, with a minimum of pretense.

Tahiti — An Island Paradise
May, 1958

I have always had a romantic interest in the South Seas — particularly in the area covering Tahiti, Samoa and Fiji — and in the past couple of years Mrs. Rehnborg and I have had the chance, after 40 years of wishing to do so, to visit the area, and to acquire some first hand information, as well as to develop a very sincere admiration for, and interest in, the area and its people.

The area we have grown to know better stretches from French Polynesia in the east to the beginnings of Micronesia in Fiji and New Caledonia — a distance of over 3000 miles. There are literally hundreds of islands in this expanse of the Pacific Ocean, of which the total land area is extremely small when compared to the tremendous expanse of the ocean surrounding them. Always, on these islands, one gets the effect of terrific isolation in a very great expanse of sea.

The Western world has invaded the whole area, generally to the harm of the people that the first explorers found there, beginning with Captain Cook. But the area is still predominantly "native," and perhaps even Captain Cook would recognize the present inhabitants as closely similar to those he saw when he first arrived. In the eastern part, and northward to Hawaii and southward to New Zealand, this population is predominantly Polynesian — people with glossy black wavy hair and light brown skins — and in the west are the Micronesians, who have very dark brown skin and kinky hair, with all varieties of graduated mixtures of tan and brown in between.

No one knows exactly the progression by which the Pacific islands became inhabited, or where the inhabitants came from. The whole history of the human race, it should be remembered, is many hundreds of times as long a period as that covered by all of our written histories, and during all that time there has been a slow but constant movement of many varieties of human beings over most of the surface of the earth. What we call races, for example, are merely distinct varieties of the human species developed in their specialized characteristics by isolation, and not by any absolute difference in human attributes or characteristics. When, for example, we speak of a "pure" race of nationality, we do not mean what we think we do.

Far enough back in human history, any one outside an immediate human family was an enemy. Then, when men had achieved a greater degree of cooperation in groups, any one outside the group was an enemy. This natural and wild caution in dealing with unknown individuals, when intensified by geographical separation of the groups, resulted in the almost complete isolation of these groups from one another over relatively enormous periods of time. Because of forced mingling, such as occurred in the capture of "enemies" in warfare, and of migration into marginal areas between "tribes," a considerable amount of mixing took place; but essentially there were particular differences from group to group, intensified by area, climate, food, habits, and language. These various factors, however, produced variations between the separated groups of so marked a character that even in the most ancient pages of history there was recognition of substantial difference between various kinds of men from various areas.

Yet even before this there had been at first an essential sameness as generalized "humanity," and then diversification because of group isolation, with some small degree of mingling and exchanges. The so-called racial groups, which developed and were differentiated some time before the dawn of history, were all of mixed origin, but generally similar to one another within the regional group.

Take illustrations from nature. On the Galapagos Islands there are thrush, all birds of one species, which on any one of the islands are clearly different from the same species of birds on all the other islands of the group. Clearly, to the eyes of the ornithologist, they originated as one species and one variety of thrush on a much larger expanse of land, which was separated into islands as the land subsided into the sea; and the separated bird groups of the one species, isolated from other groups by the water which they did not attempt to cross by flying, in time developed by isolation into different varieties of one species. Again, on the island of Kauai in the Hawaiian group there is a central mountain which is worn by the constant erosion of rainfall into valleys separated by very sharp ridges of rock. In each of the valleys so created between ridges there is a separate variety of one species of snail, and again the variations are due to separation and isolation. To interbreed the varieties in each case produces something near the original variety from which the specialized varieties developed.

In the same way, any group of varieties of human beings can be interbred to produce a generalized type. In all probability this generalized type is very much like the original human type from which the so-called individual races developed, and they developed and differed almost entirely because of the effect of isolation in separated areas over extremely long periods of time. Perhaps the nearest thing to this remingling that we have at the present time is today's population of the Hawaiian Islands.

Many scientists have "explained" where the people of Polynesia came from, as if they had been picked up from one place and put down in another. They have been separated too short a while for their difference from other groups to be due to isolation, because the Polynesian islands have only been populated by human beings for a matter of a couple of thousand years. But wherever they started from, there should be a trail of their passing in other areas. They came from somewhere. Some scientists say that they came from Southeast Asia, and point to a group of human beings of similar type who live in the mountains between Burma, Indo-China and China. This runs into the difficulty that between Southeast Asia, and, for example, Tahiti, there is very little evidence, in the type and characteristics of the inhabitants of the intervening islands stretching over the supposed route of some 4000 miles, to indicate that the Polynesians stopped by there, as they would have in the case of migration, or that they mingled with the population which now lives there.

Other scientists insist that the Polynesians came from South America, and the book *Kon-Tiki*, which many of us have read (and which certainly deserves reading), was written partly in support of this theory. Neither theory is altogether convincing, and the movement of people may have been a more complex affair than either theory accounts for. In any case, the movement, or mixture, or both, occurred about 2000 years ago, and produced a group, or variety, of human beings unlike any group found elsewhere.

The order in which the successive invasions of the islands occurred is somewhat more precisely determined. The language spoken in Hawaii, in Tahiti, and the Tuamotus, among the Maori of New Zealand and as far west as Samoa, is so similar over the whole area that when Captain Cook in the 1700's took natives from one area to another area of the South Seas, the men he took with him were able to talk to the inhabitants of the other area.

En route to Tahiti, the Rehnborgs stop over in Honolulu, where they are greeted with flower leis.

On arriving in Papeete, Tahiti, Edith and Carl, center, receive warm welcome from their many Tahitian friends.

Among the Polynesians, who had no written language, history was stored in the minds of men. They had certain priests whose business it was to memorize (and to remember) the genealogies of the chiefs. One of the first investigators along this line of inquiry could show that the genealogy recited by the priests of Hawaii for the most recent period of approximately 900 years was different from the genealogy recited by the priests in Tahiti for the same period; while for the centuries earlier than that the genealogies were identical. The total of either list would amount, allowing some estimated figure for each generation, to about

2000 years of "history" for each group. His first finding, concerning the age of the settlement in Hawaii, has been confirmed by making a radiocarbon check of ancient campfires on the south end of the main island of Hawaii, where the Hawaiians themselves say that their ancestors first landed. The age of the carbon of these ancient campfires, by the radiocarbon method of dating, is about 900 years.

The migration of the Polynesians from island to island probably resulted from population pressure. Exactly in the same manner as a population of slipper animalcules allowed to multiply in a glass of water, a human population in a restricted area will grow until, as a group, it cannot find enough food or enough room in the area, unless some control on population is applied. The slipper animalcule has no place to go, and the whole group comes finally to the end of the food supply, and dies. A human population is able to modify this result for itself by various acts of reason. The forms of control used by the Tahitians were abortion, infanticide, internecine warfare, cannibalism, and migration. It was migration which populated the islands originally, and which spread the population from island to island.

In this process, the Polynesians became perhaps the world's most daring and successful navigators, and it was navigation by the stars. They invented a sort of "sextant" with an artificial horizon by which they could determine latitude, and they used this instrument to return home from a voyage of exploration, or in the visits and exchanges between the islands which eventually developed. The navigating instrument was made with a coconut shell. The shell was partly filled

Building a vacation home on the Rehnborgs' land at Punaauia, Tahiti, was not a complicated process. The final result, complete with pandanus roofing, had a great view of the ocean and the island of Moorea across the strait.

Mr. Rehnborg sits outside the lanai which is open to the South Sea breezes, enjoying the balmy climate.

The Rehnborgs took great pleasure in furnishing their Tahitian home with native arts and crafts, and loved the relaxed lifestyle. Mrs. Rehnborg is wearing a special headdress woven of flowers and fronds.

with water, and two holes were bored in the upper part of the shell. When the light of a chosen star, reflected from the true level surface of the enclosed water, could be seen through the other hole, the navigator had reached the parallel of latitude on which his own island lay. The shell had been calibrated at the home island at the start of the journey, and the position of a known star crossing overhead had been used to line up the sight. Therefore, a Tahitian, for example, returning from Honolulu, would know that his own island was either to the west or the east of his own position when he was able to line up the particular star to which his shell was calibrated. He would sail south from Honolulu until he had reached the meridian of his own island and of the sights of his shell, and then sail in the proper direction, either west or east, until he came to his home port.

The other population controls — abortion, infanticide, warfare, and cannibalism — sound horrible to us, but were considered both natural and necessary by the Polynesians. Human beings, like other forms of animal life, breed usually at such a rate that more individuals are born than die in any given period. The inevitable result of such a progression, however slow, in either direction, will finally result either in the extinction of the group, if the birth rate is too low, or in an absolutely unmanageable increase in population, if the birth rate is too high.

Normally, the birth rate is too high, and for that reason the world itself, as a whole, is now faced with the problem of population increase, which will have to be solved if the human race is to survive. We may find in the end that we have to use even more extreme measures than were used by the Polynesians, but at least on the islands of the Pacific the practical problem was met head-on. Birth control by other means than death to the infant was not known to the Polynesians, but abortion has always been practiced in the human race, and infanticide is the perfectly simple process of putting the infant to death. These methods were used as a matter of course, and as a matter of absolute necessity. There would otherwise simply not have been enough food for the living population.

Similarly, with cannibalism it was perfectly obvious, if one had no preconceptions, that a man was at least as good a source of meat as a pig. Pigs they had brought with them, and pigs they ate, and when the antisocial members of the group, or captured enemies, were sacrificed to the gods and then eaten, these carcasses became known as "long pig."

Warfare, in turn, was simply the "football games" of these ancient populations — a sporting event — and the slain were eaten quite as matter of factly as were the victims sacrificed to the gods. In the warfare there usually was no rancor at all. Simply, the chief of one village, over some fancied or real difference, usually not of any very serious character, would notify the chief of another village that at a certain time on the following day he and his men were going to invade and destroy the second group.

The fighting was strictly by appointment, and when it had continued long enough to satisfy the point of honor involved, the fight was discontinued by some signal from either chief, and everybody became friends again on the spot. If one of the opposing teams lived in a valley with no other outlet than the entrance held by the opposing team, the women and children would be sent out through the opposing line, and on the way out would sometimes deliver a message of friendliness from a relative in the village being evacuated to some member of the fighting team of the opposition. The whole thing was a completely sporting proposition. Nobody was ever surprised or ambushed. The fight was a scheduled event in broad daylight. Sometimes, even, if there was no pressing need for meat, and no great number of people needed to be killed to supply it, the point of honor would be settled by single combat of one champion from each of the villages, and the death of one of these champions settled the dispute in favor of the winner.

We do not have any western analogies for the culture which was developed by the Polynesians, and for their customs as a society.

As has been mentioned, there is no certainty as to where the Polynesians originated. Their own legends say they came from the east, or from the direction of South America, but there is no kind of history available, except these and other legends. They do not look like any other race. If they are a mixture, as is possible, no one knows where the melting pot for this mixture lay, or whether the islands of the Pacific were themselves the melting pot. Their languages are all so very closely related that it is virtually certain all of these groups were members of one central clan, or tribe, with a well-developed language and an advanced Stone Age culture.

Trying to find the origins of this culture, and of the developed language, and of the people themselves, constitutes a first-class mystery. All the experts on the Polynesians and their customs disagree. The best they can do in reaching an agreement is to have a fairly good notion, drawn from the Polynesians themselves, of the development of the people over the past two thousand years. This agreement extends to saying that they were governed by chiefs, but that there was not any common government for the whole racial group. There was not, frequently, even a common government for one island, although they sometimes, here and there, approached this situation. Mostly the Polynesians lived as special groups — the Samoans, the Maoris, the Tahitians, the Marquesans, and so on — with noticeable differences in their languages and in their social customs, and even in the general appearance of the people themselves. Each group was further divided into tribes, or clans, sometimes as many as the number of separate valley watershed divisions on a single island, and these tribes were rarely at peace with one another.

All the early discoverers agree that the Polynesians were a beautiful people. They were fierce, because the unending competition for room and for food made offensive and defensive warfare commonplace. They lived quite naturally and spontaneously, plagued only by their problem of finding or growing enough food for a constantly overflowing flood of population on restricted areas, and by the necessity for defending what they managed to secure against the incursions and claims of other tribes. Bitter as this struggle must have been, they did it with song and laughter, as if they were playing a game, without any apparent notion that any part of the struggle was tragic.

They lived on islands of surpassing beauty, and they themselves were beautiful. The range of temperatures in these islands is almost steadily between the low 70's and the high 80's. The air itself is like a caress. There is crystal clearness and plenty of sunshine, and on the high islands, copious rainfall in the hills, and plenty of water. Even in the low islands, or atolls, there is plenty of drinking water in the young coconut, and the sea all about for cleanliness. Very little but coconuts grows on the low islands, but the high islands are volcanic and incredibly rich, and the vegetation is lush and luxuriant.

And the people themselves are incredibly beautiful — the men of magnificent physique and the women beautiful by any standard. It is very probable that in these isolated areas, where the terms of living had balanced themselves out, that these people, living on a natural and adequate diet, and superbly healthy, did not have a single ailment of the kinds that plague the western world. No contagious or infectious diseases, not even the common cold. Dental caries was an unknown thing. Very old people wore their teeth down on rough food, but nobody lost any teeth. It is quite probable that the only disease they suffered from, and then not extensively, was filariasis, the parasite which causes

In a photo taken in Bermuda in the 50's, C.F. Rehnborg finds the fish
population as interested in him as he was in them. That the diving gear was
somewhat antiquated seemed not to bother him at all!

elephantiasis, and which is spread from person to person by bush mosquitoes.

These were the people, outstandingly attractive as human beings living lives of love and laughter and song, with vigorous dances and vigorous warfare, and a tremendous lust for living, who were found by the first of the intruders. The traders from the west brought their governments, and the governments took possession of all of Oceania for exploitation.

For very small payments, usually in the form of booze, the traders persuaded the chiefs to let them denude the high islands of their camphorwood and sandalwood. With the backing of their own governments, they moved into the lagoons of the atolls and mined the pearl shell and pearls. Among natural mineral resources, gold and manganese were discovered in Fiji, and a potash deposit near Tahiti, and these have been taken away also. The copra trade was organized and developed for the benefit of the interlopers, not the natives. Now, with many of the areas moving toward autonomy, the natives will again gain some measure of control over their own lands. They will have to develop their natural resources, and to sell their sunshine as an export, but whatever natural resources were there, are gone. Nobody replanted the camphorwood and sandalwood forests. Nobody is stopping the present exploitation of the hardwood forests on some of the islands.

In the outlying areas, such as New Zealand and Hawaii, the natives have simply been dispossessed of their lands, finally and completely. Belatedly, the governments controlling the remaining areas have begun again to consider the rights of the natives as human beings, and have put guards around these rights, such as forbidding the sale of their lands by the natives to citizens of the outside world.

But all this is very late, and it does not restore what was there before. Disease and liquor and the white man's diet have in many areas decimated the population and reduced the physical stamina of the natives. And in Tahiti there are relatively few pure Tahitians left. In the main the population is Tahitian mixed with Chinese and French and other western nationalities. The mixture has much to recommend itself in the final result, but it is not a native stock.

Summing up this line of thought, it can be said that the advent of the white man in the islands was almost an unmitigated calamity.

lothing was brought to the natives that they needed; much was taken way that they should now have. It is a complete fallacy to believe that ecause our system is ours, it is also the best for everyone else. It quite imply is not. Just as, in the name of progress, we have wrecked and lespoiled most of the natural resources of our own land, so, in combination with other westerners like ourselves, we have wrecked a beautiful and primitive native people and their culture. What we have given them of western progress — if it is indeed progress — does not fit them, and they did not need it. The whole effort, now, should be to preserve what is left.

Notes From A Trip To Europe

Mr. Rehnborg went to Europe in 1954 to investigate the possibility of selling Nutrilite in those countries. Unfortunately, difficult times in the U.S. and the maze of international regulations eventually persuaded him to retreat from his original aggressive plans. It is interesting to point out that 30 years later, in 1984, Nutrilite was finally introduced into Germany and the United Kingdom. Plans are now under way for introductions into France, Belgium and the Netherlands.

Les and I left Los Angeles at five minutes past midnight on the morning of April 7th. The first stop was Winnipeg, then the airfield in Greenland, and next Copenhagen, the whole flight taking about 24 hours. We arrived in Copenhagen at 9 o'clock on the morning of the 8th. The SAS does not merely feed you on these flights, it overfeeds you. We had berths, but it was at least two hours before the berths were made down, and we were put to bed. In those two hours we were fed a midnight snack that ran on and on, and all the schnapps that one wished to drink. We first started sight-seeing when we approached Winnipeg the next morning. It was weeks before the beginning of spring, and the weather in Winnipeg was rather cold, not far from freezing; and the country had been inundated by recent rain and melting snow and looked like a quagmire. It is almost completely flat and rather uninteresting.

Taking off from Winnipeg, we went straight northeast over the tundra country, then across Hudson's Bay and the very northern tip of Labrador, and thence to Greenland. The ice was just breaking up and the tundra country to the south was still snow and ice covered. This is the most desolate stretch of inhospitable country one can imagine Doubtless there were many hundreds of Eskimos and other inhabitants in the areas we traversed, but at 18,000 feet, the height at which we flew, such details are too small to catch the eye and the effect was of a land which had never been visited by people. There are, of course, no roads whatever, and the tundra country north of Winnipeg is the flattened surface gouged into the ancient shield of Laurentian rock by the glaciers of the ice age, so that there is nearly as much water surface in lakes as land surface. The land surface is covered by forests of spruce and jack pines, but at our height they looked more like moss than trees. There were frequent snow squalls below us over the land section of northern Canada; but beginning over the reaches of Hudson's Bay, we had clear weather all the way into Greenland and beyond so that we could see an immense vista of icy landscape. The whole area was snow-covered except where occasional bare rocks and rocky hills showed through, and from the northern tip of Labrador on across Baffin Land and other islands of the Arctic and into Greenland, the mountains grew higher and higher, and the effect was inexpressibly grand and impressive, but always inhospitable and barren.

The airport in Greenland is at the head of one of the longest fjords in the world, running inland well over a hundred miles from the coast, and as the sun sets rather late at this season of the year, we had the opportunity to see a great deal of the landscape and to take pictures of it.

The airport at the head of the fjord is also an American military base with about 3,000 men stationed there on rotation periods of a year. We were driven from the plane to the dining hall where, as usual, we were given something to eat, and the buses were run by American soldiers. The temperature was 18 above zero. I talked with one of the boys who had been there 9 months and had 3 months to go, and he said he didn't mind the climate so much as he minded the fact that there were no women, and as the Eskimos are not permitted to come to the reservation and the soldiers are not permitted to leave it, he couldn't even count Eskimo women. He said the highest temperature in summer was in the neighborhood of 45 degrees, but in spite of that temperature, there were enormous numbers of wild flowers and swarms of mosquitoes as soon as the temperature got above freezing and stayed there.

Contrary to my long-time impression, the glaciers of Greenland do not come down to the ocean except in the northern half of the island.

The fjords, of course, are the channels by which the glaciers formerly reached the sea; but at present the ice cap begins perhaps 120-130 miles from the coast, first as glacier ends in the valleys and then as deeper and deeper ice sheets that finally cover the mountains themselves, until the center of the island is completely covered with the ice cap. The coastal hills are tremendous and beautiful but barren, and they are dusted with snow, but again oddly enough there isn't a great deal of snow or rain in the area. It has a very light fall. The reason for the ice cap is that the rainfall is greater than the melting rate. Even at that the melting rate is now slightly larger than the rainfall rate so that the glaciers are receding.

Circling the field before we came in, it seemed impossible that a plane could sit down on what looked like a tiny patch of runway cut so deep between the hills at the shore of the fjord, but it came in quite easily and rolled to a stop on the snow and ice partly cleared away from the runway itself. The plane was surprisingly sure-footed, both on the field and when it rolled off the field to the spaces in front of the airfield sheds. And the hills which had looked big, but not enormous, from the air, became tremendous when viewed from below.

I don't see how the boys stationed there put up with it, because it is as cheerless as anything I have ever seen. They even had a movie theatre but it had burned down. The only thing that looked comfortable at all was the building maintained by the airline to debark its passengers for the 45 minutes to an hour that we stayed at the airfield. The building contains a curio shop, but the curios all come from America or from Denmark. I found one single thing in the whole room that had been made by a native, a little statue of an Eskimo woman carved by an Eskimo from a walrus tooth, and I bought it, which left them with nothing made by natives. The women who sold it to me said she had become very attached to it and was sorry to see it go.

The plane had been refueled and we took off just as night was falling, somewhere between 8:30 and 9:00 local time. It became dark as we reached the edge of the ice cap, and from then we flew through the night until we flew over the northern part of Denmark in the morning. It never got entirely dark, however, because the sun was near enough to the horizon in the north at midnight to keep the sky gray.

In Copenhagen we drove at once to the Codan Hotel, where we had very nice rooms on the waterfront. Copenhagen is a lovely city and the people are delightful. We stayed in Copenhagen for two days until Monday the 10th, when we took the plane to Frankfurt. These two days were entirely given to sight-seeing except that we confirmed again that Copenhagen or Denmark at least does not represent any immediate opportunity for us because of its governmental form. It is a strictly socialist state and everything is regulated even down to the dosage of vitamins that an individual may take without orders from a physician; but we saw also what is evident throughout Europe, and that is that a public understanding of the subject of vitamins is about at the stage it was in the United States twenty years ago. The best products offered are about on a par with the One-a-Day brand here, small dosages of a restricted number of factors. The general idea of a wide range of factors, and specifically that the wide range is needed in nutrition, has not yet penetrated. It is Germany, together with the fact that Germany now ranks third among the trading nations of the world, that represents our tremendous opportunity. The market is there and nobody has started to develop it, not even any local firms and certainly none from our side of the water.

We made a motor tour of the island on which Copenhagen is located, visiting Helsingor (which is the Elsinore of Shakespeare's Hamlet) and having lunch at the hotel I visited once before, the Storekro, which means big inn, which was the high point of gastronomic delight this time as it was the time before. The food is strictly scrumptious. We had a guide supplied by the hotel whose English was as bad as my Danish would have been if I had tried it. But I already knew the points we saw so that I was able to act as interpreter. We found beautiful weather in Denmark, which followed us for the rest of the trip, as we did not even see rain during all the time we were there. Spring had begun to arrive in Denmark. Most of the trees were still bare, although there were some flower, but the air was crisp and rather cold. Our next stop was Frankfurt.

We were met Sunday afternoon at the Frankfurt airport in the company car, which is a Mercedes-Benz 220, a very nice car indeed as it should be, costing about $5,400 U.S. in Germany, which would even be a high price in the United States.

Before leaving Frankfurt we took a few days off and borrowed a car to make a trip down the autobahn and east of Heidelberg into the country so that we could see some areas which were not commonly visited by the tourist routes. The most interesting part was a visit to an 800-year-old town named Bad Wimpfel on the Neckar River east of Heidelberg, which was the high point of our European trip. It was built around an old keep or tower on a bluff overlooking a bend in the Neckar, and our hotel practically hung over the river. The town was old and very interesting indeed. The trains and canal boats went past the hotel, and I am continually amazed at what the Germans have done to these rivers. Normally, they would not be extremely deep and probably ran over rapids, but the Germans have put in check dams and locks at regular intervals all the way up the Rhine and all the ay up these branches, and the rivers are actually canals with flowing water which handle a tremendous amount of traffic.

After returning to Frankfurt we went on to Belgium, and rejoined the courier to make several preliminary investigations, and a short time later I flew down to meet him at Brussels. We found the Belgian government as easy to deal with as the German government had been difficult. They were enthusiastically willing to make it very easy indeed for us to get to introduce our product into Belgium, and we have every prospect of doing so because Soors on later investigation turned out to be quite competent to handle the details of the business, at least in the beginning, especially with the help of his wife, who is a most remarkable young woman. While there Les and I were driven by Soors over to The Hague to see the most promising of the several shipbuilding companies we contacted with reference to a research boat, with the idea of seeing whether they could build a sailing vessel of smaller size to enable us to tackle the deal without the tremendous expense involved in getting a motor vessel. They referred us in turn to a firm in Amsterdam, to which we drove, and they gave a tentative price for a 130-foot boat of approximately $300,000 which we will now use as a starting point to compare similar shipyards in the United States. I might add that subsequently we have got in touch with the Alden Company of Boston with regard to this.

After a few days in Belgium, we drove down to Paris. We stayed at the Claridge Hotel on the Champs d'Elysees near the Arc de Triomphe. We saw the usual tourist attractions, the Eiffel Tower, The Louvre, Versailles and several night clubs. It was springtime in Paris and the

weather was beautiful, and altogether it was even lovelier than I ha̶
been led to expect. Particularly, we did not find it staggeringly expensiv̶
because, being under the care of a French-speaking couple, we probabl̶
fared about as well as any French group would have fared and did no̶
pay tourist prices for everything we wanted or saw. The suite at the hote̶
which we occupied, however, was about the last word. I have never see̶r
anything quite so gorgeously supplied as that suite. It was o̶:
tremendous size, some 75 feet long and about 50 feet wide, for thre̶e
rooms and a few service rooms. All of it cost somewhat less than to sta̶y
in a very much smaller suite at the Waldorf. On May 1st, I flew Avianca̶
by way of Madrid and Lisbon and the Canaries to Bermuda where I met
Mrs. Rehnborg. Les stayed with the Soors family to return to Brussels
and then to continue his trip through other parts of Europe. Les' trip of
course is reported separately.

Summarizing, I would say that we should go at once into Germany
and Belgium with the idea subsequently of either going into Scandi-
navia and other countries such as Switzerland directly, or by way of our
establishments in Belgium and Germany. I think that our immediate
plans should include details of arrangements for going into Belgium and
Germany, and since we have to wait for a certain length of time still for
development of the product which is to be sold, there will be time to
investigate further the personnel which is to be trained and to make
another trip to arrange the details. Immediately, however, I think we
should prepare the literature which is to be used in Belgium and
Germany and to bring our representative home, both because his work
in Germany can be considered to be completed and because he can
supervise here the preparation of this literature by overseeing the
translation and retranslation through local agencies.

* * * * * * * * *

We have seen four countries, and in each I have gotten the impression of insularity. We read in our papers of the affairs of Europe, and get
the impression that the countries, as whole populations, are keenly
aware of their own nearness and interdependence, and are conscious
that Western Europe is the economic unit we know it is. Actually what
we are reading are the reports of the activities of chancelleries and
legislative bodies in the various countries.

In each country the man in the street seems blissfully unaware that
any country other than his own exists. He speaks no language but that

f his own country, usually, and foreigners are foreigners from wherever they may come. He is solely concerned with the persons and events of his own neighborhood, but of course, as we do, he reads the papers and knows there are larger international events.

This, of course, also describes our own man in the street, but we have the partial excuse that our area is continent-wide and separated from other areas by oceans, and that therefore the international events are distant in fact, not remote because they are ignored.

I feel the elation of a discoverer in having it dawn on me that people are much alike everywhere, and that the difference in reading about various peoples and seeing them lies in the fact that one does not have enough imagination, without actually seeing them, to make the population live and breathe and go about its daily affairs.

But even after seeing them, I am still amazed that so many varying peoples can live on such small areas, all highly civilized, for so many centuries, without devising and using some common language for communication between various populations. Only the exceptional individual in each population takes the trouble or accepts the responsibility for making the contracts outside the borders of his own country which are made by using the language of the other country in addition to his own — and yet it is almost an axiom of history that common language does promote amity between the countries using the language.

Travel Notes From A Trip To Micronesia

July 1970

This trip was undertaken when C.F. Rehnborg was 83 years of age and it was the last major long-distance traveling that he did. His keen interest in everything around him, and his observations about the areas in which he traveled, were characteristic of his immense enjoyment of life.

It is now near the end of our visit to Truk and we are about to go on tomorrow afternoon to Saipan, and after that to Yap and Koror, and finally to Guam where we will stay and from which we will go to Japan. Then the tour will continue back to Honolulu by way of Ponape without us. Ponape we are sorry to miss, but it is not anything that makes me feel disturbed because it is an island which has about 300 to 400 inches of rain per year, and the fair weather does not last for very long at a time.

Truk is the name of the lagoon here which contains a number of islands, each of several hundred acres. The name applies to the whole group throughout; Lagoon, was also the name of the various islands. While they have different names, they are not commonly used. We went yesterday from this island to another at the other side of the lagoon. We could see, as we did when we came in on the plane, that it is in fact an almost continuous lagoon extending in a general oval of 40 miles in diameter.

During World War II the Japanese kept their fleet in this lagoon, and we made it very difficult for them to do anything else. They didn't know where our fleet was, and we didn't let them know. But finally after we had bombed them almost as badly here as they bombed us at Honolulu, they had to get out, or felt that they did, and look for our fleet. They found it in the Philippines, and they came to our position at the end of the strait in such a manner that each ship coming through had to meet the American fleet as a lone ship. In military problems it is called "crossing the T." We practically destroyed every ship in the Japanese fleet and, a few days later when we bombed Japan with the first of the atom bombs, they were quite ready to surrender and did so when the second bomb was dropped. One of the members of our tour group is a man who was in the last war, I would say "up to his chin," and he has it very well organized in his memory. He is as interested in Truk as any place because, of course, in the wartime he never saw it.

Yesterday at this distant island we went to — it was private property — we met the girl who is the daughter of the owner and she gave us permission to use it. Everybody on the boat except a very few of us had snorkel gear, and so they all went over the side and onto the shore as soon as they arrived. I stayed on the boat because it takes practically a whole ship's crew to get me in the water and out of it again.

The island was a Japanese refuge of one kind or another, and on the shore where the boat went in they had left a very large crane on a very large buoy. This was used to bring out and put into the various vessels their heavy equipment and replacements when the Japanese fleet was in Truk. Before they left it this was one of the things that was shot by the American invaders and left where it was sunk. It makes a very picturesque addition to the scenery, but it was definitely not a useful part of a swimming expedition.

The water, however, was absolutely wonderful. It was clear blue and extended near the island to depths of up to 100 feet. There was much water of a depth of say 15 feet, which was used by our group for their underwater explorations. All the people on the boat that had snorkeling equipment were very good at using it. There were even a father and a son whose hobby was taking underwater photographs. They used all their equipment and were of interest to everyone else down in the water with them.

This is the most beautiful place to which we have come. It is just as hot, nearly, as any other place because it is so near the equator, but it is a tremendous sight. This type of lagoon, 40 miles in diameter, does not occur anyplace else, apparently. A very large island with mountains sank here and became a number of islands in a very large lagoon, because the lagoon built up from the former level of the islands and finally enclosed them all. It is not anything I know much about, except that the land sank here and the water rose, by whatever system it is ascribed to.

For example, when the last Ice Age ended, the water that was in the continental glaciers came back into the sea, and this amounted to approximately as much as from 400 to 600 feet increase in the sea level. The island that resulted here left hills sticking up, but the original reef around the very large island, which was there when all of this started, already had a coral reef which was increasingly submerged as the level of the water rose over perhaps 1,000 to 2,000 years.

At the end, the lagoon reefs around the original large island were the same reefs that are around the very large group of islands that are here now, and it was only the reef near the sea on these islands that was encouraged by the conditions to grow further. The result is a very large lagoon enclosing the group of islands, none of which at the present time have full-grown reefs, but there is the peculiarity that the ocean swell is entirely lacking. There are waves kicked up by breezes, but they are waves of from say 3 to 5 feet. The swells of the deep ocean don't come through the lagoon entrances.

Today we are going to go on our last sail on the boat we used yesterday. I forgot to mention that it is a trimaran, about 60 feet long — but, of course, very wide since it has three hulls and very fast because the catamaran shape goes through the water faster than a beamed boat shape. The water is not shoved away from the hull, except for a very small number of inches, because the supporting hulls are narrow and very deep. This one goes down something over three feet under the water, and the three hulls create less fluid friction with the water at any speed than would the same amount of cargo space in a standard-type hull.

Part VII
PERSONAL LETTERS AND MUSINGS

Sammie Is Two

Sammie is two.

Sammie is probably the only name he will get, but his real given names are Carl Reinhold. When he was born (by Caesarean section) Rada, the nurse, brought him down from the operating room and laid him on the bench in the nursery beside a little "premie," and there Sammie's nearly ten pounds were such an astonishing contrast to the other baby's three or so, that Rada, who always invents nicknames for the babies, called him Samson, and the name stuck. Rada also called him Mister Filthy McNasty on several subsequent occasions which do not need describing in detail, but that name was allowed to lapse by neglect.

That morning, too, I saw Rada several times manipulating one of Sammie's ears, but it didn't change it any. Sammie had apparently spent part of his latest weeks before the doctors lifted him from his cozy nest putting the best part of his weight on that ear, because it was quite definitely the sort of ear that mauling makes for pugs and wrestlers. He still has it. I call it his cauliflower ear, and I suspect I love its divergence from normal far more than I would a perfectly formed ear. To me it has always seemed so exactly in keeping with his masculinity. Only one person has ever mistaken him for a girl, and that was when he was very small, and I, of course, thought that woman somewhat weak-minded or else poor of sight.

Sammie has hair so blond that it is like white gold. For a long time it curled in little waves all over his head, but when he had a little boy haircut, which was soon, all that was left was just a suggestion of a wave. When he was walking, and wearing blue corduroy overalls and polo shirt, the baby haircut didn't match the rest of him, but it was a jolt to lose those tumbled curls. Sammie has blue eyes, verging on hazel, and a beautiful long head, high above the ears but without any exaggerations of contour. The proportions of his head are so balanced, in fact, that one does not get the impression of a skull or bony frame so much as the sense of a delicately fashioned case for a thinking machine, almost fragile of structure and translucent of texture, so that his cobwebby hair seems like the light of his mind.

And the mind is there. I have the deep conviction that he will be a notable personage. I do not mean that he will be of necessity notably

good or bad, or a giant or pygmy in commerce, but just that he will have
a mind so high and deep that it can hold great subjects in true
proportion, and illuminate deep convictions so that other people can
comprehend them. Such a mind is too large for politics or religions of
formal types. It is of necessity free from stereotyped beliefs and
unreasoning prejudices. One can watch very readily that even this small
mite of a Sammie at two can distinguish between just and orderly
discipline and what, apparently, he considers to be unreasonable interference. He is perfectly amenable to ordered discipline, but reacts
vehemently to "interference" — especially unnecessary orders. Even the
adult who gives them can see, on reflection, that they were in fact not
necessary. Sammie says so by doing carefully, exactly what he has been
ordered not to do. But sometimes disobedience is mischief, and then he
looks to see how you are taking it, and says gravely, "No do dat," and
actually stops doing it.

Sallie and her tribe came home from China two days before
Christmas. Some two weeks earlier we had a letter saying they were
coming, and Sammie's pet game became the detailed account of how the
boat would dock at San Pedro, and on it would be "Sayee, Fooey, Moan,
Choey, Fran, Wang, and Ki." Actually, however, they found the boat
would be a matter of nine days at San Francisco, so they all came down
by train, and I went up and met them. Now the only "big boat" that
Sammie knows are the two dismantled hulks which are anchored off the
coast in the summer for fishing barges, and which are now tied up near
the Arches for storage and repairs, and he points out the larger of those,
when we pass, as the boat that brought Sallie and Fuzzie and Melon and
Chuppie and Wang and Kyle and Sara Frances.

When Sallie's letter came, she asked if we could spare the kiddie
koop for Sara Frances. Sammie had been using it ever since he came
home at two weeks of age, and we had not even considered promoting
him to the big bed, but now we decided the request was a good reason, so
we dispossessed him at once and I took the koop to the shop and painted
it. Sammie was fascinated with the big bed, especially as a place to
bounce, but it was a job getting him to lie somewhere on top of it, big as it
was. He sleeps usually lying on his stomach, and in the koop he edged
forward like a little grub until the top of his head touched the screen at
the top. Now there was no limit except the wall at the head of the bed,
and sometimes he would toss a little first, so that he was not pointed at

the top of the bed, and then he would hitch and hitch until at last he went over the edge.

The first night, I put the koop mattress under the side of the bed at the top, for a soft place to fall. There was no sound from Sammie's room, but some time in the night I woke and went in to look at him. He wasn't in the bed, so I looked down at the side, and there he was, knee and chest with his elbows close at his sides for warmth, his feet under a chair and his head under the bed. He had dropped about three feet to the mattress on the floor, but instead of making any outcry had accepted it as part of the new adventure and made the best of the new position. So funny and so pathetic. If I had not been concerned because it was so chilly I would have waked his mother to see it, but I took him up and tucked him back, and put more things in line to keep him from getting off again. Now he has learned more, and stays, not put, but at least on top of the bed. Furthermore, he takes Teddy Bear who arrived Christmas morning to bed with him, and making Teddy go to sleep somehow puts Sammie to sleep as well.

A Letter to Sam, Written from Greece

Athens, September 26, 195:

Dear Sambo:

When you and I come next to Greece, with Edith's permission yo
and I alone will visit the monastery at Mt. Athos, in the north of Greece
where women are not permitted to enter. Your mother says that an;
organization of males so superior they rule out women is doomed to
failure, and for proof points out that Mt. Athos has not grown, but stood
still, in all the centuries since it was founded.

We came here from Israel on the 24th. That first evening we went to
a performance of Hippolytus by Euripides, done in the ancient manner.
I had never seen is so, and it was interesting to watch, but the dialogue
was all Greek to me. Enclosed is my seat check. How would you like to
find your way by directions written like that?

Yesterday we "did" the Acropolis, and today we went to ancient
Corinth. They are, of course, complete ruins (man-made). I gather the
two greatest calamities ever to visit Greece were Maminius, the Roman
Consul who destroyed Corinth in 146 B.C., and Lord Elgin, who
despoiled the Pantheon and the Acropolis. What is left goes all the way
back to perhaps 5,000 B.C. (the Greek to 1,000 B.C.), and stirs the
imagination, but whatever is spoiled was spoiled by men, from the
Christians who defaced the statuary to the Turks who made lime from
all the marble which could be shattered and moved. They even tried to
get the gold out of the tiles by making a furnace of the stone Byzantine
Chapel Dofini, near Athens, but only ruined most of the mosaics. Under
the soot, one was left in the undersurface of the dome, a magnificent
portrait of Jesus as a black-eyed, black-haired, black-bearded Jew.

Nothing certain of Jesus and his times of 2,000 years ago was left in
Israel except the scenery, but I soaked myself in that for background,
and took very many pictures. All this land from Israel to Greece and all
around the Mediterranean is more desert than Southern California,
made so by the stupid humans who have lived here and removed the
forests utterly. They all admit the lands were once forested, and seem to
think nothing was lost but the trees. Instead they lost rainfall, rivers,
climate, and fertility, and now are on the edge of starvation. The Jews,
alone, have started to reforest on a grand scale.

We will have much to talk of. Tomorrow we go back to Rome, and on
the 1st start flying east to come home. We love you very, very much.

— Dad

A Letter To Sam About Writing Letters

Karachi, Pakistan — October 3, 1953

Dear Sambo:

When we got back to Rome from Egypt, Palestine, and Greece, we found not a single letter at the American Express except one from Virginia and only one letter from the Brucks at the Hotel Flora — nothing from the office, or Mrs. Cooper, or the Blades, or you. But the letter from Virginia was dated September 17th, and the letter from the Brucks the 22nd.

This left us in the middle of a guessing game. Our letter from Rome to the office had taken two weeks to get home by air mail, but the letters from Virginia and the Brucks had made the return trip in 5 days or so. Therefore, either nobody else had sent a letter, or else all the other letters were delayed.

But even if you wrote us after returning home, you still are not off scot-free. You sent two postcards from Oslo. Thereafter you were in Scotland, England, France, and Gibraltar, and a week or more on the steamer, and in New York, without sending us any further word, when only a postcard would have been sufficient — and your mother was most greviously disappointed. So here is your lecture, which please read carefully.

One of the penalties — if it is to be regarded as a penalty and not a reward — of living in a group larger than a prehistoric family in a cave, is that in the larger group, with stable government, civilized comforts, free communication, and dependence on the literature and arts and inventiveness, and their products such as agriculture and industry and commerce, every one of which is the result of community cooperative effort, it is absolutely impossible for a man to live entirely for himself, except by retiring to an island or a monastery or a cave. There he can evade — but not escape — his inescapable social and cultural obligations, because these are an integrated element of the whole complex.

The intelligent man, as compared to the boor or the dolt, not only meets his implied obligations as a member of the human group, but also considers — because it is true — that they add grace and true pleasure to the business of living.

The wisest teachers have reduced it to a simple rule — you must love men. Love in this sense has extensive implications, and one of its forms is the Golden Rule. You know what to expect of other people, and they know what to expect of you. Perhaps I have told you the Japanese word for "rude" means literally "other-than-expected," which puts it in a nutshell. And this love for other men must be selfless — not expressed for any other reward than itself — because it is a truth and not a sarcasm to say "Virtue is its own reward." It should be. And doing as you should extends to such apparent trivialities as writing a bread and butter letter to a house where you have been a guest.

Let's put it another way: Doing what you should do as a member of the human group is "selfish" to the extent that it actually benefits you more than anyone else, but it is also the basis of all the cooperative effort that makes whatever human progress there may be. The more nearly all men achieve it as individuals, the more nearly we shall approach the ideal human society.

Perhaps the highest expression of selfless love in humans is the love we sentimentally etherealize as "mother love." A woman who "mothers" a man gives more than any other human, and gives it selflessly. And Edith is your mother. I would expect it to be normal that a young man of your approximate upbringing, age, and disposition, would give a fair share of his waking thoughts to considering what form he can give to his expression of appreciation, and then act on it, even if it is only to recall what interval has elapsed since he sent a message, and what there is to report, and then to send a postcard reading "Hi, old gal, I'm fine. Lots of love. Sam."

I love you, too.

— DAD

About Quitting Smoking

October 11, 1961

Mark Twain, we are told, knew all about quitting smoking "because he had quit two hundred times." This sums it up. The person who does not form the habit because he does not finally like tobacco or respond to it has no problem. He is like the man who is temperamentally or physically a non-drinker. There is no appeal. But the compulsive smoker, like the compulsive drinker, is a biochemical slave. For him smoking is addiction to a habit-forming drug, a drug which has specific physical effects. He may refrain from smoking for shorter or longer periods, but he is not in any natural way "cured" of his addiction.

There are many ways of quitting smoking, of which a few may serve as typical examples.

One may break the habit gradually. This will mean that the smoker decides on Thursday evening that this is the last cigarette. He lasts until Saturday at noon. Then he decides he will have one to break the ever-increasing tension, and by Saturday evening he is smoking at the usual rate.

Another may decide to vary his pace. He goes without a smoke until it is a strain. Then he smokes a cigarette and starts another period of abstinence. The periods of abstinence will clearly get to be of longer and longer duration. But they don't. Instead they get shorter and shorter, until in not too long a time he is back where he started.

Still another may use the method of skipped steps. When he finds himself patting his pockets to find the pack and take one out, he now and then, perhaps every second time, stops patting and relaxes, ready to wait for the next time he feels the urge. But instead, the urges come at closer intervals, and presently he finds himself smoking, not as much, but more than before.

In all this there is the same struggle between desire and resolution which ever so long ago resulted in the philosophical conclusion that the world is ruled by good and bad gods of about equal power, and that one is under their alternate power as a pawn of fate. Actually this is rationalization, which is always bunk — man's begging off from the burden of duty to use some logical process for his decisions — the faculty which gives man the animal a control over his situation which instinct cannot, and the reason he is not merely an animal.

In the end a thing is either a rational thing to do or it is not. In a universe of order there is no dualism, no god of order and devil of disorder; and in the universe there is no disorder. The dualism exists only in the mind of man, to rationalize for himself the lack of orderliness in his own thinking; and the "orderliness" or "disorderliness" are only the plus and minus signs of a progression. In fact there is exactly one way to quit smoking:

YOU QUIT.

A Letter of Love
to Edith Rehnborg

Papeete, April 29, 1961

Sweetest darling —

It is mail day, and mail days slip up on me unexpectedly. I was just reminded when I heard the blast of a steamer in the harbor. I did not know one was due, and I do not know which one it is. I need you with me just to feel organized and in step with events.

There is so much to get onto my discs that I do not get the time to dictate it. There are enough hours in the day but not enough system to my use of time. I need to manicure my nails, but I did get my hair cut. If you were here both would have been done days ago.

Today is typically crowded. It is 9:00 a.m., so I have taken too long to dress. I dash next to Les Tropiques, where I have an appointment. Then I'll get off a few more discs. Then at 3:00 p.m. I go to see a princess, the aged daughter of Pomare V, and then with Simone to outline what has to be done at Punaauia to get it in condition by June. It has been sadly neglected, but Simone will hire the gardener or gardeners and get it done, and keep supervision of their work. I gather this is being done for you, sight unseen.

More and more, it seems to me, I realize how much I adore you, and how smooth and rational life is when we are together. I go my own way alone, and some of my events might not occur if you were along, but it is like the kid who is coursing through the neighborhood until Mama calls him home to wash behind his ears and get ready for dinner and homework. Both are fun, but home is more orderly, and much more satisfying.

I love you hugely and absorbingly, and I am lonesome. Millions of kisses and a long hug.

— Your adoring Carl

A Letter To A Granddaughter

Dearest Lisa,

This doll is Chinese, and he looks like the Chinese "boy" I had when I lived in China. He was a man, but the French call servants "garcon," which means boy, and so people who live in foreign lands have got the habit of always calling their native servants "Boys." The servants don't mind it at all; in fact, my boy called me "Master."

His name was Hua, so this doll is named Hua also. In Chinese this is written

花   and it means "flower." Imagine a man (or boy) named flower and not being bothered.

He used to take care of me as if I were a baby. When I woke up in the morning, he had already drawn my bath and put out the clothes I was to wear that day. I am quite sure that if I had allowed him to do so, he would have dressed me. No matter how late I came home in the evening, he was waiting for me, and my bed was turned down and my pajamas laid on the edge of the bed. In the mornings before he called me awake, he went out in the fields to hear the morning song of the wild birds. Usually he took his own caged bird with him so it could hear the meadowlarks also.

Once he made me a present. He bought three goldfish and a glass bowl for them to swim in. I fed them each morning and grew quite fond of them. One evening when I came home it seemed to me the fish had an odd look. I went close to them, and I saw they were not the same fish. So I called the boy and asked him what was wrong with my fish, and he said,

"Oh, master, I very sorry. This morning I have put fish in bathtub while I wash bowl. I forget I have turned wrong faucet, and water very hot. Fish have swum quick like happy, then die. I very sorry, so I buy more fish but no can find same color and master have see not same fish."

Once he told me a story about an American named George Washington. Your mommy can tell you the real story about George and the cherry tree, but this is the way Hua told it to me:

"Long time before have got one small boy name Georgie Wash. One time he papa go Ningpo more far. What time he have go, Georgie take one piece hatchet cut down chelly tree. Papa come home look-see: no have got chelly tree. Georgie papa say very loud, 'Who man cut down my chelly tree?' and Georgie say 'House boy have do.' "

So you take good care of Hua. I was very fond of him and perhaps you will be fond of him also.

— Gran'pa

Reading was very important to Rehnborg, and he read on an enormous variety of subjects. But writing was also an important activity in his life and he wrote continually as a way of disseminating information and expressing his thoughts.

Part VIII
PERSONAL BELIEFS AND PHILOSOPHY

A barefooted and wind-tousled Carl Rehnborg is enjoying one of his favorite pastimes . . . sailing California waters near Newport Beach aboard his 30-foot P.C. sailboat, the SCANDAL. Much of his inspiration was drawn from the sea.

Existence — The First and Greatest Wonder

Written Approximately 1960

The first and greatest of the wonders is the wonder of existence. I take it as obvious and needless to argue that perception of the exterior universe, however subjectively our impressions of it are formed, is adequate evidence that it objectively exists.

But consider the odds involved in having the gift of existence as an individual. The tree outside my window is called a Saint John's Bread tree. Year after year it bears thousands of pods of bean-like seeds which fall to the paved walk and street below the tree, to be gathered up by the street-cleaning machine and conveyed to the city dump, and no one of them ever becomes another tree.

In fact if only two of its seeds became new trees, and each new tree produced two more always, in time the descendants of this one tree would cover the surface of the earth's land to the exclusion of everything else. The chance of any one seed becoming a tree, therefore, is almost vanishingly small, and the same thing is true of the many things which live.

Your mother had the potential capacity to produce many thousands of ova, each capable of becoming such an individual as you are, and your father, embracing your mother in love, expended millions of millions of spermatozoa, each adequate to fertilize an ovum to produce a human entity, and yet you are the only result. The odds of one particular ovum being fertilized by the specific spermatozoon which produced you for your individual destiny are as one to a number outside of actual comprehension by a human mind.

Have you ever looked out at your world and inside at yourself, and given thanks that you were granted the right, by a god or by a statistical inevitability, of becoming and living and thinking for your term of years in this amazing universe?

Reflections On Living and Dying

February 19, 1964

When I was an adolescent of about seventeen, like all other adolescents who have ever been, I knew virtually everything. In time, like all
the other adolescents, I recovered as the immensity and complexity of
the universe penetrated the cocoon in which young human beings live
until about that age.

Now, however, the feeling of knowing more than I should keep
entirely to myself has begun again to assert itself; this time, because I
have passed the point in time where seventeen became seventy-one, and
for the years between I have absorbed impressions and reached conclusions which seem to myself to have significance, even if not fully in
agreement with majority opinion. Perhaps in reaching this point of
view, it helps to be at least immodest enough to feel that I have been
using a good mind through the years, with which to do the observing
and concluding, and to feel that modesty, unless it is due to an actual
sense of inferiority, is largely a pretense in any case.

It seems to me, as a first conclusion, that when one does something
happens which is very similar to the ordinary departures an individual
makes daily during a lifetime, whether he leaves home to go to school or
to go to the office, or makes his farewells more elaborately to go on a
journey of days or weeks or even longer. Quite certainly, however,
departures are more carelessly arranged when one goes away forever, if
only because one does not usually plan for the event called death. In our
own lives we almost but not quite get around to visiting an old friend or
to writing him a letter, only to have someone tell us or to read in the
paper that he is dead. Moreover, he did not say goodbye.

This is altogether wrong from an emotional standpoint, as well as
very wasteful from the standpoint of the human interests involved. Any
man or woman of standard intelligence accumulates some store of non-
scientific values of the sort that basically affect our common human
destiny, and then, so to speak, dies intestate merely because this
individual set of opinions has not been put into the record to make it
tangible. It is storing a valuable sort of human value in leaky vessels.
Perhaps a particular human being does not have more than a little to
contribute, but even that little should be contributed by giving it expression. Then, since one does not know quite exactly the date of his final

eparture, at least one can make a sort of guess based on common human experience, and then, if the record has been compiled earlier than necessary, there is a gain in being able to revise the record now and then to include new insights.

Personally I do not consider that death, which is the absolutely inevitable final episode in the life of a human being, as of all other animals, is in any way gruesome. Further, I would like to say goodbye to my family and my friends, if only to tell them how much more I love them than it was conventional to show, and how honored and enriched I was to have them for my associates. The individual comes into the organization we call human society when he is born, and steps out of it again when he dies. Before that he is not known or imagined. After that he is sooner or later forgotten completely, and should be, except to the extent that he had value to his friends or added love and a bit of knowledge to the assets of the society. As a consequence, since I cannot stick around for the decades and centuries it will take for some of the concepts of the human race to be sufficiently investigated to permit human knowledge to reach provisional conclusions, I choose for my own satisfaction to outline various convictions I have, either as donations to knowledge or to controversy, as a sort of accounting for what I have done with the privilege of living, because I have had a full and eventful life and I have enjoyed it completely, and, except for a very few, have loved my fellow travelers.

With the sort of knowledge which I think should be saved more systematically by individual contributions, is the range of thought which deals with the values in human society, referred to above as non-scientific — the individual's responses to the universe and the concept by which human beings account for the facts of the universe. For example, one may accept that the only physical entities in the universe are the constituents of the atoms which comprise the 'things' we 'see,' and yet adjust to the objects of everyday experience as easily as did the most primitive member of a human society.

Again, one may comprehend that the process of thought itself is a matter of physics and chemistry and yet see that the 'mind' of man has organized the very sciences which have disclosed this fact; or that man's religious beliefs or 'explanations' of reality may be subjective and mythological and egocentric, and yet also perceive that these beliefs are related to the social customs which point man's development to higher

An excellent mariner, Rehnborg loved the sea and during his lifetime owned a number of sailboats and yachts. Here he has taken the wheel of the Cynjo, a 48-foot teakwood ketch. At his right is the skipper, Thor Millard, and at his left is his brother-in-law, F.F. "Fuzzy" Vaughn. Other friends and sailing buddies are in the background.

and higher levels or values; or that man's philosophies can envision higher levels for society as increasingly mechanistic and materialistic, and yet hold firmly to the conviction that man must and will always be greater than his machines. This is finally the search for the 'why' rather than merely the 'how' of what we feel we know on the ideal level, both during and after we have explored our knowledge on the physical level, such as asking why an electrical impulse in a nerve fiber can become a thought.

Whenever we watch — or even consider — the occurrence we call death, whether at a lower level in the incredible numbers of microscopic entities involved in eating and drinking our foods, or the hordes of planktonic forms engulfed by a baleen whale, and animals eating other animals in all the water of the earth, and all the fowls and animals killed deliberately to provide our tables, or the hundreds of other kinds of terminations of the metabolic process we call living, it is born in on us hat to the highest degree of probability death is an end, whether of a plant or an animal, and including human animals.

In the process of life, materials flow into and out of an organism, and during a lifetime the organism may ingest or consume many times the volume of materials comprising that organism at any given moment in time. But when death supervenes, the flow stops and the collected materials on hand dissipate. In a broad sense the atoms of all the available and required materials are used over and over again by a succession of living forms. The number of separate atoms entering it is of the order of the numbers of individuals who have existed on the earth or of the stars visible in the universe of galaxies. The individual is merely an arrangement and rearrangement of these atoms, and living is a chemical process involving the atoms as physical entities and does not infer any special or metaphysical state of the atoms.

Because of the numbers of atoms involved in any one organization of a human being, for example, it is exceedingly probable that in the body of any given human individual, at any given time, there are atoms of elements which at some time have been part of the body of every human being who has lived long enough ago for his materials to have been disseminated completely over the earth's surface.

There is nothing disturbing in itself about the thought of death as an end, and a dissolution, any more than there is in the thought of sleep, except that each human being has an importance to himself which rebels vehemently from the thought of not awakening — of not being an observer of the events of tomorrow and tomorrow — of being soon forgotten by all but a few; of eventually being forgotten by all as completely as if he had never existed. Yet each of us will be forgotten in time just as each of us has forgotten the lamb who supplied the chop we had for dinner one evening a year ago, or the slave who held the stirrup for Ghengis Khan as that noted figure mounted his horse — and even Ghengis Khan is remembered not as a human being but as a notable historical figure. Certainly if death is the end of one's existence, and the beginning of non-existence, it is a completely dreamless sleep and therefore an untroubled sleep.

The grief we experience and show at the end of the life of one we love is evidence that we shrewdly suspect death is in fact an end. It is a goodbye forever, not a departure on a journey with a finite term, and the grief is felt only by those left behind; for the one who has left it is the peace of nothingness. Just as most of us cling to the beliefs arising from dreams that we dream, that our consciousness is a separate entity from our physical bodies, such a seer as Gautama called the nothingness a desirable end. He even suggested that freedom from desire is an escape from living.

If such ideas have a depressing effect, they should not. There is wonder and adventure in the highest degree in most of the elements of this affair of being a part of life in the universe, but man has a distaste for looking at facts objectively, and some notable thinkers, such as this same Gautama, have refused entirely to see any part of the human relationship to the rest of the universe in an objective light, and man as an integrated part of the universal whole.

They — and we — are more inclined to assume that man is an extremely important and differentiated part of the universe, and related to it mostly by the fact of being in it as a spectator. But instead and in fact, man is an integrated part of the universe, in and of it, made of the same materials and obeying the same natural laws as all the rest of the universe, and a result of the same total evolutionary development as the galaxies themselves.

C.F. Rehnborg's Legacy

To those who knew him, C.F. Rehnborg was a very special person. His charisma was such that one was instantly drawn to him with an instinctive feeling that here was an extraordinary human being. Whether one was part of a group of five or five thousand, he had the unique ability to make each person in the group feel that he was intensely aware of and interested in him or her individually. When he spoke, he captivated his audiences as few people have ever done.

C.F. Rehnborg, as he preferred to be known, had a splendid intellect, a profound store of knowledge about a great variety of subjects, and a never-ending curiosity about everything in the universe. Yet he was direct and almost childlike in his approach to life and people, and children adored him because he spoke to them as equals, never 'talking down' to them.

Above all else, one felt the love and caring for people that emanated from this remarkable man, and that was manifested in his words and deeds. He was a man who truly lived as he believed in his mind and heart. And in so doing, he left a legacy to his family, friends, and associates — stemming not only from his achievements in the nutritional field but also from his beliefs and the personal examples he set through his life and work.

In his book, JESUS AND THE NEW AGE OF FAITH, which was written over a forty-year period of intermittent study and research, Mr. Rehnborg expressed his concern that men and women should 'know the truth, and the truth will make them free.' In his characteristic fashion, he tried to help them understand truth as he conceived it to be. Following are excerpts from his book which illustrate his reasoning and provide valuable insights into his complex personality.

Excerpts From "Jesus and the New Age of Faith"

Jesus . . . taught success and achievement as attainable individual goals, and He taught the manner of living which produced achievement. All the thousands of inspirational books which fill libraries and bookstores are, in the final analysis, adaptations of what Jesus taught, and of what He taught more completely and in far fewer words:

THAT WHAT MAN WOULD HAVE, HE COULD HAVE.

The most clearly outstanding characteristic of Jesus as a man was the serenity and consciousness of power He displayed. That He sought nothing for Himself but spent His whole being in love and service for mankind is the final stamp of His greatness; and that death was His only reward for His teaching from the men He tried to teach, stamps His life and sayings with immortality.

Many men believe that what Jesus taught will one day become the sum of the motivations of humanity and bring about the Rule of God He foretold; but meanwhile, any man can live by those rules and complete and fulfill all that his own life may mean to himself and to his fellows.

* * * * * * * * *

The earth is not the center of the universe, but a minutely small part of it, and there is no God but God. Jesus was veritably a Son of God, but so also is every man. The way on which Jesus made trail for us is open to every man. It is a universe of marvels, to be lived in freely and confidently and bravely. There is no simplest thing in it that is not marvelous and ultimately without discoverable limit to its infinity.

* * * * * * * * *

All science admits, and Jesus knew, there are qualities in the human mind beyond and above the mechanism of the brain by which they are evidenced in the world, and these qualities are related to the Infinite Mind that we can name, but cannot define, as God. Jesus said, "God is Good, God is Love, God is a Spirit, and God is Father to Mankind," leaving nothing whatever to be added. Not only that, but he left this simplified concept in a form entirely comprehensible to all manner of men — subject only to acceptance or rejection, but magnetic with the impulse to accept it.

* * * * * * * * *

When Jesus moved about the countryside of Galilee, in the early days of His teaching, He was not teaching specifically the Jewish or Greek or Buddhist or Christian or any other kind of organic ritual religion. He was teaching the basic religion that underlies them all: That God is One, that we are to love this God utterly and to love other men as we love ourselves, that God is Father to man; that because this is true man may have whatever he will.

This is called the 'Miracle of Believing' to which all men can subscribe, in which all good can be received merely by the one act of preparing to receive it . . .

* * * * * * * * * *

Jesus said if men loved God wholly, and loved other men as they loved themselves and as they loved God, there would be no evil anywhere. This is obviously true, and it could not happen in a universe that was maleficient or merely neutral. It could only happen in a universe that was beneficient. Jesus said, moreover, whatever men would have they could have, for the reason that the God of the Universe was Love and bore to the essence of men the relationship best pictured as that of Father and child. This characteristic of the universe can be demonstrated to be true — and it could not be true in an aimless universe or in a directionless or meaningless universe. It can only happen if there is a beneficient Creator and Ruler, and if He does actually have a relationship to men, His creatures.

* * * * * * * * * *

Again and again, Jesus told individuals that their own faith was what brought about a desired result. Never did Jesus say He himself had answered the asker's prayer, but that it was the Power of God. He taught, in nearly the same words over and over again, "As ye believe, so shall it be." In homely words, Jesus would have had little use for those who go to church to pray for rain and leave their umbrellas at home.

Every moment of his life of which we have any sure record shows Jesus living as he taught and as He told others to live: with courage and nothing else — never with fear but always with faith. It is unjust to the magnificent Jesus to imply that he had foreknowledge of inevitable success and an assurance of miracles, and therefore had no cause to fear. He had the same causes for fear as have all other men. He said to those of little faith that they should trust in the Father, and He himself believed it, lived it, and told all others to do the same. He never for one moment let fear enter any facet of his mind or being. Why can we not believe Him?

* * * * * * * * * *

Although the principles of Jesus have grown slowly into the consciousness of peoples, they did not come into being slowly. They were exploded by Jesus into an unready world; yet in the one moment they were uttered and almost carelessly entrusted to the uncertain human memories of his disciples, each concept of principle began to sweep existing human ideals to a plane of aspiration higher than men had theretofore known — higher than men have yet been able to attain. Nevertheless, the course of history of the past nineteen hundred years indicates clearly that the principles actually charted a course that mankind has approximately followed, and continues to follow in its development.

* * * * * * * * *

Once we recognize that doctrines do not come from God but from men, we are really ready to listen to Jesus. When Jesus said the Pharisees bound the souls of men with rules, in effect he urged all men to forget such rules, of whatever brand of religion, and to look for the rules of God as we can see them every day, everywhere, in the natural order.

* * * * * * * * *

To ask for what one desires, as Jesus said we might, does not come about through any violation of the natural order of things. It is part of the natural order: the universe is made that way. If one follows the Law of Love in his dealings with men (or even if one does not), and if one knows what he wants, then inevitably and certainly life orders itself in such a manner that the desired thing simply happens.

* * * * * * * * *

The resources of the universe were infinite, and just as a human father made the benefits at his control free for the good of his children, so also the Father of all men made the resources of the universe free to mankind, His children. Not only happiness, but every other desirable thing was free to all men for the asking.

But note: for the asking. Not supplication, not lazy wishing, but asking, which implies a readiness to receive. And to a readiness to receive there are unexpected consequences: one must use what has been asked for. Those of us who attend church, and who repeat ... the words "Give us this day our needs for the day . . . and do not let us be subjected to temptation," do so perfunctorily, without particular heed to the meaning of the words and their implications.

But if we ask with consciousness of the meaning, and by intent, we thereupon learn new things concerning law and relationship. The words of this prayer ascribed to Jesus come alive. We get our needs for the day, nd more, to be used. And if we do not use it but sit on it like a miser, we accumulate tokens of work done that do us no good but simply wait to be released to go to work again. If we ask with intent not to be subjected to temptation, we are not subjected to temptation; on the contrary, we cannot even overtake temptation. But do not think this will be productive of sanctimoniousness or of self-esteem. It is supremely enlightened selfishness, and we will see it as such. No good we do is, or can be, completely "un-self-ish." Even philanthropy makes the giver feel good, or he would not be philanthropic. We ourselves are the chief gainers.

* * * * * * * * *

Jesus said, "Ask and ye shall receive; seek and ye shall find; knock and the door will be opened to you. For it is he who asks who receives; and he who seeks who finds; and he who knocks to whom the door is opened."

The great changes are to come about, not by inertia but by action; and the action must first proceed from men as individuals, and then from men in groups. Jesus consistently followed the idea that the Rule of God was within the hearts of men who heard and acted, and that in a society made up of such men no social ills could exist.

Let us recognize the obvious truth of what He believed and taught, and help it to come about — and live rich and full lives because we so believe and act, knowing that all the problems have answers, and that the problems may receive their answers in a world conditioned to seek them — and willing to believe that it shall receive them.

* * * * * * * * *

Worship is nothing else but the practice of God's Law of Love, and the service of this love extends over every second of our conscious living. It is not something done at intervals in a church.

* * * * * * * * *

Jesus made it his main point that love should be a habit of behavior, so that worship in temple and synagogue was not to be a visit to a filling station. The Laws of God were the laws of living, and the feeling of communication with the Source was a continuing experience, not a cyclic filling and emptying of a man's "soul." Jesus said the Laws of God were the only possible laws of human conduct — that, literally and exactly, to use them was "life" and to neglect them was the road to destruction. This observation does not have a specific place in time. It does not, for

example, refer to AD 29 alone, but to all times and all places, and applie
sharply to our own times.

* * * * * * * * * *

Above all, Jesus had a perfect mind. His logic was flawless. His grasp
of essentials was never in the slightest degree confused. He said instantly
all that could be said on the point at issue and in the fewest possible
words of the utmost simplicity. He arrived at once at conclusions that
he never had occasion to modify later in any particular, and one may
critically examine what he said without ever being able to add to or
subtract from his final meaning. He never compromised.

* * * * * * * * * *

We instinctively resent perfection in a man, not because it is wrong
but because we regard it as so manifestly impossible. Ordinary men,
when told of another who does not drink or lie or cheat, who conducts
himself with unfailing kindness and consideration towards others, half
jokingly and half earnestly ask what his secret vices may be. This is the
result of experience. No man is in any degree proud of shortcomings in
himself; and no man is unconscious of the many shortcomings in
himself. In retrospect, his life is always filled with things he wishes he
had not done, and things he should have done and did not.

But we are yet able to realize that unlike all other men of whom there
is record, Jesus actually was a full and perfect man. We can see Jesus
knew this of himself, as He shows by what He says and does, and still
we feel no instinctive resentment or disbelief. This is homage to a man
who practiced fully what He taught through all His life. There is no
difficulty in seeing why His followers made Jesus divine. They knew no
other way to account for Him in terms of ordinary men than to ascribe a
different origin, and the idea of divinity . . . was then an accepted part of
their ideas concerning unusual men.

* * * * * * * * * *

If the essence of the philosophy of Jesus can be put into small
compass, it would be about as follows:

There is a world, or universe, in which we exist. There is a power, or
logos, or Spirit we call God, "on earth as it is in heaven," which is the
cause and meaning of the universe, and which is "like a Father" to the
spirits of men.

The Laws of God control every manifestation of reality and are immanent, eternal, and universal. Men may offend these laws, but cannot change them. Offense is a self-inflicted deprivation, and adjustment to the laws is harmony. The greatest of the laws for men is in the Shema, not because it is Jewish, but because it is true: The Lord our God is One God, and you must love the Lord your God with your whole heart, and with your whole soul, and with your whole mind. And the second law is equal to it: You must love your neighbor as yourself.

When these laws are part of your faith and control your behavior, you are utterly at harmony with the universe. But God is greater than to require obedience for favor: He sends his rain on the just and the unjust. He makes his sun to shine on the good and the evil. He makes the resources of his universe free to all men His children, only asking love for Himself, but rewarding men's love for other men; for it is a universe of Law, and therefore a universe of cause and effect. It is a universe in which you may have whatsoever you desire, and therefore a universe in which there need be no concern or apprehension for the future, so that life should be lived with hope and confidence, never with fear.